BELLE J. BE

MY FRIENDS,
THE APES

With Illustrations

BOSTON
LITTLE, BROWN AND COMPANY · 1949

Published August 1942
Reprinted June 1943
Reprinted January 1944
Reprinted March 1949

PRINTED IN THE UNITED STATES OF AMERICA

BY BELLE J. BENCHLEY

MY LIFE IN A MAN-MADE JUNGLE
MY FRIENDS, THE APES
MY ANIMAL BABIES

Photo E. H. Bold

Ngagi at the Salt Box

TO

DR. HARRY MILTON WEGEFORTH

*President and Founder of
the Zoological Society of San Diego
with my deepest appreciation and gratitude*

INTRODUCTION

WHEN they neared the edge of the jungle the great
beasts paused, restrained by the will of their leader and
their own inherited terror of the unknown. Far out in
the light of the open lands they saw those for whom they
were seeking: others of their own band who, weary of
damp, dripping darkness, coarse food and low tunnels,
had overcome their submissive acceptance of discomfort
and their fear of change. They had followed the rebel of
their number who had urged them ever more strongly
to venture with him into that inviting world just beyond
the border of their jungle sanctuary.

Suddenly one of the explorers stood erect upon his
short heavy legs and raised his mighty arms until they
were at right angles to his enormous torso. Then, turning
to face his former master, he began to beat the familiar
challenge of the jungle upon his broad breast.

The deep-set eyes of the leader, still in the shadowy
forest, glared from under heavy brows as he watched,
glared with a mixture of hatred and longing. For the
first time he refused to recognize or respond to the
friendly defiance of one he had loved. Wheeling, with
the remnant of his followers at his heels, he led the way
back into the silence and stagnation of the jungles, the
home his ancestors had chosen. There no danger lurked!
Even killer beasts would not willingly enter that rain-
drenched hideout which through centuries had sheltered

the cautious black beasts. There, he knew, could be found the coarse food upon which he and his kind had learned to subsist. He greatly preferred the familiarity of the home of his forebears. He had none of that burning desire for change and improvement which had driven his comrades forth.

My own imagination has always painted such a scene of the separation of the animal kingdom into its species and kinds, a picture formed perhaps when I first learned of the theory of the development of species and the survival of the fittest. Actually, we know that no such definite event or movement brought about by the will of a single creature took place, but that changing conditions of the earth, dire necessity, or at times too easy living for some, must have gradually destroyed those who were too highly specialized to adapt themselves, while others, more capable of change and endurance, lived on and grew into creatures capable of coping with their surroundings.

Since Darwin first stated simply and boldly the theory that popularly speaking bears his name, it has been the subject of frequent arguments, as many of them based upon misunderstanding as upon blind religious beliefs. Almost daily I am asked by visitors to the San Diego Zoo if my experience has taught me that man really *did* descend from monkeys. The deprecating air with which the remark is so often made, as though the speaker were either facetiously playing up to a pseudo scientist or giving me credit for too much intelligence to believe such a ridiculous theory, makes me long to retort, "Well, that isn't what Darwin believed, but if he had had a chance to compare some people with some of my monkeys, I am sure he would have said intentionally just that — *man descended*." The speaker, not Darwin, is wrong.

Although most scientists graphically depict as a tree the development of the species, to me it has always seemed a long and arduous road beginning with the first simple cell which, by dividing itself into two living parts, performed the initial miracle of reproduction. Along that different highway through time and space, I always hear the tread of weary feet; some, finding the road too hard, perish by the wayside; others stop or turn aside into pleasant openings which indicate easy living; but no matter how many hesitate, some are always going on to emerge at last in what scientists picturesquely call the "dawn of civilization." In advance of all is the weak and probably terrified creature called "man."

Having at last thrown off the shackles of the jungle, the adventurous primitive man found himself able to stand erect and walk upon his two feet, bearing burdens or his helpless young in his arms. But with his advance he lost something of his capacity to endure an existence of constant fear, the rigors of a natural environment, and something of his power to defend himself against wild beasts. So he sought supplementary means of protecting himself and his dependents. His intellect, sharpened by necessity, discovered ways of fashioning weapons and shelters until, with these tools, he became the strongest of all creatures and was able to lead all others into his life as he chose. First he selected those most useful to him, making them produce his food and his clothing and even his rude shelters. He made of them his slaves, his friends, and some of them he worshiped as his gods. Wherever we follow the history of man we find, in his rude shelters, on the walls of his caves, buried in his graves, and finally in his words, first oral (as legend) and then written the story of his association with animals. Man alone of all the creatures can leave a written record of himself and his accomplishments for the guidance of those who follow.

At last, man progressed to that degree of civilization which enabled him to become interested in creatures not to use them for his ends but with what we call scientific interest in the creatures themselves; and so he went out into the world and brought back to his dwelling places beasts from far away. There has never been a civilization in which some crude form of zoo or menagerie has not flourished.

As travel facilities shrunk the limits of the unknown parts of the earth, the creatures called apes became more and more interesting to him. He searched not only the wild for signs of them and their habits, but the literature of past civilizations to find out what they had known about these creatures that were now so fascinating to him.

In early writings, five hundred years before the birth of Christ, we find the first mention of a gorilla in an account written by one Hanno, who made a journey down the west coast of Africa. In the fourth century B.C., Aristotle compiled our oldest *Natural History* and in it he uses the term *Ape*, carefully explaining that monkeys and baboons, which he also described, are "tailless apes."

Early pictures and descriptions are confined largely to African species and are exceedingly meager. I believe this is due as much to an attempt to emphasize the manlike qualities as to poor drawing technique.

During the early voyages succeeding the discovery of America, precious metals and stones were the temptation for the explorers and their high commands, not animal treasures. So only slight mention is made of the wild life of newly discovered lands. Even the people inhabiting them counted only in so much as they satisfied the demands of the discoverers, or made conquest and possession easy or difficult.

Much misinformation and legend still surround the anthropoid apes in the wild. People, on the whole, like to believe strange tales. They prefer crediting the mysterious to learning by patient personal observation, when possible, or by annotating the observations of others whose reports are reliable. Travelers, knowing how audiences enjoy the sensational, frequently embroider fact with fantastic details or put an occult interpretation upon phenomena which they have witnessed and have failed to understand clearly.

The first sight of any great ape swinging by his giant arms from the branches overhead in a shadowy jungle, or stealing silently through the mists of his forest home, must be a terrifying one even to those seeking him. With his gigantic size and near human shape, his tearing strength and wordless screaming, he may well look like something part human, part beast. We cannot wonder that he was endowed with supernatural origin by the savages dwelling in adjacent territory, and that he was avoided rather than sought. Reports of these terrifying creatures coming to the early explorers prompted them to press on into the unknown. Few, upon their return to their homes, did anything to dispel the air of mystery and horror surrounding the great apes. Perhaps they were too filled with horror themselves to be calm when depicting what they had seen.

Gradually, however, a few facts became known. In a natural history brought out by Buffon in 1776, a variety of species of great apes became recognizable.

[xi]

Then the lack of power of speech was established as an essential difference between the ape and savage man. Although it was then impossible to bring back living specimens, due to slowness and difficulty of transportation and to other causes, some of the early explorers succeeded in returning with preserved scientific specimens. In this way scientists learned a great deal about the anatomy of the anthropoids and classification into genera and species became possible.

The men of science have agreed, even in their first classifications, to designate as *primates* the highest of the creatures preceding man. Today, the word primate has been enlarged in meaning to include man himself. It also embraces lower orders of monkeys, baboons and lemurs. The scientific term *anthropoid ape* is drawn from two languages: the Greek *anthropoid*, meaning like a man, and the old English *apen*, meaning to imitate. An anthropoid ape is an imitator of man in his physical form. Scientifically, anthropoid and ape are interchangeable words, but the word ape should never be applied to any creature other than an anthropoid.

There are four types of anthropoid apes: the *gibbon*, the *orang-utan*, the *chimpanzee* and the *gorilla*. For many years, the species were confused with each other, especially the chimpanzee of West Africa and the orang-utan of Asia. Both were called by the same name, orang-utan or pongo. With the eventual discovery of the gorilla and the classification of gibbons as apes rather than as monkeys, the four types of mock-men were complete.

In the chapters that follow, I shall introduce the four types, not in the order in which I myself met them but according to the way in which science has at present

[xii]

classified them in relationship with man. I shall begin with the apes farthest removed from man, that is, with the gibbon, whose race is divided into two families, the siamang or pouched gibbon, and the larger and more numerous group of several species designated by the name *Hylobates*, which means *Walking on the Trees*. I can think of nothing more appropriate to call the gibbon.

The orang-utan, somewhat nearer man than the gibbon, is known in Malayan as *The Man of the Woods*. Both the gibbon and the orang-utan are geographically confined to the southeastern parts of Asia, in territories which are overlapping. Gibbons are still numerous throughout a wide area, but the orang-utan is scarce and is restricted almost entirely to the islands of Borneo and Sumatra.

The two remaining great types are the chimpanzee and the gorilla. They are indigenous to the tropical belt of the so-called "dark continent." Like the native people of Southern and Central Africa, these mock-men are black-skinned. The chimpanzee, distributed throughout the tropical west-coast region, is the best known of all the anthropoid apes. His most commonly used scientific name — *Pan satyrus* — implies his manlike qualities; *Pan*, god of the woods, and *satyr*, part man. I frequently designate the chimpanzee to myself as the "half-man."

The gorilla, last to be discovered and identified by modern science, dwells within a territory ranging from the lowlands and jungles of the west coast of Africa through French Equatorial Africa and high up in the mountains of the Belgian Congo. The lowland gorilla was known long before the monster of the mountains appeared. But the natives knew and spoke of Ingagi, the giant Hairy Man, whom they glimpsed on the fringe of the forests at rare intervals.

No word or picture could ever give you the feeling toward the great apes that is produced upon you by personal acquaintance and friendship with them. At most I can only try to convey what I myself have come to feel and understand about them. I shall do my best to bring you face to face with these apes, not as scientific groups but as individuals, creatures to be known and singled out even from their cage-mates. I will tell you how they look and act and something about their characters, and I hope you will like them and pity them and laugh with them and with me, until suddenly you will find yourself knowing them as they are; not as low, hideous caricatures of man, but as magnificent animals — noble, loyal and affectionate — virtues to which neither man nor any single beast can lay sole claim. Who has not seen them in his dog, his horse or other pet? And I have recognized them in the behavior of almost every one of the wild beasts gathered together under the care of the staff at the zoo. It is only when we try to raise the beast to the level of man that he fails us and only then that we fail him.

Once again I must frankly confess that this is not a scientific book written for scientists. It is a simple, perhaps sentimental account of my own adventures with the apes, our "next of kin." I have learned through personal association what I really know about my friends, the apes, and I have, to my own satisfaction, both confirmed and contradicted some of the published findings of our greatest scientists. If I think I have a deeper understanding than some others, it is because I have had a day-by-day association with these creatures, at times a joyful, happy association, but sometimes one of trouble and care. I have had rare opportunities; for those I am thankful. If the sharing leads you to delve more deeply into science than in this simple volume, you will find many great books to give you much that you would like to know.

It is my hope that, just as my associates in the zoo have often been urged forward along a new road to higher learning, so may I open for you a door into a new, rich territory you might not otherwise have found. But primarily these tales are intended to give you simple, transient pleasure. And so now let's go down to the ape cages.

Contents

Illustrations

PART ONE

HE WHO WALKS ON THE TREES

CHAPTER I

Gibby — The Tale of a Tyrant

THE ONLY way properly to introduce a gibbon would be to stand at a great circus microphone and cry in stentorian tones: "La-a-adddie-e-es and Ge-entleme-en! Yo-o-u-u-u-ur atte-entio-on Pl-l-l-eas-s-se! We are about to present in the center ring the tiniest of the near-human midgets — the daintiest, the most bewitching, the most daring of aerialists — that superb artist of the air, the original lady of the flying trapeze — Ma-ada-ame Gibbo-o-on A-a-ape! She will now startle you with her death-defying leaps through almost boundless space. She will execute a series of giant swings and aerial somersaults such as have never been equaled. Ladies and Gentlemen, *Madame Gibbon!*"

(I always seem to hear the roll of drums when a gibbon springs out into the air with destination to me unknown.)

But I had no circus announcer to acquaint me with the miracle that was a gibbon. I was the new bookkeeper who had been at the zoo a few weeks. Finding the continuous life in an office stifling, and the bookkeeping with which I was only vaguely familiar terrifying and dreadfully exhausting, I had finally found a noon hour which I could spend out of doors in the beautiful little institution of which I had so lately become a part.

[3]

I obeyed an impulse most zoo visitors share of not spending much time at one cage but trying to see as many things as I could in my limited time. I was wholly unequipped by training for life in the zoo, even unprepared by experience for a real bookkeeping job. Circumstances had plunged me into a new world of business because of the necessity of supporting myself and a young son. And now I found myself in the world of science as well. It was fortunate that I discovered in the natural wild life about me the joy and inspiration that I did, otherwise the burden of the job I had undertaken surely would have been too great.

I had become convinced by indisputable evidence that anyone who worked in a zoo was automatically considered by the general public as an authority upon every scientific subject and that, in order to become a competent zoo worker, I must inform myself as rapidly as possible upon our own collection and allied creatures. Thus I might eventually learn to answer the telephone intelligently and at least a portion of the questions.

I knew, also, that I should have to learn much, especially about our own collection, from personal observation. Our library was then almost nonexistent. So from the very beginning of my employment in 1925 "knowing the animals" was an important though self-imposed part of my job.

There was another reason for becoming acquainted with the animals. I was sure that I should be a better bookkeeper if I should learn the needs of the creatures around which my staggering array of accounts were compiled. I felt I could make wiser purchases, more intelligently distribute the meager zoo funds and better evaluate the requirements of the entire organization if I knew all about the zoo. So day by day as I could, I,

[4]

who had never been more than a casual zoo visitor, wandered from cage to cage asking questions from the animal keepers, who were impressed with the curiosity of the new bookkeeper, as I found later. I watched, and studied, and tried to understand.

I do not quite remember the day when I stood and read the sign on the gibbon cage, which was: —

GIBBONS
Hylobates lar
Hylobates muelleri
EASTERN ASIA

If it had been more detailed and explicit, as I now try to make our signs, I doubt that it would have meant any more to me than it did. Anthropoid apes were something of which I had heard, of course, and in some dim way I had connected them with Darwin's theory of the Descent of Man, but that is all. I was instantly attracted to these thickly furred monkeys with their small black faces, closely enfolded in a soft fur ruff like an infant's hood. I kept planning to go to the library and borrow a good natural history from which to read about some of my favorite creatures. I thought of such a book lightly, as if it were an easy thing to find and use.

To my great joy I was beginning to find a great deal that was fine and uplifting in the surroundings and work of a zoo. I began to be ashamed of the half-joking manner in which I had approached my position of book-keeper there, and of the way in which I had reacted to the teasing of my friends when they heard of my appointment. Day by day, as the office job became less overpowering, I found more than relaxation in the few minutes I could afford to spend at the cages. Suddenly, without having realized it, I found myself drawn back again and again to some cages, where I would linger for longer periods than at others. The reasons for this attraction were varying. In some instances it was the reaction of the animals to me that made me return. In the case of the gibbons it was the physical beauty of the inhabitants. They were such sleek, well-clothed creatures! Their excellent health was plainly evident to my eyes, trained only by my association with farm animals and domestic pets. Neither then, early in my zoo life, nor since, after becoming the head of the staff with the responsibility of watching, studying and caring for the animals, have I ever lost the keen joy of just seeing a gibbon.

But among the things that interested me in this cage was why these two small monkeys should be housed here away from the others, instead of in the large group of monkey cages partly inhabited by all sorts of small and large carnivores. Right at the first I had taken this for granted. Later I put it down to the expediency that had prompted much of the placement of our small and somewhat helter-skelter display.

One of the gibbons was darker than the other and had white hands and feet. The soft little ruff around his face was light, also. The one with the white hands and feet was almost always high up on a narrow shelf in a back corner of the cage. The other moved about frequently and I seldom saw her in the same spot more than once. In my ignorance, I attached little significance to either fact.

As time went on, I made note of several facts, one the complete absence of tail and the extreme length of their arms and hands. Their faces were soft, dull black and they had very small ischial callosities, such as are

[6]

The Grace and Beauty
That Is a Gibbon

A Gift from Marquess Hachisuka

Mother and Baby Gibbon

Primo, Our Baby Gibbon,
Has Refreshments

present on the rumps of most small monkeys and baboons.

One day as I approached that cage, with no intention of stopping, the light-colored one, until then sitting on the floor, suddenly stood very erect and with her hands held high above her head ran toward me with incredible swiftness. She jumped up on an angle iron three feet off the floor of her cage with as little apparent effort as if she had been wound up and the spring had been suddenly released. Without pausing, she leaped backward and up to a bar several feet away, but she reached out with her hand and over it she went with one swing, her arm stretched at full length. This swing brought her nearly to the top of the fifteen-foot cage, where she stopped on a four-inch post supporting a bar without any effort or need to balance herself.

Nothing I had seen in the cage heretofore had prepared me for the grace, speed and precision of this act. In that one second I formed an opinion that I have never changed: that the most amazing thing about the gibbon is not the way it moves, but the way it stops. One second all was power and speed, the next a complete and sudden halt. Without seeming to exert herself to check the forward motion, the gibbon was completely relaxed and still. There had been no jerk or sway of body or limbs.

But I had yet more to learn of what this small, insignificant creature had to offer in the way of entertainment. I had been doing some reading, however, since the movement of the gibbon had intrigued me so greatly. I found that the gibbon, smallest of the anthropoid apes, is Asiatic in its origin; that it is a tree dweller entirely, coming to the ground only in case of emergency. It feeds upon the leaves of trees, fruits, and undoubtedly on birds' eggs and insects. It is widely distributed through the forests and jungles of Malay, Siam, up into Indo-China and islands strewn along the Asiatic Coast. Its arms are so long that they would easily drag upon the floor unless consciously held bent at wrists or elbows. I learned, too, that the gibbon is the only anthropoid which naturally walks erect, not on all fours. These gibbons vary greatly in color pattern, not only among the same species, but in the same individual during its growth to maturity.

Some of the published accounts spoke of the cry of the gibbons, especially as they travel in groups; but no words can adequately describe the song of a gibbon. And so again I had a thrill when I discovered quite by chance that the gibbon who swung and whirled so beautifully was also responsible for the ringing song I had been listening to many mornings on my way to work through the park. This song began with a few short, round notes swelling in volume until I knew a million strange, wild birds were singing in unison, but so resonant I could not locate the source.

One morning, arriving early, I walked out through the zoo before starting on my books. Gibby, as I now familiarly called her, sat in her favorite position on top of a round post. Her small, black face was lifted to the morning sky and her mouth was roundly open. She was singing her mating song, *Wau! Wau! Waaauuuu!* Faster and faster the notes poured out. She was entirely oblivious to my proximity. Her small stomach expanded and contracted rapidly like a bellows. Except for a slight quivering of her lips, her open mouth moved scarcely at all, as the ever-rising crescendo of sound came from her throat alone. But just as it reached its loudest, highest, fastest beat, the small brown body flew off the post out into space. Her hand only touching the top of the

[8]

lower bar, she leaped up high to a corner and back again; finally stopping with perfect precision as the last note fell, she leaped back on top of her post again. Not until she had launched her body into space, had her mate joined the chorus with a softer, clearer, more musical note, but actually nothing like the peal of music of the female.

Gibby seemed to take her singing with the air of a serious duty and visitors often considered it mournful. To me, gibbons in repose always look a little sad; their eyes are large, their faces wrinkled on each side of the nostrils and mouth. They are reported to live in family groups, which may join temporarily, during a forced trek for food, into a larger body which has no close adherence; for gibbons are not essentially gregarious. Living as they do in tree tops, both their feet and hands are grasping organs. Their long fingers can tightly clasp a fair-sized limb. I have never seen them lose a hold or slip off a bar once it is grasped. Their thumbs, far down on the side of the slender hand, look weak and lie close against it paralleling the fingers; an opposed, protruding thumb might catch a knot and be injured or retard progress. Their feet are as long and slender as their hands, the toes are almost as long as the fingers. And while they usually travel with their strong, well-developed arms, the feet can easily grasp a branch to furnish aid in moving. They seldom if ever carry anything in their hands, but use the feet instead, keeping the hands free for rapid motion in case of emergency. The great toe is placed far down on the inner side of the foot. It is wide, well-opposed and the nail is much flatter and broader than those on the fingers and other toes.

The bony structure of the gibbon reveals its relationship to the human being, especially in infancy. The head is very like that of a newborn child and, while it keeps

[9]

its round, full shape through life, it does not grow in proportion to the growth of the body, there is no forehead, and the brain of the adult is very small. The shape of the face, especially about the mouth and chin, is very like that of a diminutive human being.

I was greatly pleased the day Gibby first stretched out her hand to me in recognition of a familiar person. It was not just a begging gesture such as she gave to the general public. I rushed away to get something for her and here my study helped a little. I began to gather leaves for her and found that she was especially fond of the leaves and blossoms of the bougainvillea, and would gobble them greedily.

I was so delighted with my new friend that I failed to notice that high up in his perpetual corner, Billy, her cage-mate, never stirred, but watched with hungry eyes the food that Gibby received. When I did notice him one day, I went to that end of the cage, for I thought he was shy, and coaxed him to put out his hand. Darting fearful glances over his shoulder, he finally extended it. I imagined he was afraid of me, but suddenly a ball of brown fury struck him to the ground and together the two gibbons rolled over and over, silent but struggling fiercely. The fight lasted only a minute, but I was terribly frightened for I knew it was my fault; that I had tempted Billy beyond his power to resist. He alone had taken the punishment his past experiences led him to fear.

I was not yet accustomed to the sort of control exercised in an animal cage by the powerful, mentally or physically, against the weak, and to me the condition was horrible. I sought our foreman, Norman Johnson, and told him my experience.

"Yes," said he, "I think we ought to stop feeding in that cage. It often leads to fighting."

[10]

"How does he live?" I asked.

"Oh," said Norman, "we just give them so much food she is so busy that he gets all he wants and there is always some left. At night we feed them separately, and as long as no visitor tries to feed him, they are both all right. She loves him in her way and he is used to it, for they lived together several years before we bought them."

A sign prohibiting feeding was installed, but did not stop it. Several years passed and the situation became no better. Then our veterinarian decided that Billy should be protected in some way and that he could easily anesthetize Gibby and extract her long canine teeth. This program met with approval and Dr. Whiting and the keeper of the monkeys, Henry Newmeyer, went in to catch Gibby. Usually she would walk right up to Henry, but this morning apparently her intuition told her something was amiss, and she refused to come down. After everything else had failed, Henry took a net and tried to catch her in it. Up to this moment Billy had sat on his shelf, an interested spectator of the proceedings. He had thought perhaps Gibby was in for some treat she would not share with him and he was taking it philosophically. The net put an entirely different appearance on the matter. Suddenly, without warning, Billy entered the affair. He watched until Henry, in his efforts to net Gibby, was close to him — facing the other way. Then he dropped. Henry said he didn't know at first what hit him, nor that he had been hurt. He felt the shock of a heavy blow against his shoulder and it was gone. Blood spurted from his chest and neck where the two long, sharp canine teeth had slashed into his flesh, exceedingly deep and uncomfortably near the throat. Billy, high upon his corner shelf, looked down upon the havoc he had wrought. He had saved his overbearing mate at the sacrifice of his kind keeper. How human! I think my pity for Billy was well tempered with contempt after that, for I had a long way to go before I reached my present understanding of these near human creatures. At that time gibbons were still pretty much monkeys to me.

In spite of Gibby's overbearing manner to Billy we, at one period of her life with us, introduced two quite small siamangs into her cage. These two — christened Amos and Andy by the zoo men — were at the time of their arrival the only siamangs exhibited in America and so they were very precious to me. For several months they had been in a cage adjoining the one where Billy and Gibby were living. Gibby had reached her long, slender fingers through the wire netting and had touched them in a friendly fashion. The babies clung to each other constantly, apparently feeling very small and strange in this big, New World zoo, and I believe that something in their helpless baby whimpering and their dependence upon each other roused the mother instinct in Gibby.

Finally, by the simple process of removing the wire between the cages one night after they had been closed up, we turned them in together. It was rather laughable. We were all out to see them greet each other, but so accustomed were they to the division that it was several hours before they realized that they could do more than touch each other across the barrier that had been between them. Suddenly Gibby realized that she could swing and run much more freely than before, and as she entered the forbidden territory, both little siamangs scampered to the farthest corner.

Soon they realized that the intruder was none other than the kind gibbon who had been patting them through the fence, and they snuggled up close to her. I never saw her hold them or permit them really to cling to her, but they lost their dependence upon each other and would sit close to Gibby, sharing her food and learning from her how to enjoy the big cage. We felt sure there would be no danger from Billy that she could not handle. And we were correct. If possible, she exercised greater control over him than ever, for even when her canine teeth which we finally had removed were missing, she was his moral superior. He was never permitted to share her joy in the two black babies for she was extremely jealous of any attention he paid them. They lived there harmoniously until late in the fall of 1931, when we had to make way for the great gorilla cage and the space their cage occupied had to be used. The four gibbons were caught and placed in a fine, big cage for the small monkey group. There they fought each other and made trouble for us. They became very morose and we hurried the completion of a new gibbon cage which was also under construction. But long before we could move them into it, we found that first Billy and then one of the little siamangs was ill. Soon Billy died of a severe cold. The two siamangs did not long survive him. Only Gibby, the valiant and strong, was able to be shifted about from cage to cage; hating it as much as the others. But she had an unconquerable spirit which lasted until the end of her long life of fifteen years in our zoo, which was finally ended by a malignant growth in the colon.

Many zoos have had gibbons and have found, as we have here, that they are a most uncertain exhibit. Many times with everything in their favor they seem unable to survive; while again with little to comfort them, no skill in handling and poor food and accommodations, they live persistently. I am sure that the most amazing gibbon on record is the one in the Philadelphia Zoo which I believe was put, as a temporary measure at first, in a small corner cage in the reptile house. It was warm there. There were jungle scenes around him prepared as settings for tropical reptiles, into which the gibbon could look; he apparently found life cozy and perfectly satisfactory. When I made my first official visit to the Philadelphia Zoo, I noticed him with a little pity. The cage was separated from the rest of the house and, what is more important, from the public by a glass partition. He had shelves and bars; not much room to swing in, but apparently all that he wanted. He had at that time been there twenty-three years. I expected constantly to hear of his death, but he actually lived for something like thirty-one years, and established a record that will last perhaps for all time for longevity under conditions that most people would have considered impossible.

Following the deaths of Billy and the little siamangs in 1932, Gibby was the only representative of the smallest of the apes in our zoo for several years. She seemed happy enough without gibbon companionship, and yet the one comparatively small animal did look lonesome in the large cage. But our efforts to obtain another gibbon always failed, and so because, like the gibbon, they are fond of climbing and swinging through the trees, we finally put a spider monkey from South America in the cage. The differences and similarities between the two are amazing. Both are long-armed and agile climbers, but where every movement of a gibbon is filled with grace and beauty, the spider monkey is always funny, even when he is sad and lonely or ill. Except for his big, bloated abdomen and small round head, he is all angles, like the stick-man children draw. The coarse hair sticks out always in the wrong places. This little fellow had bandy legs and a tail too long for beauty, but just right for utility. He was as fast on his bars as the gibbon, but he sprawled, slipped and leaped wildly. He would step up to run along on the bar and at the next step, his whole body would drop to catch at the last possible second by the very end of his long prehensile tail. The spiders are noisy and full of quarrelsome good nature, all squealing and struggling together by tails, feet, hands, and teeth one minute, and the next hugging each other in a frenzy of affection. And this clown was the creature we put in the cage with Gibby, the lovely, singing, graceful aerialist. But strange to say, she liked him. She bullied him, loved him, raced around the cage with him and tormented him. She browbeat him about his food. But there was no cause to pity him for they were, to all intents and purposes, good, friendly companions.

I thought that the idea had been an excellent one until one day when, as Gibby was swinging back and forth across her cage on bamboo poles, the spider monkey, which had been squatting on a shelf, suddenly uncurled his tail from around his feet, stood up and, reaching out with his tail, dropped full length. Then, with no apparent effort, he swung his body up to grasp the pole with his hands. He swung along with his tail, hands and feet, grasping the bar with one after the other in no particular order. I stood there laughing at him and mentally contrasting his awkward antics with Gibby's grace. At the same time I admired his skill just as one admires that of the clown aerialist high up in the circus who is frequently the star. Suddenly I became conscious of a conversation going on beside me. One visitor said to another, "How do you suppose it happened? Poor thing!

It seems quite used to getting along without it." I turned to see what they were looking at. They, too, were staring at the queer cage-mates. Then one of the speakers turned to me and asked, "How did the other poor little fellow lose his tail?"

Just another idea that hadn't been so good. I changed the signs on the cage to be more explicit, but I always had a feeling that people were being confused by the queer combination, especially after one of the many fake explorers who periodically spring up around all zoos stood by the cage and told me he had seen spider monkeys and gibbons mating in Malaya and felt sure they interbreed frequently. He didn't seem to think it necessary to make an explanation of how the little American monkeys happened to be at liberty in large numbers on the wrong side of the Pacific Ocean.

Gibbons are not often in the animal market, especially on the Pacific Coast, and for years we had no opportunity to obtain any more suitable companion for Gibby. She was happy, however, never failing to sing her morning song. Her spider-monkey companion filled all her needs for companionship except in singing.

In 1936 we sent an expedition to the Orient ourselves. Dr. Wegeforth, President of our organization, and Mr. "Si" Perkins, our herpetologist, went together. All was excitement and anticipation. Return passage for the Pacific Coast is always difficult to arrange. Several times Mr. Perkins was disappointed but finally he was on the water, coming home. Dr. Wegeforth, having become ill, could not wait to return with him. "Si" air-mailed a long list of specimens so that I could get permits for entry and arrange quarantine, but of all the creatures on his long list of specimens, the item that excited me most was sixteen gibbons.

[16]

Ralph Virden, for many years our building superintendent in charge of maintenance, was working hard to get the cages ready, especially the fine, big new cages for the gibbons. In it the houses were so arranged that each gibbon would have a small sleeping room for himself. High bars of inch pipe criss-crossed the exhibition cage. On the intersections small platforms, such as gibbons love to sit upon, were in place. Little corner shelves would permit them to arrange themselves like ornaments on an old-fashioned whatnot. A tiny pool was ready for them and we could hardly wait until the sixteen gibbons would be turned into it. The cage was just the size of the gorilla cage — a fine, big, roomy place, crowning the hill where the anthropoid apes were housed.

When Mr. Perkins arrived, we had our first disappointment. Some of the gibbons had been put on the boat for him at Singapore. They had all been ill when they arrived at his point of embarkation, Surabaya. And so, although he hurriedly did what he could for them and kept them alive for several days, he had arrived with only nine gibbons and two siamangs. One of these was the most woebegone creature I have ever met. The skin was rubbed off her back and pulled off her arms and chest. She held tenderly in her arms an engaging, saucy young siamang, nearly grown, who, Mr. Perkins informed us, was her daughter. The old one's teeth were worn down to the gums, as many Oriental specimens' are, from gnawing on cocoanuts. She gazed out at us, her mouth drawn down, her eyes mournful.

Among the others were a mated pair of gray gibbons and an adult golden gibbon, the handsomest one I have ever seen. The rest were tiny things not more than two or three years old. All held out their arms to Mr. Perkins and, although he was ill and injured, he petted each one,

[17]

talked to it, and saw that it was properly fed before he left for home at nearly daybreak.

We were all tired, cold, but jubilant, when we too went home; but after breakfast and perhaps a bath, each hurried back to see how the new treasures looked by daylight. I drove into the zoo through the main gate and thought I would make a circle past the monkey cages. Stopping a second at our new gibbon cage, in which Gibby was already much at home, in my mind's eye I saw the bars filled with our new gibbons, eleven of them. As I stopped, Gibby, high on the topmost shelf, raised her face, and, opening her mouth, began her morning song. Up it rose in the accustomed crescendo and, with the loudest, highest note she was off in her wild swing through the cage.

Suddenly, almost in midair, she paused and, swinging up to the bar, cocked her head and listened. High and clear, from the hill off to the south where the hospital stands, there came an answering cry. One of the new gibbons had heard her song over the tops of the tall eucalyptus trees and was calling to her. Gibby sang again, just a few sharp experimental notes. Louder came back the answering song. Gibby could not believe her ears. She had been in her cage with that chattering imbecile of a spider monkey, silent or whimpering, so long she must have thought she was the last gibbon in the world. Once more she sang, then paused to make sure of the response, which grew louder and louder, as though other gibbons were joining the first. Gibby was silent, but off she went into the air in such a rush of action as I have never seen her equal. Around and up and down; finally stopping at last on the highest shelf in the corner of the cage, closest to the spot whence the sound had come, she turned her face to the hospital and sang and

[18]

sang, never pausing to hear an answer. Her song was not to the morning light and sunshine, but to her own across the forests that separated her from them.

You can imagine our eagerness to see her with them all, but to our amazement, when we put them in the cage with her, her terror knew no bounds. She rushed at the newcomers, biting and striking like a released fury. It was undoubtedly an act of defense, but whatever its nature, the newcomers retired, slashed and bleeding, and later refused to return to the cage with such a fury.

Gibby did not like any one of the new gibbons; she emerged from self-induced battle with several cuts and a bad opinion of her own kind generally. It was, I suppose, the first time in her career in captivity that anyone ever talked back to her. The little black siamangs had bowed to her maturity and had possibly appealed to her sense of protection. The supine Billy had never dared oppose her, but when she threatened he fled in shrinking terror, and so for the four years that I saw them together, he never suffered real injury from her.

Both she and the gibbons she had attacked had to go to the hospital for repairs. Gibby, always difficult to catch since the time we had pulled her teeth, now at last came to us willingly, her hands held out as though for help. She was brought back from the hospital as soon as her cuts, all of which were superficial, were cared for. But Gibby remained hidden within the sleeping room she had chosen because none of the new gibbons remaining in the cage would enter it. There she permitted us to pet and comfort her. I shall never forget how she whimpered her meek little song to me there in the deep shadows when each morning I went in to see her. She preferred any sort of company to that of gibbons of any species. When finally she did venture timidly out into the big cage her obvious fear of the other gibbons made her an easy victim of their attack. After a fair trial at the combination Gibby was taken out of that cage forever, and her first victims were returned to the group.

The days of Gibby had gone on here in the zoo fifteen years when the veterinarian came in one day and said, "That old gibbon is really sick. She has some sort of growth in the rectum and apparently it is of a malignant nature. She suffers a good deal with it and there are other abscesses which seem secondary, but I cannot tell the nature of the trouble just yet." The end came rather abruptly, for he soon determined that there was little that could be done for Gibby and so she went to sleep.

CHAPTER II

Amos and Andy; Old Mom and Blackie

THE pleasure I found in Gibby and even the less responsive Billy roused in me the desire for more gibbons. In fact, looking back upon my first years in the zoo I realize that I was always wanting something until finally I became reconciled to receive and exhibit the specimens the public most wanted and that fitted best with our methods and type of exhibit. If I had been given free rein at selecting specimens I would probably have had few well-rounded groups and a great helter-skelter exhibit of unrelated specimens. But in those first years I was sure nothing would make me completely happy but a few additional gibbons, and especially some of the second of the gibbon families, the siamangs.

Siamangs are always jet black and are reported to be numerous in the forests of Sumatra. Their hair is long and silky. They have strange pouches beneath their chins which, connected by small openings into the larynx, can be distended to the size of a soft baseball when the animal is excited. When he howls or when he wishes to groom or clean the wrinkled skin which makes up the outer surface of this sac, he inflates it with air from the trachea.

The living habits of the siamangs are much the same as those of the family of *Hylobates* with whom they oc-

[21]

cupy overlapping territories. Siamangs are much larger than the ordinary gibbon, being somewhat like tiny chimpanzees in form and appearance. Their habits and activities are typical of the gibbon. They are rarely shown in zoos, and I longed to see some. I was ecstatically happy, therefore, when, in 1928, a returning collector brought us two youngsters possibly a year and a half old.

They were so jet black that one of the boys in the monkey yard immediately dubbed them the Gold Dust Twins, but eventually they became known permanently as Amos and Andy. Neither at the time of their arrival nor later was I ever able to tell them apart, and apparently they never learned to distinguish their names, for both, so far as I could tell, answered to either name.

They sat facing each other with their arms clasped. If one moved a few steps, the other also ran to that spot. When they ate, each unclasped one arm but they remained sitting side by side with the inner arm clasping the little mate. As soon as the meal was over, they immediately turned their little faces together again and cuddled down in each other's arms. It was my first experience with any baby gibbons and I did not realize that they should still have been with their mothers. They did not need to be held constantly, but to have the comforting warmth of a mother's body against which to press their little stomachs, and her thick fur coat into which to twine their baby fingers when they felt very small and tired and alone. Apparently each feared to let the other one out of arm's reach lest he completely disappear.

The complete dependence upon each other and their pathetic clinging lasted until they became inmates of the cage occupied by Billy and Gibby. Then they adopted Gibby as their somewhat aloof and impersonal fostermother and became independent creatures developing along fairly normal lines.

These two tiny siamangs made only the slight whimpering sounds that all baby gibbons make. It is a quivering little noise, as though they fear to release the great volume of music they hold in their throats. I found them quite as docile as anyone would wish a gibbon to be. I wooed their confidence by imitating their own baby noises, which from their response to me might have been the way their mother called them. After they had been in the zoo a week or two, they would stand up at my first quavering "*woooo-oo*" and run as fast as their little legs could fly, straight to me. I fed them gruel when the men were busy and they ate politely out of the spoon, taking bites turn and turn about. We fed them cereals, baked potatoes, bananas and leafy vegetables, with bread and milk. As they grew older, we saw them catch spiders and bugs and we found they would accept meal worms.

Their little throat pouches, of which I had heard, were never extended, but the areas under their tiny chins were wrinkled like deflated balloons. They were probably a little less than two years old when they arrived, and had been here nearly two years before I ever saw these pouches fully distended. To accomplish this they put up their little chins and injected air into the laryngeal sac until it looked like a small black-rubber football. They would scratch this distended surface and then permit it to become deflated again. I always hoped vainly that this might be the beginning of a song.

One day, while I was across the wide canyon that separated the monkey mesa from the elephant corral, I heard the gray gibbons begin to sing. The two little siamangs had been put in a big cage adjoining the one

[23]

which housed Gibby and her mate, Billy. Suddenly, as Gibby sang, Billy joined in. Then I heard a most peculiar sound: a harsh note mingled with a deep bark like that of a large excited dog. It was a strange jumble of sounds that even yet — after all the years I have heard it — I am unable to describe clearly. I rushed back to the monkey cage and could see the two little black gibbons up on a shelf in the corner of their cage, sitting very close together, their faces toward each other, chins up, sacs extended, barking and whooping together in queer medley. Gibby had stopped her own song to hear them, but so absorbed were they in the grand song they were singing that they were not conscious of her silence. My coming, alas, did attract their attention. Their chins drooped — yes, gibbons do have chins; their sacs shriveled into oblivion, and the two of them dropped off their shelves and ran toward me, arms outstretched.

This was my experience time after time, and so I never really did get to hear their song and watch the performance. Whenever I approached them they seemed to feel that I wished to stop the noise. Other gibbons we have since owned glance at me and go on with their caroling, but this business of singing on two keys at once was a serious affair requiring the entire attention of one small gibbon to keep it at a maximum of decency.

Amos and Andy did not live long enough to satisfy my curiosity about their song making for, as I have said, they and the hapless Billy succumbed to the difficulties of life in the zoo, leaving the solitary Gibby to carry on the traditions of the gibbon family. You can realize how glad I was that included in the big shipment that Mr. Perkins brought back from India, in 1936, we had two siamangs.

They were perhaps the most spectacular of all his gibbons. To our great regret, they were not a pair but an aged mother and a grown young daughter. I have never seen a more wilful child or a more abjectly patient mother. Old Mom became her name at once, for that is the favorite zoo name at San Diego for any old female animal with grown children. I suppose the name originally became popular through the stories of Old Mom, the famous circus elephant who was a character known to every man who came to work at the zoo via the circus.

Poor Old Mom! She was the largest gibbon I have ever seen. Stooping down to peer into the box, I was convinced that she was as large as a small chimpanzee. Her straggling forelocks hung over her forehead in a discouraged fashion. She had been in the crate so long, bracing herself against the rough seas, that she feared to stand erect without something to hold to. Her posture was a crouch with bent knees which made her body seem out of all proportion to her short legs. The hair on her chest and stomach was short, smooth and thick, and that on her back was completely worn off in spots.

She kept up a constant moaning and each time I approached her, I was reminded of a dear old colored maid who whined just that way, and I wondered if Old Mom didn't have what Rascoe used to call the "misery." Mom seemed to feel that she and I were kindred spirits and would wail louder and louder as I drew nearer, especially with offerings of food.

We found almost at once that she could not be fitted into the cage with the other gibbons until she was in better health. So we took her out of the cage and moved her back to the hospital. She had some difficulty eating because of her teeth, worn as they were from opening cocoanuts. She would scrape at carrots and apples with the stumps and then put them down, terribly discouraged. She missed her daughter. So Blackie was moved up to stay with her. She suffered from dysentery and finally Dr. Wegeforth suggested a little paregoric. The effect was magical. She began to improve and before long was eating greedily. Almost every day I visited her with a small offering of some food, which she accepted and soon came to expect.

She was, I am sure, the saddest creature I have ever known, and the high spirits of her daughter, Blackie, were the greatest contrast imaginable. Blackie was extremely fond of Mr. Perkins, who had cultivated her friendship all the time he had been detained in Surabaya awaiting transportation home. He also paid them much attention after they arrived here. When he would go into the cage with them, Old Mom would welcome him by holding out her hand. But when Blackie saw him open the door, she would rush to the top of the cage, swinging full length with her arms, kicking and grabbing at him with her feet in the way that gibbons often fight. She was rough-and-tumble, pulling hair, strangling him by clasping both feet about his throat. The more roughly he battled with her, the better she liked it. At times he had a difficult time getting away from her, but with all her roughness she played fair and never bit. Now and then she would open her mouth as though to take hold of him, as most young animals do, but one cross word was sufficient to change her mind.

When I began to make friends with her, Blackie thought she could rough me up as she did Mr. Perkins. So I never entered the cage until she had become accustomed to holding my hand or letting me rub her stomach or back without any rough stuff. Then a few times I went in and held her in my arms and tried to make her a gentle pet. Blackie, however, was not a ladylike gibbon. She was all tomboy, and if she could not bat me around and pull down my long hair and smash my glasses, according to her standards we just were not playing.

At times I became very impatient with both gibbons because of the mother's self-sacrificing character. I would go to a good deal of trouble to bring something that Mom needed and then Blackie would gobble her share and reach over and take Mom's away from her. Because of the difficulty she experienced in eating, which made it slow, there was always the greater share of hers lost. I often took them eggs, especially if I could rob a bantam's nest without being caught. Mom loved eggs and ate them carefully by breaking a small, neat hole, not spilling a drop. Blackie broke hers carelessly and drank them down, letting much escape on the floor or shelf. Then she would grab her mother's and drink it from the neat little hole.

Finally, Mom and Blackie went back to the big gibbon cage and fitted in fairly well. I was to hear plenty of siamang singing now that I had acquired two adults. But even after hearing the small Amos and Andy make their infantile attempts at siamang vocalizing, I was totally unprepared for the lack of harmony and their peculiarities of conduct during their choral offerings. Crowded together, facing each other, as the former babies used to sit, the two large gibbons filled the twenty-inch–square perch completely. Their faces held close together, their mouths on a level, their chins raised and their laryngeal pouches widely extended and inflated they uttered first the high note, then the low muffled one. Drowned out now was the old gibbon chorus of the million wild birds singing. Their first medley of sound grew in volume until you were sure that a large, assorted pack of hounds was baying in unison.

I was always drawn to the cage when I heard them begin, and if the gibbons, especially siamangs, are vocalizing you cannot fail to hear them. People rush from every part of the zoo as they run after a fire siren, and I have never become so familiar with it that I can resist the temptation if I am near. Like the baby siamangs we first exhibited, these two mature specimens take their caroling seriously; and strange to say, the other gibbons also show them proper respect; when Mom and Blackie start yodeling, the others in the cage huddle down in corners or on shelves at the farthest end. As their vocalization gains in volume, all sounds in the cage are hushed. The other gibbons, with the exception of our old female Gibby, have never sung with the siamangs, although the two black gibbons have never left their seats or threatened the others as far as I can ascertain.

When Mom and Blackie were put back into the big cage again, there were nine other gibbons there in one big group. Among them were four tiny fellows still in the whimpering stage — if they opened their mouths to sing. When the adult gibbons started singing, these babies would, with the first note, rush together and huddle down in a pile, their arms encircling each other's small bodies, holding them in a compact little group. When the old gray gibbons would finish their song and swing wildly out into space, these four tiny ones would cower down as though they knew they had no place in this adult orgy. But as Old Mom got over the nostalgia from which she apparently suffered on her arrival, she and her daughter became the prima donnas of the chorus and gradually even the loudest singers recognized their own inadequacy and hushed their voices as though they,

[28]

like ourselves, could not believe that such a raucous medley of bass, alto and high soprano could possibly come from one pair of throats, even augmented by the extensile gular sacs.

At first I could think of nothing to which I could liken this noise, or the serious attitude and complete absorption of the singers in what they were doing. Finally after several weeks I recalled the memory I had been striving for. In my girlhood, my first schoolteaching was in a small Indian school in the mountains of my home county. At our mountain dances, we had a one-man orchestra in the person of a large and talented Indian. This man, by means of mechanical devices, played a mouth organ supported by a frame over his shoulders, while with his feet he beat loudly and constantly upon a deep-voiced drum. His hands were not idle for while he thus played the air and beat out the rhythm for us to dance by, he managed a harmonious, if a little monotonous, accompaniment to his solo parts upon a guitar or banjo loudly strummed with steel hooks attached to each finger and thumb. His absorption, his serious hard work and something of the medley of sounds was not unlike the combination of many of the tones produced by the hardworking gibbons.

Sometimes I decide that there is no subject completely finished as long as you work in a zoo, for every day is a new one of learning and experience. One day, after I had written all I knew about the song of the siamang and the manuscript had already gone to the publisher, one of the most interesting and inspiring experiences of my life occurred. And so the book had to be opened, and a page inserted, especially about Blackie and her strange vocalizing.

Standing by the gibbon cage one early morning, talk-

[29]

ing to the primate keeper about some aggravating colds among the anthropoid apes, I turned in time to see Nelson Eddy, the singer, standing almost beside me. Since there were few persons in the grounds I spoke to him and invited him inside the guard fence to have a closer look at my friends.

We walked slowly down the line of giant cages toward the gorillas but just as we reached the gorilla cage the gibbons in the first cage burst into their morning song. Without a word Mr. Eddy and I turned and hastened in that direction. With the rare understanding we find now and then among strangers to the zoo, Mr. Eddy made no rush toward the cage, but kept back close to the guard fence some twelve feet away and moved so silently that he did not disturb the singers or attract their attention in any way.

He was entranced, as most people are, by the volume and sweetness of the gibbons' clear notes and then we spoke quietly of the peculiar combination of sounds produced by Blackie who, with her pouch roundly expanded, raised her chin and barked and boomed at the same time. Mr. Eddy was one of the few persons I have met who saw nothing funny or doleful in the performance but accepted it as an interesting and habitual combination of sounds for which nature had fitted the gibbon. As he spoke of the resonant booming I realized I was listening to an expert on vocalization and tone control, for Mr. Eddy explained that she actually made only one type of sound which she first emitted through her opened mouth, then forced through the stretched skin of the laryngeal pouch. This had a tendency to muffle and deepen the sound and at the same time to give it the resonance associated with such instruments as the drum. Then Nelson Eddy, with a complete lack of self-consciousness that was both boyish and charming, inflated his cheeks and boomed, then opened his mouth with the barking sound; an excellent imitation of the combination of sounds of the siamang.

I am not judging the perfection of his performance by my own standard, however, for Blackie stopped her song and looked in every direction, cocking her head first one way and then the other, every sense alert. For the imitation, like the original siamang cry, seemed to fill the air rather than to come from any definite source. And then once more Blackie sang ecstatically and listened, and Mr. Eddy answered her. So, between them both, Mr. Eddy and my beautiful Blackie, I had the chance to hear, not the lonely chorus of one single siamang, but the full conception of the cry, and the call and answer as it should be made.

Now I must confess that following Mr. Eddy's directions, I am practising and do manage a feeble imitation to which Blackie has been very kind, for she now and then stops a second to give me a chance to be heard. Needless to say, Mr. Eddy did not stop with Blackie's song, but imitated also the full round bugle tones of the other gibbons. They, like Blackie, appreciated that they were listening to the work of a master and after a few minutes of silence they threw themselves with all their might into their efforts at singing, and Mr. Eddy, accepting the fact that they, too, were masters of the art of gibbon caroling, stood with me, enjoying such a chorus as the zoo seldom hears.

One by one most of the gibbons had to be moved out of the cage or were disposed of. Finally only Mom and Blackie and the four babies were left. Blackie in turn teased and roughhoused them. She tantalized old

[31]

Mom until the poor creature would stay in her house for hours, dreading the rough-and-tumble play of the rampant youngster, who was by now fully as large, if not as heavy, as her mother.

I had continued my efforts to help in the rehabilitation of Mom and long after all of the others had forgotten to bring her delicacies or give her special attention, she seemed to watch for my coming from her favorite seat high in the southwest corner of her cage. If I appeared to be driving by without stopping, she would set up such a wail that the whole primate mesa could hear it. And if I stopped and walked inside the guard fence surrounding the cage, she would climb down and, her long arms limp at her sides or waving about her head, shuffle toward me uttering her most mournful and eerie cries. People hearing her always laughed or thought Mom was angry or afraid until they would see her stretch her long arms out to clasp them around any part of my body she could reach. I tried always to have something in my pocket or in my car for her, which she remained always willing to share with greedy and curious Blackie. Her own eager wail of joy at seeing me was that of an adoring chum. She wanted my attention and my petting. Her teeth barely showed above the gums; her lower jaw protruded far past the upper jaw like that of some old witch. Her chin almost touched her flat nose when she closed her toothless jaws. Old Mom, funny to everyone else, was as pathetic and pitiful an old crone as ever I have seen.

No matter how much fighting there was in the gibbon cage, and gibbons do not live harmoniously in large groups, none of the others ever had trouble with Old Mom. They knew she was old and helpless, and even when Blackie, who was not averse to starting a quarrel, would run to her mother's arms for comfort and protection, the others never molested the old gibbon.

Blackie was the only one I ever saw really abuse her, although the others finally followed Blackie's lead in grabbing food out of the poor old creature's hands. She would sit and gnaw with her stumps of teeth upon carrot or dry bread while all the choice bits went to the more agile ones. Even when we fed her by hand and inside the house, she would not try to protect herself.

After four years in the zoo, Old Mom again began to show signs of failing health; her coat of hair, which was never very good, became thin and short, with no luster at all; she lost weight and the old dysentery returned, and it seemed impossible to check. She seemed to fear the other gibbons, even her own daughter, more and more, and refused to leave her room. Alone she was even more unhappy and, in our attempt to do everything we could for her, we put her in a group of new gibbon youngsters which had just arrived from Java. We hoped she might become interested in them, but Mom was past being interested in anything except her own misery. She wailed at me, but did not want me to give her food, just to rub her chest and let her hold on to me. Finally the poor old thing was taken to the hospital for more intensive medical treatment, provided we could find what ailed her. And there we had to make the always difficult decision that nothing could be done for "Old Mom" but let her go quietly and easily to sleep.

During the last two years of Mom's life, Blackie seemed to have lost any filial affection. But when we took Mom out of the cage, Blackie, who was really adult, became suddenly much more sedate than she had ever been. She sings almost daily and even though alone, her mixed chorus still confounds us with its volume and dissonance. But she has lost some of the stimulation she seemed to receive from association with another of her family.

She has been famous for several years as the Flying Gray Ghost, a name she earned by her remarkable performance when, dressed in a sack, she flung herself madly through the air, chasing the small gibbons who fled through the cage in apparent terror. The terror, however, I am firmly convinced, was largely assumed or imaginary; for just as I can remember my own delightful childish nervous chills when I was being chased by some of the older girls and boys, pretending to be mysterious monsters, and my real fear being that they would not catch me, so have the other smaller gibbons in the cage seemed to pretend to fear Blackie as the Gray Ghost until at times their fear became almost actual.

The Gray Ghost play, which started quite by accident, went on for several years. It was always good to draw a large crowd of shouting, laughing zoo visitors. The little gibbons seemed to know how much fun they were giving others, for the larger and noisier the crowd the wilder and faster became the play, and the more daring and longer the flying leaps of the Gray Ghost as she swung about the open spaces in the cage from pole to bar, her arms extended through small holes in the sack, her head completely covered and just the tips of her long toes visible below the open end. We never understood how she kept her perfect direction and precision, for she never missed a bar or pole in even the wildest of the swings. The weight of the sack, which was considerable, seemed no handicap, as she was always equal to producing the extra power required to carry her with her accustomed speed over any distance.

This particular game seemed to bring out the most of Blackie's histrionic talents, and her pleasure in them. Sometimes at the loudest burst of laughter, she would swing to the top of one of the vertical poles and, whirling rapidly, slip from the top of the cage down to the floor; lying flat she might hesitate a second, looking precisely like a bundle of old sacks; then lifting the bottom of the sack she would peer out at her audience satisfied, as though called to the footlights for a bow. Then back she would duck into her ghost disguise and on with the game. But after a time the gibbons themselves seemed to grow tired of the play. The smaller ones were growing up and could no longer pretend to be afraid of a Gray Ghost that all knew too well was only their rough-and-tumble Blackie dressed in a sack with the corners cut out. I personally had begun to feel that Blackie took advantage of the play to handle her cage-mates with a roughness that was intended to hurt. They appeared to realize that she was taking advantage of them, also, and after one or two especially mean tricks the others ganged up on her and repaid her in kind. So we had trouble in the gibbon cage. Finally, after one or two Ghost plays ended in a free-for-all fight as children's pillow fights are apt to do, we ceased to provide the costume and the game came to an end.

Our problem after the death of Old Mom had become to provide a suitable mate for Blackie. We have had orders for male siamangs on file with several dealers for a period of three years. One tiny male was brought in for us. He was suffering from a severe cold on arrival. The cold progressed into pneumonia within a day or two and proved fatal. He was here only long enough to arouse our sympathy for his forlorn baby misery. Blackie doesn't know how near she came to having a playmate of her own species. On two recent trips to the Orient we have intended to bring back a male siamang without being able to do so.

But if there is any human heart in which hope springs eternal, it surely is that of a zoo director; so every time we send a collector out into the field I warn him that he must not dare to return and face me and Blackie without a suitor for her hand. Blackie is now just in her magnificent prime, the sturdiest, glossiest, longest-haired and most beautiful gibbon I have ever seen. She gives every promise of living long and furnishing plenty of entertainment for the visitors, providing exercise and diversion for such of her cage-mates as can continue to live in peace with her in the once haunted territory of the old Gray Ghost.

CHAPTER III

The Family Life of Gibbons

As I have said, we built a huge gibbon cage with high hopes of keeping a large and varied collection of gibbons of different sizes and ages in it. But upon bringing over a collection of eleven, made up of three species, we found at once that gibbons are creatures with established habits that cannot be trifled with. Even in captivity, they were determined to live in small family groups the way their ancestors had done. Perhaps the modern prototype of the fabled ancient Amazons is the adult female gibbon, the most jealous and domineering female in the world. Her mate is her own possession; she refuses to share his slightest attention with any other creature, and he is abject in his obedience to her will. Billy, while not the same species of gibbon as our famous Gibby, nevertheless was Gibby's mate, whether through voluntary selection or circumstances, and he never ventured either to assert his independence in the slightest degree or pay the least attention to any other creature within the zoo.

The first difficulty in our big group came, as we realized within a few days, because among them we had a true mated pair of gray gibbons. These two caused several hideous fights which left themselves and others torn and bleeding. A gibbon fight is so fierce and sudden that it cannot be anticipated or stopped as such trouble can in any other group of animals in the zoo. When we finally were able to net the two partners and move them out into another smaller cage, we found that the real cause of trouble had, temporarily at least, been removed.

The names of animals in the zoo seem to spring up from nowhere. Suddenly we were calling the male of this pair "Harry." Harry and his nameless mate were really devoted, spending much of their time sitting close together, swinging wildly through the bars together, singing their songs and copulating often. After we realized their devotion to each other we hoped that they might in time have young. When more than a year had passed with no sign of the approach of a blessed event we decided to experiment. So we caught the female and placed her temporarily in a hospital cage and put our mature Gibby in the cage with the male. They were of the same species, and Gibby and Harry's true nameless mate were also almost identical in coloring. But Harry would not go near Gibby. So far as we could see they never sat any closer together than the size of the cage made necessary. Neither sang or enjoyed food in the presence of the other and since Gibby, already getting old and sensitive to cold, retired almost as soon as the sun went down, Harry refused to go into the sleeping quarters at all. He sat, knees drawn up, arms wrapped around them and his head buried on his knees, a round, egg-shaped bundle out in rain and cold.

This combination of animals seeming so completely hopeless, we decided to make at least two of them happy by putting the true pair together; and so late in the spring we took Gibby away and again gave Harry the mate whom presumably he had chosen either from the large number brought into the Surabaya Zoo or in the jungles of Java before they were captured.

And it was to this pair within a few weeks of this

reunion that Primo, our precious baby gibbon, was born. Our surprise was complete. Not one of us had suspected such an event was approaching, and had rather attributed the female gibbon's depressed and poor condition to the fact that she had been separated from Harry rather than to any physical reason. Perhaps if we had known the birth was so imminent we would have made a fatal mistake by separating them again. But since they were together when the young was born, had shared in the rites of birth, and since the father was obviously so genuinely interested and happy over the birth of his son, we decided to be very watchful rather than suddenly to remove the baby from the cage. And so the baby grew and learned all the lessons of gibbon lore possible in captivity from both parents. His mother early shared the care with the father and permitted the father to play with his son and teach him the necessary gibbon tricks. Primo swung from the top of the cage when he was very young, and frequently the father would approach the mother and child as the baby was swinging just above her head, ready at any time to put his little clinging feet upon her head and shoulders for support. Taking hold of the legs or slender body, Harry would swing and pull his son, testing the grasping power of those fragile-looking hands. Sometimes he even went so far as to frighten Primo with a sudden jerk. This usually resulted in a real show of temper and the little fellow would kick at his father, striking out with his little feet straight at his father's face, squeaking and whining to the mother for help.

Unless the play was too prolonged she paid no attention, for this part of the infant's training seemed to be the father's duty, although I never saw him carry the baby.

The perfect harmony between these two mated gibbons convinced me that it was the difference in species and lack of real understanding which made Gibby such an abusive cage-mate to the patient Billy. For even after the baby was large enough to be completely weaned and thus shared the family meals, neither Harry nor Primo's mother ever showed any sign of resenting anything that Primo took or was fed as a special treat by the members of the zoo staff. Primo was so sure of his own place in the family and his parents' complete absorption in him that he would many times reach up and take bites almost out of the very mouth of either father or mother. He never was hurt by either parent, and his prowess in making his first complete journey across the cage was a memorable event to his parents as well as to us.

His father had been very hostile to me, which I had perhaps wrongfully attributed to the fact that he had gashed my finger badly and felt that I feared and disliked him. But as time went on we realized he was a very queer gibbon and that whenever a woman visitor to the zoo would pay any attention to him he would talk to her in soft little chirping notes, grimace at her cordially and do everything in his power to entice her within reach of his long arms. His attentions to me were just the same as toward others. People always exclaimed at his affection for me, but I had learned from several experiences which came after my first encounter that his blandishments were no sign of friendly interest. I had seen him chirp to a lady, and then turn and peer at her roguishly from between his legs, coaxing her with a sex display that she did not recognize, close enough either to turn and catch her or her clothes, or spray her with urine if she could not be reached otherwise. Two or three very unhappy experiences in close proximity to

Harry's cage made me very careful never to pause there even to show off the baby gibbon. Once when a friend stood close, admiring the beautiful family group, I warned her several times not to approach too near.

"Oh, he is so sweet and friendly," she said. "I am not afraid of gibbons."

The words were scarcely out of her mouth when one clutch of his strong hand pulled almost the entire bunch of lovely flowers off her new spring hat.

It was difficult to translate his overtures, which appeared so friendly, into menacing gestures, and at times even I relaxed my vigilance. But one creature which had no delusions as to the character of Harry was Ngagi, one of our gorillas. Ngagi apparently saw through his attempts to attract us with his friendly actions.

Once, as I walked in the narrow aisle between the gorilla cage and the one containing the gibbon family, Harry leaped about ten feet across the cage and dropped from above to thrust his arm through the wire and grab and tear the lace off my sleeve. Another time he snatched a few strands of hair, pulling it viciously. But never again did he threaten me without my being warned. Each time he started to strike, Ngagi would rush at that side of the cage, grunting in his most threatening manner. Harry did not mistake the menace in the deep-throated gorilla sound, and I have seen him hesitate and swing away from the wire more than once when Ngagi rushed to my defense. I felt that if he could have come to grips with the agile gibbon he would have torn him to pieces in order to protect me. Otherwise I have never seen the gorillas pay the slightest attention to the gibbon except on the occasion of the baby's birth. Then Ngagi was most interested and spent the afternoon watching the family group next door.

[41]

We thought for some time that it was women only whom Harry hated so intensely, but he has also struck several of the men although he had permitted Moore to enter the cage freely and made no attempt to snatch or injure him. For weeks and weeks he had permitted Emily De Konza, our technician at the hospital, to feed him from her hands. I had warned her, but Emily is one of those rare people who apparently have absolutely no fear of injury and who believe implicitly animals will not hurt them. This feeling has no real foundation in fact, however, for wild animals are wild animals and people must understand that sometimes elements over which neither the animal nor the person has any control enter into the situation. At times animals, even the gentlest of wild creatures, do not want to be handled, and such moods are to the cautious and careful animal keeper evident and unmistakable. Unfortunately, many times trainers must do their work no matter what mood the creature is in, but in zoos it is never necessary to take any real chance with an irritated and hostile animal for safety devices are always supplied for all such emergencies. After, as I say, Harry had encouraged Emily with his friendly advances until she felt sure our warning was founded in misunderstanding, she entered his cage. He came toward her, whining, his hands extended in his usual manner. Suddenly, without warning, he sprang upon her, lacerating her hands and the muscles of the abdomen extensively, so that many stitches were required, and barely failing to enter the abdominal cavity, which might have been of serious consequence. If help had not been handy he might have easily injured her critically, for because of his exceedingly long canines, and strong hands and feet, it was impossible for her to free herself.

* * *

Our little gibbon was the first to be born — in 1938 — and live for any length of time in an American collection. The birth of Primo and the success we were having in exhibiting a comparatively large collection of gibbons in out-of-door surroundings stimulated interest among zoos. Many of them began acquiring gibbons in larger numbers and insisting upon pairs. Scientific institutions have been striving to arrange an expedition into gibbon territory for more extensive observation than has ever been made before. Soon after the arrival of our large group in 1936, a formidable group of men representing leading institutions made a joint expedition. The field work was undertaken in the heart of the gibbon country in Northern Thailand (Siam) where gibbons were not too much encroached upon by civilization.

Groups of gibbons were located in suitable areas and then carefully studied from well-placed blinds or shelters through powerful glasses. Still and motion pictures to confirm his records and to provide further material for study were also made by the observer. And more important, one by one the groups he was noting were collected in their entirety so that sex, size and relationship as observed might be submitted to further proof and examination.

My pleasure in talking with two of these men and in comparing our gibbon family in the zoo with gibbon families observed in the wild has been very great. Dr. Harold J. Coolidge, Jr., and Dr. C. R. Carpenter, have visited our collection since and have found much of interest and value to add to their field work. My own background for success with a gibbon group has increased immeasurably and we hope greatly that one more chance at raising a baby gibbon will be given us.

The many papers which have been published as a result of this expedition have given to those who are interested a picture of this tiny anthropoid which is perhaps the most complete study ever made of any single species in the wild. This was the first time that comparative study of the social behavior of a given species has not lagged far behind comparative anatomical study, and thus forms a new and, from the standpoint of man's development, most valuable basis of study.

But it is the careful observation as recorded and published by Dr. C. R. Carpenter which has given to scientist and layman alike a fascinating story of family life that he saw over a period of weeks; and weeks of the most intense observational study. His ability to interpret what he saw into life history was proven by the analysis of the groups which were collected for study. If his findings are used by zoos in preparing gibbon exhibits it will become possible, no doubt, not only to exhibit interesting groups of these fascinating creatures but to have them develop into small units of families such as he observed in the wilds of Thailand.

After talking with him and reading his reports I can readily understand our own mistake in keeping large, mixed groups of individuals together in a limited space, for in the wild each individual family has a large area of several thousand acres. This territory, with its fruit and other food upon which gibbons live, is respected by other gibbons as a private domain. There the one family follows the same trails through the tops of the trees day by day as accurately as the gorillas follow the tunnels. Gradually Dr. Carpenter was able to see and distinguish the network of paths through the tree tops by the worn branches, which each gibbon grasped with his hand as he passed. He saw the mothers — cautiously proceeding at a slightly slower pace, hampered by the clinging arms of their children — follow their mates and the juveniles of the group. Always the small group seemed to be made up of the father, the mother and the children of various ages, up to a size that would indicate young maturity. Once or twice he discovered a young male living on the edges of two such family groups, too old and mature to live longer in the family to which he had been born, yet loath to sever himself completely from all connection with it, endeavoring, apparently, to enter also into some sort of relationship with another group.

As I read this interesting account I was reminded of some of the stories of ancient times and Bible days when the oldest born son of the family went off into the world to seek his fortune and find himself a mate, and establish, perhaps in very close proximity to the territory in which he had been born, his future domain. For thus does the young gibbon establish his own pathway through the tree tops, his own food trees and sleeping tree, with its well-protected crotches in which he can form himself into the compact ovoid shape in which gibbons sleep, and finally bring forth in the jungle another gibbon group.

I have looked back upon the care and responsibility that both the father and mother gibbon seemed to feel toward their offspring with much greater understanding than I had before. Many times, I saw our baby gibbon struggling out of his mother's arms, and playing about her while she was apparently completely oblivious of his presence, just as did the wild babies under the observation of Dr. Carpenter. But if a truck made more noise than usual, or a peacock screamed near by, her long arm would reach out as though without her volition, and gather the little one to her. Then, with Primo, she would swing to the top of the cage.

Again, as the baby grew and was more and more bold

in his reaching out into the unknown, imitating his father as he swung across a ten-foot space, I have seen the mother grab him and hold him tight just at the second that his little arms were too tired and his fingers too weak to grasp the big round bamboo pipes any longer. And after reading Dr. Carpenter's amazing account of family life I realize how much of this was her instinct which had been brought down from those days in the wild when the preservation of the species depended upon the constant protection of the weak young from the dangers and pitfalls of aerial passage.

And Dr. Carpenter tells of how even when the baby was old enough to travel part of the distance alone, the parents, usually the mother, would, when the journey included some extremely hazardous plunge of forty or more feet from one tree to another, reach out her arms with the same apparent listlessness I have seen so often and gather the youngster to her and, carrying it on her back or in her arms, make the leap with much more evident caution and care than the others.

Also he writes of how she would hold down the limb to help the baby make the jump that the adults and juveniles of greater age could make with ease. Never did little Primo fall, at least to our knowledge, although the baby chimpanzee in the next cage fell twice from a high bar in the trapeze. This was surprising to me because several gibbons had come into our collection with stiff or crippled joints and Primo's mother had one arm which she always favored. Although she could extend it and use it, seldom did she even pick up anything with it. She carried it held close in the curve of her body helping herself along with her other arm and useful feet.

In the scientific findings of the Asiatic expedition of 1937 was a report on healed bone injuries which were quite prevalent among the collected specimens. This would indicate not only falling, but perhaps so much speed and power that at times their slender bones could not stand the strain put on them, especially if shrubbery should entangle a long arm or hand as the swift passage from one hold to another was made.

The family life as it was studied in the wild and that went on in our own cage of gibbons is apparently organized very much like that of the typical human family so far as the make-up is concerned. Parents, chosen by each other, live together in apparently monogamous conditions; their children seem to be born one at a time and live with them until fully mature and able to shift for and protect themselves against ordinary encounters.

Our own gibbon family was composed of such evidently normal individuals that it seems almost criminal that circumstances should have combined to break the family up. When the mated pair of gibbons were taken out of the big gibbon cage they were placed, merely as an emergency measure, in a cage which was one of the earliest built in the zoo. It did not conform either in design or size to the rest of the anthropoid cages. It had long been slated for remodeling but we waited until we thought the gibbon baby was sufficiently mature to be moved out and put in another cage. In catching them, however, the mother's arm was injured and so, instead of keeping them in an isolation cage inside the monkey yard, we took them up to the hospital for treatment. Her arm gave her considerable trouble, becoming badly infected and crippling her so that she was unable to swing about with little Primo, teaching him to leap long distances through the air by swinging from the short rope that hung from their ceiling. Primo missed the crowd of visitors for whom he loved to perform, but as often as I went to the hospital to see him he would fly to the wire side of the cage and reach out his little arms for the treats of fruits and crackers I took him. As his father had always prevented my doing this while they were out in the big cage, I was greatly surprised that he was willing for the infant to touch me there in the hospital yard.

When it became obvious that the mother was suffering from too much confinement and not doing well at the hospital, we took her down into one of the exhibition cages at the monkey yard, but to our chagrin not only she but the baby began to fail rapidly. Careful attention was given them. There is nothing more disheartening than to see a gibbon failing in health. There seems to be no fight in a sick gibbon, no wish to get well; the patient little face, always sad, looks out dolefully from the thick ruff of fur. The gibbon mother of Primo would willingly accept everything that we could do for her, and then turn away with an utterly hopeless expression.

And so just a few weeks before Primo's second birthday she lay dead on her bed of clean straw and sacks. Cuddled close against her was the tiny Primo, also very ill, and Harry sitting in the doorway, first looking at his family, then wildly swinging up around the big tree and back again to sit looking at the ruin of his happy life. Within two days the baby Primo was gone. Autopsies showed that in both cases the cause of death was bacillary colitis and appendicitis, probably contracted first by the mother, weakened by her infected arm, and then transmitted to the little chap who ran to her to be cuddled and comforted, and who still curled up to sleep at night in the space between her bended legs and body, completely concealed in an egglike oval.

Harry, husky and normal, apparently resisted completely the infection that wiped out his family. We have not as yet found an acceptable mate although we have tried him with several adult female gibbons. Because of his record of fertility and his active, strong body, we should like to find him one he would like so that we might perhaps have a real gibbon family growing up in the zoo to enlighten us further on this interesting creature, which not only stands erect in the posture of man, but conducts his family life upon the pattern decreed by the highest form of civilization — the monogamous family group.

CHAPTER IV

Gibbons Here and There

SOME of the gibbons I have known even right here in the zoo have had so little need of my attention that they may well be called mere acquaintances rather than friends. For during the past few years I have known that it is impossible to carry on the program which has come to be my share of the zoo work and steadily increase my already large circle of intimates. There never seems to be any from whom I can separate myself willingly, for of all the many compensations offered a person who works in a zoo, to me the personal contact with the animals has always been the greatest. I am so thankful that it was my privilege to start in a small zoo and grow up with it under a progressive person like Dr. Harry Wegeforth. Having founded the zoo, he seemed always an active part of the working staff. Each new specimen we acquired meant we had earned it in some way, and had made some sacrifice for it.

But as our collection grew and the show improved, the number of visitors multiplied, and more funds became available for operation and expansion. Our growing reputation for raising babies and exhibiting well–cared-for specimens has made it increasingly easy to obtain donations and rare specimens at rock-bottom prices. So there has seemed to grow up a large group of specimens in which I feel great interest, but with which my personal contacts are far too slight for them to become my intimates.

I was more chagrined than I would have believed to find many specimens in the zoo, instead of a few scattered ones, which loved their keepers better than they did me. Some of them even seemed to regard me only as one of the more regular habitués of the zoo. And while this is, of course, a most natural state of affairs, considering our rapid growth, it is difficult to be completely reconciled to it. I shall always know I am missing a great deal of the joy I might have, but because of this I can speak with a somewhat reluctant objectivity of some tiny gibbons which have lately come into my family of ape men. The beneficial effect of this casual contact has been that I have grieved less when something has happened to these babies, or parting has become necessary, than I am wont to do, and while they enjoy the casual contacts with me, they fail to miss me or feel hurt when I am so busy I must pass them by quickly.

Following our success with our gibbon family and the fair luck in exhibiting a group of several species together in a complete out-of-door installation, and as a result of the many interesting publications of the Asiatic expedition, many importers began trying to bring in gibbons. Suddenly, from being almost entirely unknown in markets, gibbons became frequent quotations.

Because of trading off or moving those which would not live in the big cage in which we housed our 1936 shipment, we had only four gibbons in our once big group, and our experience with these had convinced Dr. Harry that only by obtaining a large number of real infants could we ever hope to fill a large cage with many gibbons. He felt they might grow and be an excellent show until they became mature when we would have to replace them. So one day when I told him a big Oriental shipment had just arrived in Los Angeles and that it was supposed to contain many young gibbons, although he was not well his face lighted up and his eyes gleamed with their old eagerness.

"All right," he said, "let's go see them!"

So we planned to start out on one of our old-time shopping expeditions such as we used to indulge in before the zoo was so large that I was too busy and he too ill to hop in a car and drive hundreds of miles any day we felt like it.

Bright and early the next morning, long before the importers expected any customers, Dr. Harry and I drew up at their front door and plowed our way through the combination of cage scrapings, sweeping compounds, and the helter-skelter of utensils with which every animal man is familiar.

Dr. Wegeforth, an inveterate bargain hunter, loved to look over a big shipment without a high-pressure salesman for a guide. He had thus discovered many rare bargains tucked away in corners some of which even the salesmen had not appreciated and therefore had not intended to show him. I have always said that no one will ever know how many lives of rare, interesting little creatures the Doctor saved by discovering them hidden away while it was still possible to save them from a death through ignorance or neglect.

The caretaker called for his employers, but before they could be found Doctor and I had wandered through the shop, looked over most of the birds, and were poking our noses into some of the small, tightly closed heated quarters "out back" where the really rare things usually are found.

[52]

A Wriggling Armful — My New Baby Gibbons

And there, in a close, stuffy enclosure, we found a bunch of baby gibbons. They were all of the species *Hylobates lar*, a gibbon of several colors ranging from jet black to silver, and commonly called the "white-handed" gibbon. Some of them were so young that their little faces were seal brown instead of black. They had been carefully divided into cages according to their color rather than their congeniality. The color had been considered by the importer as the distinction between species and he had so informed the dealers.

There was only one cage of the black color phase: two jet-black fuzzy babies with white gloves and stockings and a lovely white ruff around the pathetic little black faces. They crouched on a shelf in their cage, clinging desperately to each other for comfort, and each showed evidence of cold. Here the proprietress discovered us and began in her friendly, genial way to call attention to their good points, pulling them out of the cage and into her arms, holding them tight and wiping their little noses to cover up the colds which we would know enough to expect might result from their long trip and changed environment. She assured us that they were all over their colds. Just another drop or two of eucalyptus oil on their foreheads was all they needed. This treatment solved a question that had been puzzling me: how they had become so greasy and unhappily sticky about their little faces.

Having petted and cuddled them a few minutes, we passed to the next cage where two silvery babies, so light in color that their white hands and feet were not differentiated from their bodies, were cuddling close together. But as our guide reached out to open that door, a bundle of frantic white fur, with grabbing, striking hands and feet, tiny white teeth showing, prepared in its

[53]

baby way to defend itself. My quick judgment was that either it had been freshly caught just before the long sea voyage began, and the busy caretaker had had no opportunity to gain its confidence, or it was one of the rare little fellows that would never completely accept the friendship of man, but remain always on the defensive — always dreading the touch of the grasping human hand.

But it, like so many of the more aggressive animals, was clean and trim, in fine physical condition, and gave promise of making an excellent long-lived active exhibit. Doctor and I had already made up our mind (which was always one mind when we were out after specimens, for neither possessed what is known as sales resistance upon which to depend) that we would, if we could obtain anything like a reasonable price quotation, purchase some of the little gibbons. And so without permitting her to distress the youngsters further, we studied this white group very carefully for symptoms of colds or of the digestive ailments to which newly imported specimens often are subject.

Leaving the gibbon group, we went through the entire shipment of monkeys and animals, looking casually at some cunning bear cubs which we did not need but always enjoyed, checked up on birds which we had noted as desirable on the way up, and unexpectedly found ourselves in a long, recently built house heated to a temperature of nearly ninety degrees and distinctly smelling of snakes. There we found a fine group of monitor lizards, large skinks, and a few Indian turtles to swell the Doctor's collection. These we purchased, and then, of one accord, turned back into the storeroom proper.

Four cages of the tiny apes had now been brought out

of their heated overnight quarters and there the babies were contentedly eating breakfast in their cages up on the shelves behind the counters, ready for the day's business.

"Well, what do you want for them?" asked the Doctor.

Our dealer had not yet made up her mind as to whether or not we were in a buying mood or "just looking." She stuttered over her price and looked for some little clue from her husband. He was in the back office, poring ostentatiously over a bill of lading.

Now, I had bought gibbons once or twice from dealers and had looked longingly many more times at the few gibbon quotations among many price lists, but Doctor Harry had spent much time in real gibbon country; he had been instrumental in getting together our original collection of gibbons and he knew all of the markets and zoos in the native home of the tiny manlike apes that walk on the trees.

We both knew the costs of shipping, the losses en route and also the losses still to come through the long trying months that would pass before we could say, "These are acclimated." The Doctor knew that ordinarily I was the conservative one of the two. He had, in fact, frequently teased me because of what he called my "Scotch" frugality, and would add, "Why if I left her alone for a couple of years, she would pay the national debt." But he knew, also, on this day that I wanted them all, and he knew that I knew we were both very extravagant in buying any of them. But now as I looked at his indifferent back, walking out through the screen door, I thought, "It would serve him right if I bought every one. I bet that is just what he hopes I may do." But I knew, too, better than he, the details of what I was going to need my money for, and how much remained in our animal fund.

Finally I said, "You can send down the two little black ones — and don't you put a single drop of eucalyptus oil in their noses either; they are mine now. Well, send two of the little white ones; I want that spunky one, so send the meek little one with it."

I anticipated that I would just adopt those two little black chaps and have them for my very own babies for a while, particularly if their colds hung on.

When they arrived, Dr. Schroeder decided that we had better keep them down in the isolation cages in the monkey yard. It was bright and sunny there, protected from the wind; they would have lots of exercise and the expert care and handling of the men who specialized in the care of apes, and they were easily accessible to him.

So all four gibbons were released into a really large cage facing south, with bamboo poles crisscrossing it from shelf to wire sides, with short ropes dangling from the ceiling and a nice warm sunny shelf on which to stretch out. It was closed tightly behind them so that there was no draft, and they now had nothing to do but eat and grow fat and lazy and play with each other and beg for our attention. They made faces at the Indian sacred monkeys in the cage nearest their home, and huddled quickly into a big black-and-white ball at the approach of visitors or any unknown noise.

Each day we saw their eyes become brighter, their noses drier, their coats cleaner. They took much interest in grooming themselves, and soon were reaching out their tiny white hands for bits of fruit or a little petting; all, I mean, but the spunky one. He continued his defiant attitude, and now I was sure it was fear that made him put up the best show of ferocity he could. When he thought someone was really going to take hold of him, his tiny heart would beat so that you could see it. I hoped day after day that he was going to accept me when I whimpered a shaking little *"Whooo-oo"* to him, imitating the mother gibbon call that I had heard our mother use so effectively to call her little son, Primo. But all my efforts were unsuccessful. The two black babies came into my arms as long as I wanted them, but little Crosspatch swung from the top of his cage, striking at all of us with his dangling feet and showing his teeth viciously in the most terrifying grimace he could manage.

But alas for my excellent intentions of cuddling and petting them. I found the late summer and early fall so crowded with activities, talks, extra work because of vacations for the staff, and preparations to send our head keeper to Africa, that I had no regular time for this pleasant though unimportant duty. Furthermore, I disliked the thought of exciting the wild one which made us all reluctant about entering the cage. Meanwhile the treatment prescribed by Dr. Schroeder was doing its work well. Fresh air, cleanliness, proper diet, and above all their playful exercise was making perfect zoo specimens of all. Common sense dictates that it is only when they actually need nursing that handling and unnatural attention should be imposed upon them.

We had, soon after their arrival, a most interesting occurrence. Like all Americans interested in animals we had been wondering what was happening to European zoos during the holocaust raging there, and in spite of cheerful reports of the care of animals in zoos, and the need to keep the normal, healthy entertainment offered by zoos alive, we knew that there must naturally be almost overwhelming difficulties to face. Suddenly we had one direct contact with the London Zoo, in which

[57]

we were most interested, through a letter from a private school in Ventura County, California. This letter inquired of us in great detail concerning the care and housing of a gibbon, or perhaps a pair of gibbons. The master of the school had learned from a friend in England that the London Zoo was no longer able to care for a pair of young gibbons which she had been boarding there and she had been forced to take them out of the zoo and care for them at her home herself. Being confronted with many difficulties, not the least of which was the safety of herself and her charges, her thoughts turned to her friends in America as a refuge for her pets. The letter closed with the question, "If we receive these gibbons and find we cannot care for them, will you accept them at your zoo?"

We gave the school all the advice and help we could and assured them of our willingness to give the gibbons a permanent home if they could not care for them. All of this had occurred just after we had made our purchase, but as weeks and months had passed we almost forgot about the expected arrival of the refugee pets. Then we received a letter saying that the two gibbons had been shipped to California via Canada, but that the male had died en route, and the female, Etam (the name meaning black), had arrived at the school, and seemed to be doing well in the cage. She was happy to be established, enjoyed the children about her and was friendly, and the letter closed by reminding us of our promise to take her if the need arose. Now with the closing of the school year and the summer-school term, the masters found that the gibbon was not happy, was probably lonely. She was difficult to keep caged, and they felt that the winter would be too cold for her. They were anxious to bring her down before the new students arrived at the opening of the fall term. They knew it would create an unhappy disturbance to part with Etam after the new children had grown to know and love her.

Therefore, we were not surprised one day to receive a telephone call from the school that Etam — beautifully black and shiny, and nearly adult though not very large — was on her way down to live in the zoo. She was quite friendly, knew her name, and was willing to be friends with us if we were not too familiar. Her arrival, coming after the death of the mother gibbon and our darling Primo, we hoped might make a happy solution of our pressing problem as to what to do with Harry, our forlorn father. But he treated Etam with such profound indifference that he did not even try to hurt her. At first she feared him; then, finding he paid no attention to her, she tried in her gentle way to be friends.

The first time I saw Etam and Harry sitting close together on a shelf, I was mistakenly elated. He left her side immediately to grimace and beckon to me. And even though I walked directly past the cage to a point where I could see what effect my intentional snub had upon him, Harry did not return to her. He ignored her efforts to play or to attract him. She often chased him playfully around the tree as he swung for exercise, but he went indifferently upon his own way. Although she seemed to take some comfort from his presence in the cage, he did not notice her. So the winter months passed, with Etam and the little ones in true gibbon fashion spending their nights in the open and refusing the shelter offered, but appearing to suffer little from cold or exposure.

It was late in the spring that the little black gibbon which had suffered most from cold and illness upon his arrival showed symptoms of real dysentery and other disease. He alone of all of them had not attained a thick, glossy coat and a robust, childish love for play. He wanted to sit on a shelf and be cuddled like a baby, although he had been as large as the others when he arrived.

Our foggy spring mornings, in that long period when we always feel as though summer will never come, proved too much for him. While the winter had probably weakened him, it was the waiting for summer that put an end to his short little life. His little cold nose had always been far too moist for health, and his tiny black face was usually dirty, so that while he never appeared to be seriously ill, it was not a great surprise one day when Moore called me to say he was lying lifeless on the shelf when he had arrived at the zoo.

The other little black one had already adjusted himself perfectly in the group of white ones. He was from the start an aggressive chap who never seemed to miss the clinging arms of his little countryman. Now he alternately plays with the other gibbons in the cage, or comes to the fence to tempt zoo visitors beyond their powers of resistance into giving him a bit of forbidden food.

We finally were convinced that Harry and Etam were not congenial. So as we needed the cage room for some new, rare Luton monkeys, we put Etam in the cage with the babies and took Harry back to the hospital where he knew the attendants, and better still, where they understood his unfriendly and sometimes obscene advances for what they were.

But Etam cared nothing for the cage of babies; in fact she hated and feared them. She paid no attention to them, white or black, and her timid demeanor toward them tempted them to abuse her, just as children will persecute a timid newcomer. Poor little exile, Etam was one more convincing proof of my theory that a single animal raised almost entirely as a pet does not make a happy or healthy member of a wild zoo group. Although she finally became partially adjusted to life with other gibbons, we may sometime be forced to find a better location for her where once more she will have as much personal attention as she has a right to expect, provided she does not, because of her lack of activity, aggressiveness and appetite, slip away to the land where gibbons sleep forever.

Recently, drawn by a rare and wonderful birth of a red Luton monkey baby, I hurried by the high arched cage in the monkey yard where our little gibbons live. I had not stopped at that cage for a long time and intended to go right by, but I realized that a long black arm ending in a white hand was stretched far out to reach me. I stopped, and although I had been listening with pleasure to their full-toned voices answering the song of what I have been calling the "big gibbons," I was amazed when I realized that it had been just two years since the four little chaps had tempted Dr. Harry and me to bring them home with us, and that they were no longer frail, whimpering little *wau-waus* but husky, strong, agile, nearly grown gibbons who might, if they had remained in their native India, have been taking care of themselves among their family of bigger sisters and brothers, following where the father and the mother, with undoubtedly a new baby, white or black, in her arms, swung wildly through the trees along their own food lanes, each in its acknowledged territory. Perhaps each might be beginning to join the family vocal chorus or reaching for the bitter blue plum or teasing the new baby out of its mother's arms. In the case of Etam, the oldest of the group, she might by now from the edge of her own family's territory be shyly accepting the amorous advances of some young male gibbon, forced by maturity from his family group. There, on the dividing line between two family tracts, might thus be formed a new family of gibbons.

But this mental adventuring into the wild land of gibbon life does not mean I feel any regret that these fine young beauties are housed in my own beautiful zoo. As they swing from tree to rope and up over a big high pole following each burst of joyous singing, they leave me no room to doubt that their life is full and happy and complete. They feel no need to glance behind to see if an enemy is near; they join no hurried rush for wild figs and plums lest other creatures steal their living from them. This is no place for slips and broken bones; each youngster is perfection so far as his physical appearance goes, as he spends his time swinging and singing as he who walks on the trees has done from time immemorial.

PART TWO
THE MAN OF THE WOODS

CHAPTER V

Maggie – An Immigrant Child Grows Up

UNLIKE my first meeting with the gibbon, my introduction to the orang-utan was, strange to say, through Lesson Eleven in the old *California State Series Third Reader*. Although I had not actually recalled the story itself for many years, nevertheless I realized when I met my first orang-utan in person that during the time since I was nine years old the orang had been to me the creature pictured in the reading lesson. I like to think charitably of the people who prepared that lesson. It was anonymous and consequently is put down in my own mind to the credit of the committee preparing state textbooks. Perhaps it was intended not to convey any valuable scientific information, but to be a drill in words and expression. I know, of course, that in that far-distant day the knowledge of all great apes was most inaccurate and far from complete.

Within the past three years, the very same old reader I had used as a child came into my hands. Immediately I remembered the story and turned eagerly to it. I was surprised that my memory had so accurately retained the facts as stated in the tale, even to the tantrums of the young ape when denied fulfillment of his wishes. As a child I read the account with much greater charity than now as a zoo attendant, when I could see plainly between

[65]

the lines the pleasure derived by the crew and passengers from teasing the cunning, emotional little ape on the voyage from his Oriental home to London.

I had formed an opinion of the orang as a mischievous, husky, agile and actually drunken little rowdy. The story enlarged upon his queer appetites, his fondness for "spirits" which led him to obtain by stealth the Captain's brandy. He ate meat, both raw and cooked, drank tea, coffee and wine (I was too young to wonder who made the tea and coffee and wine for him in his treetop home) and, to the writer's surprise, he preferred fruit.

But with all of its false impressions, there was much truth in the lesson. I was better prepared for my meeting with our first orangs because I knew that they were strong, agile and persistent, that they would roll over and over in fits of temper, bumping their heads and crying loudly to get their own way about things. I knew that they would cling to you tenaciously with feet and hands, that they loved to wrap up in clothes or cloth, that they could outclimb any man that ever lived, that they could not stand a great deal of cold, and readily accepted human friendship.

The little orang, in the book, whom the sailors called by the name Pongo, arrived in London in 1818 and unfortunately died after a few months of the cold, damp London climate. Today, of course, I am inclined to think that it was Pongo's very poor diet, the teasing it endured, and the exposure it suffered on the trip especially in the vicinity of the Cape of Good Hope, which ruined any prospect of the London Zoo's successful care of it. I am assuming that there was some kind of an animal collection in London at that time, although the Zoological Garden as we now know it was not in existence until ten years later.

[66]

Ragged, Windswept Beggars — Maggie and Mike

Bunnell Photo Shop

Jiggs Dressed in Henry's Cap and Glasses

Bunnell Photo Shop

The Man of the Woods Makes a Nest

Except to say he was three feet in height, the little ape's physical appearance was left to the child's imagination.

In March, 1928, late one afternoon, there rolled into our grounds a small sedan driven by a young man to whom we had given several thousand dollars and a liberal expense allowance to make a collection for us in the Orient. His appearance was most unexpected. We had been hoping soon to hear when he would arrive and what he was bringing with him. We need to know this in advance in order to get proper permits for a large shipment. When we asked in amazement how it happened he was in our midst so suddenly and inquired as to the whereabouts of the collection, he had a story ready. The night before he was to sail from Singapore a fire had broken out and burned all of the fine collection he had gathered for us; that he had all that was left in the car with him.

A large box behind his seat contained two little bears and a gray gibbon. Smaller crates held a few birds, and on the seat beside him, just like two shy foreign children, sat two very young orangs. The smaller could not have been much more than a year old, and was clinging tightly with both arms around the body of the larger. He was naked except for a few long, straggling red hairs; his little abdomen was distended until the reddish-black skin was a streaked blue. He looked up at me out of the most innocent black eyes, slanting in his small face like those of a Chinese doll. The other orang, perhaps a year older, was covered with long, red hair, coarse and not very thick, and she held the baby against her side astride her hip much as I have seen older children lug a too heavy baby. She was not so shy but appeared just as innocent.

[67]

They were partly covered with an old quilt or robe, which had begun to slide off as the car stopped.

Thus Maggie and the baby who would always be "Little Jiggs" came into the life of the San Diego Zoo. They were the first live orang-utans I had ever seen. Whatever the truth about the collection, this young man seemed truly to be fond of these tiny creatures, and it was evident that both of them loved him greatly. They reached their long arms after him as he left the car and cried when he refused to turn back.

We put them in a very warm inner room inside the yard of the small primate cages and hurriedly collected bedding and utensils for them while their supper was being cooked in the café kitchen. During the voyage, the young man had had the cook aboard ship prepare cereals for them and he had taught them to eat from a bowl with a spoon.

I was prouder than the occasion warranted when each in turn took my extended hand and came readily into my arms. I was to learn that aboard ship they had been everybody's pet and had lost all fear of strangers. I was just one more kind and safe human being to them. During the day, they were exhibited in a cage with the two little bear companions of their long trip westward, and at night they were brought into the room inside the feed house where they could not escape and would not suffer with cold.

As they had been trained to eat like children, we hastily built a small, *stout* table, and two heavy, substantial chairs. The very first day after they arrived, I went to a toy shop and bought two little red chairs to be used at meal time. Maggie looked at Little Jiggs's chair and simply reached over and took it apart. Then she tried to chew up the pieces. As all of the sleeping quarters of the monkey cages have a downstairs and an upstairs apartment, we put the bedding for the two orangs upstairs where they could sleep away from all drafts.

On the second night, Henry Newmeyer, the primate keeper, called me to come and see what they had done, and I found that upon being put up in the little loft of the sleeping quarters, Maggie had proceeded to throw down to the floor below first the nice, clean hay and then all of the big sacks we had prepared for them. When we walked in, she had two of the big gunny sacks spread down on the hay which she had distributed evenly over the floor. The first two sacks had been quite accurately laid, one above the other, and Maggie stood in the center of the upper sack holding a third one by the corners. Then, as we watched, she raised her long and, I had already discovered, very strong arms, shook the third sack and brought it down, backing up so she could lay it straight on top of the others.

Henry and I were completely fascinated by Maggie's handy and human treatment of the bed covering. Not until she was entirely satisfied did she climb into the loft, where Little Jiggs was whimpering, and drag him out carelessly. He did not require much pulling. He was eager to come, and it required little effort for Maggie to push him down in a heap in the middle of the three sacks, after which she covered him with the remaining fourth one. When he was right in the center of the "bed," completely hidden, Maggie crawled in beside him. She was quiet for a second, then sat bolt upright. As she did so, she pulled the covers off Little Jiggs. Seeing they were both uncovered, she got up, made him get up, and repeated the whole process — even to stirring up and smoothing all the hay again.

A second time, and a third, Henry and I watched her repeat the scene. Finally, as though in disgust, she took the largest sack of all, put it over her head, shawl fashion, and curled up in the bed, now completely disordered. As she closed her eyes, it was obvious that in her feminine mind she was blaming Little Jiggs for the failure of her efforts at orderly living. With complete indifference, he cuddled down close to her and soon both were asleep.

I cannot say how many times in the next four or five months I went out in the late afternoon to see Maggie and Little Jiggs go to bed. Sometimes they were already asleep and if my coming aroused them, the innocent, trusting little Orientals would peer out from under their blankets, sleepy-eyed. Once, with the fantastic idea of improving their condition, I took down to the zoo an old comforter filled with soft, thick cotton batting. I have always been thankful it was not filled with down or feathers. Maggie stayed up a good part of the night taking it apart. Cotton filled the place. Fine particles of the batting were sprinkled through their long red hair, and actually they looked as though they had been masquerading as Santa Clauses in a snowstorm. They had had a most enjoyable time. Henry, to my deep gratitude, said nothing; he just looked first at Maggie and then at me, as though not knowing whom to blame.

As soon as their furniture was built, we took the two little orangs out into the garden each afternoon, where visitors could watch them eat their lunch of a bottle of milk and a bowl of oatmeal or rice pudding. The tiny Jiggs was not much interested in food. He should have been nursing his mother yet, no doubt. So Maggie frequently ate her own portion and a large part of his. He required much loving and cuddling, and usually would run to the arms of someone he knew and loved long before the luncheon was over.

Sometimes, for publicity purposes, or as a special favor, we would permit children to hold the two babies and eat with them. Hundreds of feet of motion pictures were taken of them and I shall always regret that one taken by Fred Lewis could not have been in color. It was on a stretch of green lawn and Maggie was especially mischievous that day. Every few minutes she would catch Henry with his attention off her table manners and steal a sly bite from Jiggs's bowl or a swig of milk from his bottle. Finally, Little Jiggs — all pretense of eating past — climbed cautiously out of his chair to the table, slid down the leg, hobbled over on all fours to Norman Johnson, our head keeper, and climbed up Norman's long legs into his arms. Jiggs's apparent confidence of the welcome he would receive and the way Norman tenderly gathered up the little fellow and put his cheek solicitously down against the round little crown elicited great applause from the crowd.

Maggie had even then one comical habit she retains to this very day. When she drinks from a bottle, she holds it upside down until every possible drop has drained into her extended lower lip. But she never gives up hope that a small amount may be left. When all fluid has ceased to trickle out, she takes the bottle and looks through it; but still not convinced, she closes first one eye and then the other, peering into the top of the empty bottle with each in turn. It is one of her best stunts and never fails to get hearty clapping, which she enjoys tremendously.

The cunning Little Jiggs was doomed to an early death. He was ill often at first. He suffered with dysentery, colds, and other baby ailments. We tried all our skill in taking proper care of him until, eventually, toward the end of summer, we felt that he was really coming through. Then one morning Henry reported that Jiggs was not well. He didn't have any appetite, and although he had a fever for a day or two he was listless and dull-eyed. Each day we could see that he was failing. He coughed and apparently suffered some distress in his stomach. Nothing we could devise or suggest did any good. This was one of the most heartbreaking periods of my long life in the zoo.

Jiggs became more and more childlike as he grew weaker; there was little left of him except the distended abdomen and the clinging fingers. He whimpered imploringly to each of us and, although we could do nothing for him, he loved to have us hold him in our arms. When one morning Henry came to tell me he was gone, I felt relief that his suffering was over. Autopsy revealed that he had a big wad of gum, paper and all, in his stomach. How he obtained it under Henry's watchful eye, we never knew. He could not rid himself of it as an older, stronger ape might have done.

Maggie missed him greatly. So, naturally, we gave her more attention than ever. Henry often took her at night in his car down to his house in the extreme west end of the zoo. She became so spoiled that no one could make her mind but Henry, who was always very strict with her and never let her learn that her hands were stronger than his. She listened for his first step in the morning, and if he did not come directly to her cage she would howl and scream — pausing frequently to listen for some result. If he started toward her cage she would stop. Many times, just for fun, he would turn suddenly away, stepping loudly so she would know it. Such a storm of protest that would arouse! Maggie would bang her head hard against the wall or upon the floor; she would roll and scream in a spasm of rage, stopping now and then to listen. As I could never resist her blandishments, she would have been unmanageable by the time she was three years old if her training had been my concern.

Finally, another Jiggs came to live in the zoo, this time an old and dangerous female, a movie actress accustomed to fighting for her rights. Within a few months we were convinced that she was a criminal because the hands of men had made her so, and not because of any natural viciousness. But until we were sure of this we did not put her in the cage with Maggie. Then they lived together five years, and during that time Jiggs never hurt Maggie willfully. Once or twice when she was too aggravating, Jiggs would hold her so tight that it hurt for punishment, but there was never a bite or real fight between them. Maggie was a tease and a persistent, trying one. Jiggs was old and sometimes grew impatient with Maggie's perpetual tagging and constant interference with her own lazy contentment.

Like most orang-utans, Maggie was — I should say "is" for Maggie is still with us — very clean inside her sleeping quarters. She waits until turned out to evacuate, even when, because of repairs, she must be kept inside many hours. In the mornings, she rushes, as soon as released, to the top of the cage for this obligation. She will not permit any filth to touch her body or hair if she can help it. This habit is not only Maggie's; it is so common to our orangs that I feel very sorry for those which must be shipped long distances. Fortunately orangs drink little water so that their feces are firm, almost like those of many rodents and ungulates, which makes life in crates easier than otherwise it would be.

Before I came to work in the zoo, an orang had been exhibited for a short time and had become famous for his nest-building ability. Remnants of some of the nests built in the trees by this "Wild Man of Borneo," as he was known, were still in existence when Maggie arrived. I was eager to try her in a tree while it was still safe to turn her loose.

One dull day, when there were few visitors in the zoo, I coaxed Henry to release her hand near a young but sturdy black-acacia tree. She needed no hint, but encircling the trunk with hands and feet just as the natives climb cocoanut palms, up she went to the first branch. She pulled at the limb a little and then, finding it a poor weak one, she climbed down again and went up the next tree. She tried several before finding one to her liking. The trunk divided at about eight feet into two limbs of almost equal size that were not too close together. She placed one foot on the inner side of each branch, and, spread-eagling as much as it permitted, she pushed with all her might as though testing the strength of the crotch. Satisfied, she climbed out a little way, reached for the end of a small branch, and bent it over into the crotch. She mashed it down as well as she could without completely breaking the branch. She repeated this two or three times, each time trampling the small twigs and foliage into a compact mass at the bottom of the crotch. She pulled off a few small limbs which seemed to be in the way, but not enough to expose her nest to too much sunshine or the people below. She climbed much higher and farther out on the limbs to break off the real material for making the nest big and roomy and safe. She tramped around and around making it fairly symmetrical and quite strong. Such a nest, connected to the living tree as it was by the first broken but not severed limbs, would last for a long time; and orangs, it is reported, do build for a certain permanency, raising their young in one nest to which they return as a family group day after day for months at a time. This demonstration of mechanical ability was very wonderful to me at the time. I have since become convinced that it is characteristic of orangs and is not the mechanical genius of one or two specimens. We have demonstrated it time after time with others young enough to be turned loose in the grounds.

Maggie is a perfect specimen physically and has always been. Her illnesses have been only slight colds or rare attacks of constipation. She is co-operative and easily cared for. In the twelve years she has lived in the zoo, she has been a constant source of joy to us all. She has some very human traits; among them is an insatiable curiosity which often gets her into trouble and exasperates her keeper. Our building superintendent, Ralph Virden, whose years in this capacity have taught him exactly the requirements of animal enclosures for safety and endurance, pronounces himself baffled at times as to how to confine our Maggie safely. She has never permitted herself to be held in her sleeping room by any mechanical device such as ratchet or drop bars, and has been known to exert such strength and cunning that she has slipped padlocked bars out of their grooves far enough to get a door open and get out. All of us agree with the keeper who said: "Maggie! Oh well, I expect to come in any morning and find Moore locked up and Maggie out swabbing the cage."

Maggie is good for at least one laugh every day. A few highlights stand out, perhaps none more strongly than her actions when she first saw Mike, the big, young

[75]

male orang-utan with which we replaced Jiggs, the old female who "brought Maggie up."

Mike was so thin and doubled up that it was almost impossible to determine, by peering into the crate in which he arrived, whether or not he was well and whole. But on the morning after his arrival, we moved the crate to the safety door leading into Maggie's cage and turned him in. He was so shy and suspicious that it took him nearly an hour to emerge. Meanwhile Maggie was registering indignation because she was kept locked in her sleeping room while interesting noises were going on outside. Finally Mike ventured out and, half crawling, half whirling, he got across the twenty-foot cage and climbed up into the ceiling where he swung, twelve feet above the floor, suspended by unbelievably long arms and legs. Dr. Wegeforth told the men to turn Maggie out. We stood outside with a hose ready to turn on a stream of water if they should engage in real fighting.

As the door slid up, Maggie's small face appeared close to the floor. She had been crouching there trying to see under the door. The orang can move with lightning speed or with such slowness that you fail to see the motion. Slowly, inch by inch, she emerged, looking about to see what had been happening. Then she discovered the new orang. First she puffed her mouth in anger and blew noisily through her extended lips. Mike ignored her. Next she walked over to the side of the cage where he swung. Standing erect directly below him, she again filled her lips and blew. His complete lack of movement convinced her not only that he was harmless but that she was being snubbed. For the first and only time in her life, she showed signs of embarrassment. She reached one hand up toward him, raised one

[76]

Mike — Long-haired, Bewhiskered Prophet of Patience,
Is Always "Folded Up"

foot off the ground, curled her toes up gracefully and hanging onto the wire with her other hand, she wiggled and twisted, the while gazing up into Mike's face with something of admiration in her eyes, as though she were a shy and modest maiden suddenly fallen in love with an awe-inspiring suitor.

Whether from shyness or lack of interest, I do not know, but Mike paid no attention to her feminine blandishments. Maggie recognized that something else must be done. So, climbing boldly into the corner until she could touch Mike, she grabbed hold of him and then, smelling his hand, realized that the magnificent creature was of her own kind. She clung to him, trying to attract him, but at his first movement toward her she was off like the wind across the cage, the shyest bit of femininity I ever saw. Being the average male creature, Mike did not realize he was being encouraged by her retreat. So doing the obvious, he went after her. For several hours Maggie led him a merry chase. I think perhaps it has actually endured to this day. She has in turn teased and bullied him. When we have had other male orangs caged near them, she has flirted outrageously through the wires, setting the poor, faithful Mike mad with jealousy. He grinds his teeth and spits profusely, daring them to come across and fight! Once, when, in spite of our padlocks, Maggie released into her cage a magnificent young male that Osa Johnson had given us, Mike attacked him viciously, biting his leg so severely that both bones were broken. But no matter how aggravating Maggie is, Mike always forgives her, lovingly enduring her vagaries and selfishness.

Maggie is apt to take sudden and violent fancies to persons. One whom she adored was the late Mr. Robert P. Scripps, publisher and patron of our zoo. He was a

[77]

frequent visitor to the zoo whenever in San Diego, but was often away for long months at a time. Maggie had been quite young when Mr. Scripps first saw her, and he had held her and played with her in the rough-and-tumble manner she adored. I have seen her watch him coming toward the cage after an absence of almost a year and, even when he was at a distance, show by her extreme excitement that she recognized him. She would invariably start showing off for him, especially a whirling motion we call dancing, although he never fed her as a reward. As long as it was safe for us to take her out of the cage, she would hold out her arms to him, and it sometimes took force to release him from her affectionate grasp.

One day when Henry was out of the zoo on an errand, Maggie managed to get her cage opened. After wandering about the monkey yard she climbed over its gate and escaped. She had been in the zoo about a year and was still such a baby to us that we hadn't fully realized how smart she was. When Henry returned and found her missing, he searched everywhere, frantically. Finally, hoping I might have taken her out or that she might be paying me a visit, he hurried to my office at the café. Henry very often took Maggie by the hand and led her to the café in order to weigh her on some penny scales. On such visits, she thought that part of the program was to visit me in my office, sit on my desk and eat an ice-cream cone. When he learned that I had not seen her, he was convinced that she had been kidnaped. I was just as sure that nobody could have walked out our gate with Maggie without attracting attention. Wherever Maggie went, she always had a large crowd following her.

But I could think of many other dangerous things that

[78]

might happen to her. So I, too, joined the search. Luckily, as I started out I wondered if Henry had looked in his car. That was the day of open cars and the cars of the zoo employees were parked near a gate just inside the zoo fence, and about half a block from the monkey yard. I walked in that direction. Suddenly I heard an auto horn. I rushed toward the sound and there, sitting under the wheel of Henry's own car, frantically turning everything that was loose in her efforts to make it go, was Maggie. She adored riding, and Henry often took her with him. She had passed several cars very like Henry's in a row of seven or eight, and had climbed into the one she considered her own.

Sometimes we took Maggie for a ride on the bus, which runs through the grounds on an hourly schedule; to her own delight as well as that of the passengers. One of her most innocent but embarrassing pranks occurred on such a trip. The lad driving was very neat and painfully shy. He used a bit of his mother's old pink-silk underwear for a dust cloth. After wiping off the seats between trips, when no one was around, he would tuck this cloth securely under the cushion of his seat. We stopped for a few minutes at one of the cages. Maggie, who had been sitting between the driver and Henry on the front seat, was not in the least interested in the lecture. Without our noticing it, she began to explore her environment. Of course, she found the cloth.

Now, like all orangs, Maggie loves to dress up. Recognizing the dirty pink material as "clothes," she tried to put them on. Suddenly a giggle attracted the attention of Henry and the bus driver simultaneously. There sat Maggie, one long, red, hairy arm through one leg of a pair of pink-silk knickers and her small, bullet-shaped head halfway down the other leg, one eye just visible through the elastic band that held the gathers at the bottom. She knew well enough when she was in mischief! In a few minutes more, she would have succeeded in dressing herself.

But with all Maggie's likable qualities and mechanical genius, I have never thought she showed the same degree of human intelligence that Old Jiggs revealed. Maggie, of course, has had a much more limited education. She has never had to pit her wits against those of man in unfriendly contests as Jiggs had had to do. She has never been abused or forcibly coerced into doing things she hates or dreads; she has never actually been trained. Her little acting under Henry's supervision was largely developed by encouraging her to enlarge upon funny little things she did first from choice. If she found herself rewarded because of her cleverness, she was always eager to repeat. Henry made her obey him and, as long as he lived, was her master. With his very sudden death, her act was discontinued and her simple training ceased. She obeys by coming when we call her, dancing or whirling for treats we withhold, and she will enter her sleeping quarters when ordered to do so. But actually we exercise very little control over her.

Maggie is not vicious, but at times she is sly and cruel, watching a chance to nip our fingers between her tremendously strong ones in an excruciatingly painful pinch. Soon after Charley Smith arrived at the zoo to take charge of the monkey string, he had a bitter and dangerous encounter with Maggie. A substitute keeper turned her into her safety cage with her bottle of milk while preparing to shut her and Jiggs up for the night. When they tried to move her into the sleeping cage, she refused to budge. The substitute keeper, completely losing his head, grabbed her and she grabbed him. I think she might have killed him if Smith, a man with great experience — he later became our head keeper — had not gone to his rescue. As it was, both he and Smith were bitten badly and the flesh of the calf of one leg of the careless keeper was badly twisted. Orang-utans fight each other by grabbing a leg or arm and twisting the flesh off the bone. At times they will do this in play until the one being twisted will scream in sudden agony.

But only once did Maggie injure Henry. That day she reached out and took hold of his thumb between her finger and stout little thumb. She alternately pressed slightly and then released her pressure. When she felt Henry had relaxed his vigilance, she suddenly squeezed with all her might. The blood spurted from under the nail, and he eventually lost it. I did not attach any real viciousness to this act nor did Henry. It was simply her rough play and he was being treated like an equal and a brother.

We are always trying to give Maggie playthings. One day we hung a new hoop on a stout chain and swivels in her cage. She investigated at once, and, after swinging for a few minutes, started to twist the chain. I stood watching, too stupid to realize what she was doing. Suddenly I saw that the chain was beginning to spread in the links and called Henry. Before he could reach me, however, the damage was done. Maggie had let the hoop swing free. Although made from three-quarter-inch galvanized water pipe, it was warped out of shape and the second link of the chain above the hoop had parted. Maggie calmly unhooked the link, twisted it and flattened it almost into a straight piece of metal. Anyone would have doubted that it could be done with cold metal, even with the aid of a vise. Her strength and perseverance in taking apart her cage equipment is

[81]

incredible and maddening. Another proof of the strength in her slim fingers was Maggie's ability to turn on a common garden valve from which the head had been removed. Henry had taken it off because she would turn on the faucet as fast as he turned it off, thus flooding her cage. She was an interested spectator to the removal of the head. No sooner was Henry safely out of the way than she took hold of the small metal end which fitted into it, turned it with her fingers and flooded the cage with water just the same.

More recently a fine new bronze sign was put on her cage, naming the donor of the funds with which it had been built. In spite of my advice to the workmen, the bolts with which the sign was fastened to the supporting bar were placed on the side toward Maggie's cage. Although they were at least three inches from the wire, Maggie removed them all and none was ever found again. I am inclined to believe she detected some nice little hole into which she poked them. The sign wasn't up as long as it took the men to bolt it on.

Like Jiggs, from whom she had many lessons, Maggie will fish for hours with a sack or a piece of string for something which lies on the ground outside her cage. Throwing a loop of sack or ravelings over it, she draws the object as far as possible toward her. She repeats the process until she has brought it either to her or up to her cage where the floor is closest to the ground, due to its slope. Recently I saw her fish for something with a slender, pointed stick twenty inches long. I wondered where she had obtained it, and discovered that she had stripped it from a new shelf above the doors of the sleeping rooms. This plank is two-inch solid oak, bound with metal; the splinter had been pulled out of the center of the board, apparently with her teeth.

When I saw her fishing with it, I asked, "What are you doing, Maggie?"

She looked at me blankly, pointing the stick carelessly toward the sky. Finally, with great *sangfroid*, she pulled it almost into the cage, balancing it loosely in her fingers and pretending that it was something about which she knew nothing. She pretended no interest in me or the stick. To test her, I sauntered toward the gorilla cage. Her small eyes followed me without turning her head, and when she thought I was safely away she slowly, nonchalantly began to slip the pointed stick through the wire again.

"Maggie," I shouted at her, and the stick was quickly withdrawn. Finally I walked on and, for my own amusement, permitted her to continue fishing. From where I stood, pretending not to watch, I saw her poke the sharp stick several times at a peanut shell until she successfully speared it. She knows she should not beg and that people are not allowed to feed her, but she watches her chance to tempt anyone who stands out in front with a bag of peanuts or fruit.

I walked over to the refreshment stand and bought a bag of peanuts. Taking them inside the guard rail, I laid down a row of five or six along the base of her cage at the low end. She realized at once that I was offering her a real fishing job. She scurried into the sleeping room to bring out the precious tool which she had cached when she saw me returning. Being whole peanuts, of course when she poked them with the stick as she had the empty shell they rolled away. I moved them a little nearer than the hollow shell had been. Maggie drew her spear inside the cage, and, raising it, passed it out through a higher opening in the wire from which she could pierce the shell easily at a very acute

[83]

angle. I am sure not even a six-year-old child could have figured it out more quickly or as accurately as she did.

Dr. H. C. Bingham at one time did a brief experimental study on our two gorillas during the first year of their residence, and one of the experiments consisted in fishing a lure of fruit out of a long wooden box open at one end, closed at the other. In the sides and top of the box, overlapping slots had been cut. Through these the gorillas had learned to slide the fruit, holding with one hand until they could finally remove it through the open end. For a simple study in comparison of their approach to such a trial, we used the same box and the same experiment on the chimpanzees and orang-utans. Both Maggie and Jiggs refused to solve the problem properly. They tried first to pry the box off the side of the cage, then broke it apart by force and removed the fruit, a method which had never occurred to the gorillas who patiently fished out their fruit day after day until they could do it in a few seconds.

Once I saw Maggie completely lose her self-possession, an event that I never would have dreamed possible. Having climbed a tree on the edge of the mesa, she looked down into the open tiger grotto. Two great cats, traditional enemies of her race, were pacing up and down in the sunshine. Maggie, seeing them, leaped from the trees to the ground, rushed to Henry, her face pale, every hair on end, and her lips pursed out, hissing and crying. She climbed into his arms and pushed and pulled at him to get him away from that dangerous point. For several days she climbed up in the corner of her cage nearest the spot from which she had seen the tigers, and hissed and moaned in terror. Ultimately she forgot the affair. I was greatly surprised, for we had had mountain lions near her cage and she had climbed the guard rail to look at them with no sign of fear.

Maggie is not a very large female. Her big cage makes her look smaller than she really is. She was one hundred and twenty-five pounds the last time we weighed her. But she is our very own Maggie, dear to me especially because in her sullen, silent adult face I still see a cunning little black-faced new baby wrapped in a sack or shawl, looking like a tiny immigrant straight from the old country. She has a place in our hearts that is strictly her own. Our little homesick baby, she was courageous in her solicitude for the younger and more forlorn Little Jiggs. We, especially I, remember her teasing fondness for two little black bears, and I know all of the things we have been able to do with her that we have never equaled with any of her successors; such things as taking her to school and to parties for children, which have given her a real place in the community.

I know perhaps better than anyone else just what this place is, for many, many times at the close of a talk on zoo animals, someone will say, "Oh, Mrs. Benchley, won't you tell us something about Maggie?" There are hundreds of episodes to tell that people never tire of hearing repeated. One anecdote the children love concerns a bright Sunday morning when I was taking some zoo pictures with the aid of a professional photographer. We had Maggie out of her cage for some shots. She became exceedingly interested in a lady with a small child in a baby carriage. Maggie wanted to push it and the lady being willing, she did just that. She held the handle and pushed the carriage (with a little guidance) all around the monkey cages. Suddenly the baby cooed. Maggie had not realized the buggy was occupied for the

[85]

hooded top had been so turned that the child was concealed.

Maggie released her hands from the bar and walked around in front. We raised the top and Maggie looked into the big, blue eyes of a beautiful baby lying on her stomach on the white pillows, her face toward the foot of the carriage. The baby gurgled happily at Maggie, who stared back in amazement. She had never been so close to such a young child. Slowly, with every evidence that she would not hurt the baby, she extended her hand.

"Let's see what she is going to do," said the mother. "She is so gentle."

Softly Maggie touched the little upturned nose, pushed gently so that it turned up even more. The baby laughed aloud. Maggie showed all her own teeth, withdrew her long black finger and placed it gently on her own flat, sunken nostrils. I felt sure she wanted to smell the baby, but the mother's interpretation was that she was trying to show it that she, too, had a nose.

Although Mike and Maggie are both fully adult, our desire for children in their cage has not been satisfied to date. If Maggie should ever have a baby of her own, it would be a great event for the children of San Diego who have watched her grow from her own cunning infancy to her clever maturity.

CHAPTER VI

Cage-Mates

BEGINNING with Little Jiggs who came with Maggie, we have had a procession of orangs occupying our cages part of the time. Male and female, young and old, all have one trait so predominantly that I feel justified in calling it an orang characteristic. This is their flair for mechanical activity. Both Maggie and Little Jiggs, young as he was when he died, were adept in taking things apart. Orang-utans do not destroy objects in fits of erratic temper as do chimpanzees; neither do they do so accidentally because of their great strength like gorillas; they do it with a patient persistence and study that is astounding. The job is never forgotten until completed to their satisfaction. Even when Little Jiggs was ill, he played by the hour with tools and strings. He loved Henry's bunch of keys, twisting them and poking them into cracks and crevices. It was when he finally lost interest in the keys that we realized he was far gone, indeed. Maggie had amazed us not only with her bed-making and raveling-out of sacks, but with her ability to remove wires from her cage, turn on faucets, take out bolts, and move stumps — feats which required not only some study, but tremendous strength in the very ends of her long, slender fingers.

But her first real cage-mate, the big old female, Jiggs,

was even more amazing. I still believe that she was the smartest ape I ever knew, regardless of species. Her use of the principle of the lever, in which Maggie imitated her, was not aimless poking and prying for the fun of doing. It was a sure process applied to the most vulnerable part of the cage always. There was never a lost motion with Jiggs. If by chance or a trick she secured a stout bar, she would walk to the side of her cage and put the end of her lever under the largest loop in the chain link she had noted and remembered pending the time she could go to work on it. Right there, where the wires or bolts would be farthest apart, she would insert the bar until she had achieved real leverage; then she would put her entire weight, as well as her great strength, on it. She nearly escaped several times due to the carelessness of some outside workman temporarily employed in the vicinity of the cage, who had held his tool out for her to inspect and lost it because he was unaware of her great strength, or who had thoughtlessly leaned a crowbar or other tool against the wire for a minute or two. When men were working near or on their cage, Maggie and Jiggs watched constantly, pushing each other aside for the best and nearest point from which to view the operation.

One time, by dint of hard labor, Jiggs managed to pull a large pipe wrench into the cage. She could find nothing except wires to work on, which were so unsatisfactory that she had to content herself with opening and closing the jaws of the wrench by twisting the set screw. It was such fun and such a treasure that we hated to take it away from her and probably would have permitted her to play with it the rest of the day if it had not been for Maggie's curiosity. No matter what Jiggs was working with, Maggie was always interested and anxious to assist. On this occasion she was so insistent that she leaned over Jiggs's shoulder to stick her fingers so often into the fascinating play that Jiggs, at last, became impatient. Raising the heavy wrench, she nearly brained her. This use of the wrench seemed suddenly to interest Jiggs even more than screwing the puzzling tool had done. Henry had to go to Maggie's rescue. He succeeded in coaxing them into the house with an extra meal. Jiggs took her treasure in and kept her hand on it while they ate. Henry, after releasing Maggie, offered Jiggs everything he could think of in exchange for the treasure. Jiggs, knowing she had something above price, paid no attention. Henry had eventually to leave the room awhile. This made Jiggs feel she was being punished. She began to pound to get out and finally seemed to get the idea that she was being shut in because of the wrench. When Henry returned, she handed it to him and immediately turned to the door for release.

When we first placed the orang-utans, Maggie and Jiggs, in a large cage especially constructed for them, we had it equipped with two rings swung on long chains and stout swivels from the top of a pole in the exact center of the cage. These two rings were a foot in diameter and of stout steel, as were the chains. Maggie swung on them constantly. She would run around to get momentum and then swing free off the floor, becoming skilled in gaining more and more height by the use of her body. She soon learned that it was advisable to use both of the hoops at once, lest the other swing around and crack her hard little head.

Jiggs's body was too heavy to hang by her long arms, which made swinging too difficult for her. So the links meant nothing to her except something to take apart. Before long she took possession of rings and chains.

[89]

Climbing to the top of the cage, she wove the two chains back and forth through the wire mesh of the ceiling. Often she pushed a double loop through the wire mesh and left it in such a tangled knot that Henry was hours undoing it. Finally, by constant twisting, she broke links in the chain close to the hoops. The hoops dropped off, and then her real fun began. Skillfully she placed the end of each chain through the same opening in the wire, carried it across about four of the two-inch meshes, and bringing each chain down into the cage again, wrapped the two free ends around the chain just where it passed through the ceiling and began to twist. The leverage of the chains stretched the loops of flexible wire. Only the fact that it was six-gauge wire (the heaviest that is woven into chain link) saved the cage. We removed the two chains and installed larger hoops on shorter, stouter chains, covered with heavy steel pipe. This contrivance provided exercise and play for Maggie and resisted the wrecking activities of Jiggs — for about six months.

There will always be a repair job for the maintenance department at the orang cage — on hoops, or on drop bars, or on sliding doors of sleeping rooms, or on the cage itself. Maggie, by dogging Jiggs's heels and aping everything she did, learned several of her tricks that she still employs.

I never cease to be surprised at the instinct animals manifest for their own preservation. Their insistence upon fresh drinking water is one of the most universal of these. We build shallow drinking fountains with perpetual inflow in every cage. In the cage we built for the orangs, we had the fresh water bubble up from a small pipe in the center of the fountain. In our efforts to have nothing in the cage for them to destroy, we had set this pipe flush with the smooth cement bottom of the shallow basin. One day, as I stood by the cage with visitors carelessly watching the two orangs, I noticed that every few seconds a small spray of water would squirt up from the drinking basin where Jiggs sat, partly concealing it with her big body.

Walking around to that side of the cage, I watched an ingenious method of procuring fresh water. The big ape, using one flexible hand curved to fit the bottom of the basin, scooped out all the water she could, holding the forefinger of the other hand stuck down into the pipe for a stopper. When the basin was emptied, she would withdraw her finger a trifle and press it against one side of the pipe. The pressure of the water held back for several minutes caused a spurting spray. Jiggs was ready; putting her open mouth down over the spray she drank from it as long as it shot above the surface of the basin. As part fell into the basin, it was soon filled too deeply for spray. Long after her thirst was quenched, Jiggs kept on with the fountain. Maggie, hanging over her side trying to catch the spray, got one or two shots of water in her face, whether due to accident or Jiggs's design I cannot say. Later I saw Maggie practising the trick until she became as expert as Jiggs had been.

Although all orangs like to wrap themselves up, Mike, who became Jiggs's successor in the cage with Maggie, is the greatest exponent of blanket wearing I have ever known. Mike, approaching maturity when he arrived at the zoo, was thin and weak for his size. Within a few weeks after his arrival he became violently ill, suffering several hemorrhages which were finally diagnosed as resulting from bleeding ulcers and from which he was a long time recovering. In the zoo whence he came to us, he had been caged with one of the most tyrannical of female chimpanzees, and he had lived in fear of her tantrums. The cage had been small and Mike had had no chance for privacy either from his cage-mate or visitors. This experience had turned him into a retiring, shy creature, who even yet finds it hard to be under the close and intimate observation of anyone. I am sure that his habit of completely covering himself with a blanket resulted not so much from a need to protect himself from cold as from his longing for quiet and privacy.

Orang-utans are children of the heavy tropical forest, so accustomed to deep shade that they are sensitive to sunlight. Maggie covered her eyes or shaded them with her hands until Mike taught her that a sack hung over her head and shoulders furnished a far better and a much more convenient shade. So rain or shine, warm or cold weather, Maggie and Mike are usually partly wrapped in sacks. By tearing the sacks open down one side and across the end, they provide themselves with a fine, large "blanket" that is valuable in many ways. Properly stretched, blankets can be used as fishing ropes; the raveled edges catch many bits of paper or peanut shells. In truth, a big jute peanut sack lasts about two weeks. They are not permitted to carry all their bedding sacks into the outer cage; each morning they must hand them through the bars to their keeper, who hangs them for airing on the rail behind the sleeping quarters. Each ape is allowed to keep one to be used as a floor mat, blanket, or sunshade, as desired. When I see Maggie and Mike standing or walking partly erect and partly covered by their blankets, I am reminded of pictures of the inhabitants of the Mongolian Desert as they struggle across the windblown plain, ragged, quilted robes billowing out behind their bent figures.

Mike's introduction to Maggie was a turning point for the better in his theretofore disagreeable life. Mike understands her teasing and even her stubborn domination. Is she not one of his own phlegmatic, silent race, a red-haired, full-blooded mate to the Man of the Woods? When she annoys him too persistently, he pursues her through the bars at the top of the cage. He seems to have learned that if he appears to slacken in his pace or lose his desire for her, she will capitulate and permit him to catch her. It is a game of mutual deception that the two play as they turn handsprings over and over the length of the forty-foot cage, high above the floor. When Mike finally catches the little pest, he holds her tightly with his two feet and two hands. She squirms, pulls and twists until finally he releases an arm or leg or hand so that she can eventually struggle free. The silence during their physical struggle is awe-striking. Orangs are silent creatures even when two males are ready to fight to the death. Their only sound, then, is a grinding of their great teeth and a low, threatening mutter that chills you with its hideous, brutal indication of an eagerness to fight to the bitter end. The slow twisting of limbs and the pulling that is necessary to escape from the clasp and twisting of the powerful hands of an adversary is a skill learned in the physical romping of babyhood, and the silent endurance of a mere baby orang is astonishing. I have watched Maggie abuse some of the smaller apes that have been put into her cage until they finally whimpered through repressed lips; I have seen her endure silently a mauling by Jiggs which would have caused a young chimpanzee or any human child to scream for aid. Often when I have thought we

[93]

would have to interfere, the smaller orang has managed to break away, only to try at once to get a more favorable hold upon its larger adversary. So the silent struggle begins anew. This almost soundless, sweating struggle is, to me, much more hideous and deadly than the sudden fierce, angry fights of the two gorillas, which are always over before you could possibly interfere, or the noisy, haphazard, nondescript fights of the chimpanzee, or even the lightning, knifelike thrust of the flying gibbon. Any beast might turn away in horror if two of these Men of the Woods engaged seriously in a hand-to-hand struggle for survival. Older orang-utans show much patient forbearance toward the bothersome younger ones who demand their attention and cling to them constantly, sticking their fingers into everything their elders are doing.

Jiggs came to us from a moving-picture studio in Hollywood in a deal involving other animals. After years of excellent acting, she had turned vicious and began to hate man with a dangerous hate. For this reason, she was kept manacled to a steel rod in her cage. So long as her hands were free she could not be safely locked up in anything the studio had available. When she came to us, she was about ten or eleven years of age, and I knew her first as a grotesque, heavy-bodied, man-fearing creature. Miraculously, through her devotion to Henry, our primate keeper, she quickly became docile and obedient. This was a tribute to his control of animals and to his character. With Henry's death, Jiggs gradually turned again into the outlaw, hating everyone but me. When a chance came to trade her for Mike, we felt it best to accept. Thus we acquired Maggie's lean and spectacular mate.

Mike has never been a handsome orang. Although tall he stoops, keeping his face in a hollow breast sunk deep between his high narrow shoulders. Almost any male orang can double up into a small space, but Mike exceeds them all. He telescopes his long body into an unbelievably small compass.

Our anxiety to get him out of the shipping crate and into his cage made no difference to him, for after the sliding door had been raised he sat still for a very long time. Then one great red hand appeared, and literally piece by piece the big fellow emerged. With a gait which combined rolling, whirling, and crawling, he in some way reached the side of the cage and, in another second, an arm was extended which I thought would never stop short of the fifteen-foot ceiling. When the hand came to a stop, the ape stood up and it actually reached not more than ten feet above the ground. Grasping the wire of the cage, he swung his body up sideways and was soon suspended by all fours near the corner, his head still concealed between the great hairy upper arms and curved-in shoulders.

When Maggie emerged from her door, we could not tell whether Mike was looking at her or not, but with that perfection of slow motion which only an orang-utan or a sloth can encompass, he moved across the ceiling of the cage to the opposite corner. Releasing one foot and moving it as far out as he could reach, he took a firm grasp of the wire; then the arm on the same side moved into place gradually and, with no particular order in using his limbs, he crossed the ceiling.

Comparing the movements of the two manlike apes of Eastern Asia, I am reminded of the grasshopper and the heavy, fat old garden toad. One — the gibbon —

"flies" through the tops of trees, springs with grace, agility and speed incredible. The other moves laboriously, awkwardly, using all of his four limbs and turning upside-down handsprings. The individual movements of the orang-utan are of the speed of a slow-motion film but the total movement seems rapid. The round, fat, somewhat puffy body of the toad, with its four comparatively slender arms and legs at the four corners of the heavy body, and its short neck and insignificant head, is not unlike the recumbent body of a large female orang. But the limbs of the orang are much more casually attached to its body than are those of the toad. I long to see just what sort of a swivel joint gives them so much play that they can not only tie themselves up into small bundles, but disentangle themselves from the strangle holds they endure in their rough-and-tumble wrestling matches without dropping off a leg or arm as insects do. All of the manlike apes except the gorillas are characterized by pinched abdomens without hips and with no pelvic cavity; the orang is the most pinched of all. It seems impossible that blood vessels, nerves and vital organs could have sufficient space in that congested area for proper working connections.

It is reported by all observers of the orang-utan in the wild that he is a great climber, much more apt to be found in solitary conditions than other great apes. The orang, like the gibbon, moves through treetops, but he must first carefully test his strength and gather great handfuls of small branches and twigs together tightly to give his great body support. He never uses, so far as I have been able to learn, the more limber branches of trees as a swing; nor does he leap from one object to another, whether in the zoo or in the wild, as does the gibbon or even the more nearly ground-dwelling chimpanzee. Traveling high in the branches of the thick forests, he moves with caution and, considering the slowness of his individual movements, at a surprisingly rapid gait. His enormously long arms and spidery body, the strength and holding power of his long, flexible feet and toes, aid him greatly in this particular. The orang can turn giant cartwheels in the air. He can move rapidly, arm over arm, suspended at full length; or he can move forward, sideways or backward by employing all methods in no particular sequence.

He grasps his long hands firmly about the trunk of a tree and goes up with remarkable speed and agility. Upon reaching the leafy top, he is expert at concealing his body while moving soundlessly. It is said that, wounded, the orang will hastily construct a leafy platform or rough nest, and partially cover his body with broken branches and leaves; that if pursued too closely he will attack his enemy by throwing broken branches at him, or sticks which he seems able to aim with some accuracy.

But to return to Mike, I am fascinated to watch him swing around his cage, just for the pleasure of exercise. Late in the afternoon he comes to life, rapidly climbs the nearest pole to the highest bar in the maze in the top of the cage, and then around and around the cage he tears — upside down, hanging like a sloth by all fours, turning cartwheels, or swinging along by his five-foot arms. Suddenly he will seize an upright of the trapeze with one hand and one foot and, without any effort, support himself nearly erect at arm's length from the pole, whirling rapidly around the pole half a dozen times under what motor power I have never quite been able to discern. Of all the strange things Mike can do, this one is the most extraordinary. I can imagine him on

[97]

the stem of a giant bamboo or some slender palm, enjoying in solitude this same wild swing, high above lush undergrowth.

On the ground, Mike literally walks on all fours; when he stands erect, his long arms easily reach his feet. His gait is quite different from either Jiggs's or Maggie's. His hands are closed so that the knuckles of the big red fingers bear most of the weight of his body. His feet are curved inward and he whirls around completely several times in traversing half of the width of his cage. He lies often on his back, with his arms shielding his face from the light and his lower limbs bent sharply at the spread knees so that his feet are coiled against his groins.

Mike was with us for nearly two years before he ever permitted me to know that he recognized my voice; it was even longer before he would come to me to accept food. Even now Mike sometimes refuses to accept my advances, but he never fails to turn his face to me or uncover it if I am close to the cage and speak his name. He is most unselfish in his association with Maggie and shares with her any treats offered. He chews his food very slowly, as do most orangs, seeming to extract from it the last iota of pleasure. He likes particularly to retain stalks of celery, sugar cane, or banana skins until his mouth is filled with a stringy mass which he chews for hours, rolling it over and over until it is a fibrous wad which he finally takes out and pushes through the wire.

Mike shows less mechanical genius than most orangs and he seldom destroys anything except the shelves of wood in his inner quarter. However, he does interesting things with his sacks besides using them for shawls. He twists and pulls and chews until he works the hemp into long ropes, strong but ragged. These ropes he braids or weaves in and out the bars of his sleeping room or the meshes in the wire of his cage. He uses them, also, as lassoes for objects beyond his reach. But Mike's greatest achievement is spitting. I have never known an ape that could at one time produce and discharge such a great amount of saliva. This spitting is not only Mike's greatest accomplishment but his most human one. However, he has never had the offensive habit of spitting at visitors or zoo employees which is common to chimpanzees and some orangs. He sits in dignified and silent contemplation, appearing not to know that anyone is watching him, until suddenly he turns his head a little to one side, purses his lips and expectorates on the floor or ground just outside his cage. He glances in the direction of his achievement and goes back into his almost inanimate state. Secretly, he takes tremendous pride in his prowess and enjoys the hearty laughter and the comments of the crowd. As this is his one great exhibition trick, he indulges in it frequently. The only time Mike has shown the mean, sly tricks that are often accredited to his race, especially to the male, have been when he was taunted by another male.

Mike has, for the past three years, shown most of the signs of the adult orang-utan male. His face is long and narrow, with a high hump, or crest, of firm flesh, rising under his hairline and actually adding to his length. Although some males do not develop wide and somewhat pendulous cheek callosities completely hiding their small close-set ears, Mike is now gaining them quite rapidly. His chin is covered with a neat beard, much brighter in color than the rest of his auburn coat. Below this, a laryngeal sac is hugely prominent. Occasionally he experiments with his ability to inflate this sac, but his life in the cage is on the whole far too peaceful for him to have cause for real inflation. The enormous sac, which most visitors call a goiter, is connected by small openings to the larynx. Air may be forced into the sac through these openings, causing it to enlarge greatly, which it does when the orang is under tense excitement. The protuberance gives to the one blessed with it an appearance of ferocious, almost threatening, power. Mike is singularly devoid of the curiosity of his race, which is the most curious of all the great apes. Often as I think of his complete indifference even to other orang-utans and his superb self-control, I say to myself, "Here is the stuff of which Tibetan monks are made!"

When we brought Goola, a young female orang, from the Orient and introduced her into Mike's and Maggie's cage, in 1936, Mike was gentle with her although she was, and remains, a teasing pest. It was Maggie's incessant tormenting and slight hurting that eventually forced us to remove Goola. Before doing so, however, we installed a fine, young male orang that Osa Johnson had given us. Mike recognized a potential rival at once. He gritted his teeth and muttered at the mere sight of Bujang, and the hair on each of the males would rise, cheeks and gular sac were inflated, and they blew noisy breaths of hatred at each other. The two were, of course, separated at night by the two barred sleeping rooms occupied by Goola and Maggie, and neither was allowed to be in the outer cage when the other was present. Mike was there one day, and Bujang, the next.

On one of the days when Bujang was locked inside, Maggie kept working at the door which confined him.

She was greatly enamored with her new friend, and it was not difficult to understand old Mike's jealousy. Several times Moore drove her away from the door and examined it to be sure it was secure. We cannot do it ourselves, but in some way — by slightly tipping and manipulating the door — Maggie shoved it out of the steel channel in which it slides, and got it open.

Instead of Bujang's coming out, in one second Mike shoved past Maggie into the room, grabbed the innocent Bujang and dragged him forth. Bujang's leg was badly lacerated by the grasp of Mike's enormous mouth, and both bones below the knee were fractured. In spite of this, Bujang gave a good account of himself. It took heroic efforts to separate them.

Dr. Wegeforth, a famous bone surgeon, worked with Dr. Schroeder to repair the damage to Bujang's limb and each day the utmost attention was given to the wounds. The cast was cut open on each side for treatment and drainage and Bujang was a model patient, helping as much as he could. He seemed happy, maintained a keen appetite, and was always affectionate with Emily De Konza, the hospital technician and attendant. Mr. Perkins was chief daily assistant and Bujang's treatment became so systematized that as soon as he saw the crew arriving he would move off his dirty bedding onto the clean bedding and hold out his leg and arms for the controlling panels and bars with little coaxing, after the first few weeks. When the dressing was finished, he would hand out the boards and help to spread the clean serval bedding. Then, one day, when the splintered bones had almost completely knit and only a small wound remained, the hospital called me to say that Bujang was dead. I rushed over. He lay limp on the autopsy table. He was fat, had an excellent color and his leg, as I say, had almost healed. No one knew what had happened until an autopsy revealed that death was due to a sudden pneumonia attack and a blood clot in the heart.

With the elimination of both Goola and Bujang from their cage, life for Mike and Maggie settled down into the routine and somewhat humdrum affair it was before the arrival of the younger orangs. Maggie and Mike both enjoy and endure each other's presence. For the greater part of each day they lie covered with their heavy sacks, rousing only now and then — at some unusually loud noise, or at the approach of their keeper, or when some party nears the cage. But when I walk down the row at night, after the rest of the anthropoid apes have gone to sleep, I hear them stirring and grunting, murmuring to each other. So I am convinced that they are much more nocturnal in their habits than are the other great apes. This may account for the scarcity of the information that has found its way to us from the land of their origin. Orangs appear to be even more limited in number than gorillas, but this may be due to their habit of sleeping in leaf-covered nests during the usual hours of exploration. They alone of all the apes frankly enjoy covering, especially over their heads and faces, and their custom of pulling branches and leaves over their bodies, partly for protection from sun and perhaps rain, surely also has something to do with keeping them from view.

The solitary or limited family life of a zoo cage appears to have little effect on the orang. In other zoos, I have seen two or three in large exhibition cages, sitting far apart, apparently completely oblivious of the presence of each other, except for a baby held tightly in its mother's arms. The reports that they are monogamous or even nearly solitary in their native woods are probably well founded. They differ from the gibbons in that they may not even keep their young with them after a new child makes its appearance in the family.

CHAPTER VII

Orangs, Large and Small

BY THEIR destruction of Bujang and driving of Goola from the cage, Maggie and Mike seemed only to strengthen Dr. Harry's determination to exhibit a group of orangs. So on the next expedition to the Orient he made a supreme effort to obtain an exhibit similar to one of the family groups that had been collected by the firm of Louis Ruhe of Hanover, in 1927. These adult pairs, most of whom were accompanied by babies or juveniles, constituted the most extraordinary collection of apes ever brought from any jungle. The collection, I understand, consisted of twenty-seven specimens, including perhaps eight mated pairs. It was the first time that adult giant male orangs had ever been brought alive into zoos. The final outcome, however, was a tragedy. Few, if any, lived long enough to bring other young into the world, and little actual scientific work was done while they remained alive. Published reports have dwelt at some length upon the remarkable diversity in the orang's appearance, the different shapes and sizes of the cheek callosities, the length and patterns among the beards, and other hirsute adornment. If the individuals in the collection just mentioned had been more scientifically observed while in captivity and if a proper recording of their activities in the wild had been brought back with them, a much longer life and more valuable information would almost surely have been the reward. It is doubtful if such a collection will ever again be made, for the orang has already disappeared from many of his former territorial limits, and is now confined almost exclusively to Sumatra and Borneo.

Soon after Bujang's death, Dr. Harry and Karl Koch left for Calcutta, where Karl was to stop and collect specimens, bringing them back with others he would gather at Java and Singapore. The Doctor planned to go on to East Africa, help with a collection of African animals being made by our head keeper, Charley Smith, then in Nairobi, cross Africa and return home by the South Atlantic route. But illness overtook Dr. Harry. Instead of going to Africa, he was forced to take advantage of an early opportunity to return to California.

About the first words he said to me when he reached the zoo were, "Old girl, Karl Koch is bringing you the biggest orang you ever saw!" One of our standing jokes was that Doctor's eyeglasses unduly magnified animals he was purchasing. He always explained away his enthusiasm by claiming that their shrunken size on arrival was due to the hardships of the voyage to America. Another of his pleasant habits of speech was, "I have bought you . . ." He spoke of every new animal as though it were a personal gift, and I think he knew that every good addition to the zoo always did seem just that to me.

When our shipment arrived from Surabaya in the following month, it really did contain the largest and by far the most impressive orang-utan I have ever seen.

For once, Dr. Harry had not exaggerated. The two-hundred–pound beast was in a cage weighing fourteen hundred pounds. The crate was made of steel rods set in heavy steel plates, and lined with teakwood or mahogany. Outside this wood was sheet metal, but the inner walls and wooden shelves had been splintered by the teeth and hands of the orang during the forty days he spent in transit. He had bent and twisted the steel bars in the front until Karl, fearing he might reach out and injure someone, had wound a heavy chain, padlocked at the ends, back and forth across the front. A large sign had been attached to the cage, reading DANGER! KEEP AWAY! The First Officer took no chances with his crew becoming careless and standing or passing within reach of the great hands.

My eagerness to see the creature was unbounded. I stood back a foot or two from the cage and, stooping, peered in. The light was not too good and the dark-red body of the animal was curled into that small area into which an adult orang can coil; thus he was only dimly visible. Turned toward me was a black face with small, lusterless black eyes, close together and slanting. That face, with its huge callosities extending seven or eight inches beyond the cheeks on each side, its enormous fat crest like a crown high above the long face, and with a laryngeal sac like a pendulous pillow, was the most enormous and sinister object I have ever looked upon. Although I had been prepared for the orang's size, I could not believe that what I gazed upon was anything but an optical illusion. The orang's hands were held close to his body; the fingers looked as large as my own wrist. That was Katjeung. He looked at me intently, right into my eyes, and I drew back without speaking.

"Well," asked Karl, "what do you think of him?"

"I just don't believe it, Karl." And I never really did.

When Katjeung arrived in San Diego, Ralph Virden looked at him just once and went immediately to the

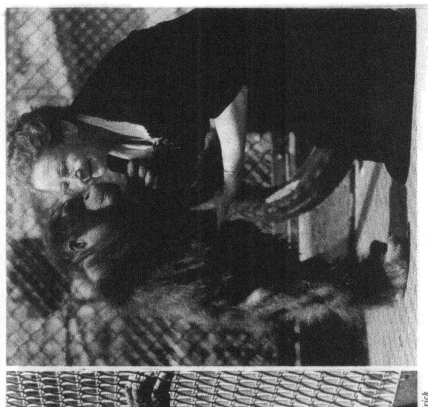

Kok-Kok Likes to Whisper His Needs

Photo E. H. Boldrick

Katjeung — Unbelievably Sinister

orang-utan cage where he welded two more heavy bars across the steel grill in the sleeping room. He put another one below the bottom of the grill to close any opening through which he might extend that enormous hand. Next a heavy chain and padlock were put in place so that Moore need not depend upon the regular locked bar to hold the door in place. Not until all this had been accomplished was the great ape taken over. Then, without haste or hurry, we permitted the animal to move straight through the safety cage into the open exhibition area. He walked with his head held far forward, his back curved over. His enormous arms supported the heavy forward part of the body as he moved across the big outer cage with the whirling motion of all great male orang-utans. Although much of his hair had been rubbed off in the crate, that about his feet hung like a skirt.

Orangs seldom appear to be excited, but if you are quite close to them and are familiar with their ways, you may recognize as a sign of excitement, fear, hatred or anger, the grinding of their great dark teeth. The great Katjeung had been raised in the Surabaya Zoo, where he had grown to this enormous stature from that of a medium-sized child in seven years. He was not excited by people. Maggie and Mike, in the cage next door, had been almost consumed with curiosity during the moving process. Maggie had climbed to the top of her cage twenty times or more during the hour of work which attended the moving of the crate: the bolting, chaining, and bracing so that escape would be impossible. All she could see was men climbing over the top of a huge, rusty-metal box, the old familiar truck, and the bars and braces she knew too well. And then while she was not looking in the right direction, the great beast emerged and whirled across the cage, mounted to a low corner shelf, and turned his face toward her and Mike. Her attention was attracted by a deep, threatening grunt from the nearly silent Mike, and the loud grinding of his teeth.

Across the three-foot alley separating the two cages, the adult males glared at each other with malice. As they eyed each other across the intervening area, I wondered if the eight-inch steel bars and six-gauge wire could keep so much murderous hatred apart.

Day after day, the grinding and spitting, the muttering of low threats, went on. The two faced each other and their malevolence increased. Maggie never let Mike forget that within sight was a rival for her affections. She would swing over to the corner nearest Katjeung the first thing in the morning and through the wire do her best to attract his attention. Mike would rush to the defense of his home life, and so the deadly grinding of broad dark teeth and sullen glaring hatred would begin and continue throughout the day. Katjeung was so filled with desire to get at Mike that for several days he repulsed all efforts to get him to eat. Finally, I had to decide to see what I could do.

In spite of my knowledge of the sly, cunning, enormous strength and swift moves which characterize the orang, I had nevertheless always loved the ape and had never felt afraid before. Now I hesitated to offer Katjeung food from my hand. I looked at his dark, hairy fingers — at least ten inches long and huge, curved a little as is characteristic. If my hands got near the wire I was sure I could not keep them from his grasp. The middle finger was gone from his left hand, but the scar was well healed and was so barely noticeable that even Karl had not yet seen the blemish.

I stooped down between the cages so as to obstruct Katjeung's view of Mike unless he moved, and for the

[108]

first time he looked straight into my eyes. Quietly I spoke to him, calling his name, and keeping my voice low as I edged a little nearer. Gradually, the gnashing and grinding of his teeth diminished. I kept talking to him, although Mike was still grinding away behind me. After a few minutes, a different expression came into Katjeung's sullen, hateful eyes; he looked at me more intently, as though listening to and studying my voice and expression. Slowly I brought my hands up and he muttered or blew audibly through his lips — not the hissing of a frightened orang, but something I had never heard before; almost like the sound of a voice, but made just with breath and lips.

I showed him a fine, large peach, broken in two, and pressed it to the wire. Slowly, suspiciously, and with no appearance of eagerness, he moved that tub-sized face forward and, extending his lips, took the peach in them. He manipulated it out of the fuzzy skin, still with his lips, and slowly ate. He took the second half in his fingers and curling the great hand around it went back to his serious contemplation of my face. He showed no interest in the other food I had brought.

Although willing to accept my offering that day and on subsequent days as a friendly overture, Katjeung did not make friends readily. But day by day I knew I was gaining ground with him, and he often moved around to face me on the shelf as I walked away. The day he climbed down off the shelf, forgetting his enemy across the narrow aisle, and followed me to the west end of the cage as I walked down toward the chimpanzees, I experienced a thrill of victory so great that it surprised me. Katjeung was now taking whatever I gave him. He would treasure it in his great hands while I was present and eat it after I had gone. On all of the occasions that

I fed him, he took the food from my hand with his lips, removed it from his mouth with his hand, and never offered to grab or touch me. I had ceased to feel in the slightest danger after the first time I fed him; I had begun to think he liked me. He never tried to put his fingers through the wires and often leaned so close that I could touch his crest or great cheek callosities.

I persisted in my attentions until, gradually, Katjeung showed plainly that he watched for me and liked my visits. He developed an appetite and began, also, to respond somewhat to the kindness and calmness of Moore, who I was sure could eventually win the affection of any ape. Katjeung spent most of his days curled up on the bench and left it only to take exercise by whirling through the maze of bars in his cage. About this time the youngster Goola, also a Borneo orang, was placed in the cage with him. At first he ignored her and then became so rough with her that we were forced to take her out. He had not forgotten his antagonism toward old Mike, but seemed to realize the impossibility of reaching him. He had lost a good deal of weight on the long trip from the Orient and during the time when he had refused to eat, but it became obvious to us all that he was regaining all that he had lost. Although the need of my daily visits had passed, I went often to his cage so that he would not lose his friendliness for me.

One day a large group of motor cops from Long Beach were in San Diego to attend the funeral of a fellow officer and called upon me at the zoo. I went down to the great apes with them and we walked within the guard fence so that they could have a good view of the great fellows. Their uniforms and badges were of immense interest to the gibbons and to Maggie, who wanted to handle everything, including their guns. Suddenly, while standing close to the corner where Katjeung had hurried to greet me, I heard once more the ominous grinding. I had not heard it for weeks. The great beast muttered, spat, and chewed. He took hold of the wire and, bracing himself, pulled it with all his might, muttering deep in his throat and grinding sickeningly. The officers had no difficulty in interpreting that noise. They hurried away, and the great hands relaxed. Katjeung looked once more into my eyes, calm and friendly. A few days later when I again went close to the cage in the company of others — this time a man and woman — the grinding recurred. I decided that Katjeung's actions were prompted by jealousy over my attentions to other people and, therefore, I would not stop at Katjeung's cage again with visitors.

Early in December, Bob Moore came to me with the worried expression that I have come to associate with trouble with the anthropoids.

"Will you look at Katjeung's pouch this morning?" he asked. "The side is swollen and the skin is shining and looks like it was blistered."

As soon as possible I went over and saw that the spot which he and Dr. Schroeder had been watching for some time was really showing evidence of being something serious and that a crisis must be approaching. The big ape, usually interested in what I was doing, gazed at me with dull eyes and kept his big arms up, partly concealing and partly supporting the heavy pouch. The skin on the entire right side was slick and showed evidence of peeling or opening; the swelling was heavy and concentrated in one area right of the center and above the largest part of the loose folds of skin.

Dr. Schroeder had already decided that surgical care was indicated. Now the big hospital cage was inspected, reinforced, and the old shipping crate in which Katjeung had made his long journey from Java was brought, cleaned, and made ready for the transfer. On December ninth, Katjeung walked willingly into it and was carried up to the hospital. There he was given an anesthetic and his condition thoroughly examined. We found a deep abscess, probably caused by some particle of foreign matter that had lodged in the huge fibrous pouch through the small openings into the throat. The wound was cleaned, packed, and the great fellow was placed in the big hospital holding crate, with its sliding panel, which would permit the attendants to hold the great arms, hands and feet tight while the proper care was given to him daily. The diagnosis that came over in the morning hospital report read ominously: "Katjeung, male orang, hospitalized 12/9: Gangrene — laryngeal ventricle."

I was deeply shocked by the appearance of the opening and the extent of the injury. I can never see such things with the eyes of a nurse or surgeon; the granulations, draining, and all of the indications of repair that nature provides mean nothing. The reports went on, and I was sure our magnificent orang was completely doomed. Dr. Schroeder assured me that Katjeung was progressing beautifully, was a model patient, and that he himself aided in keeping the wound clean and draining. Dr. Wegeforth also said he thought I need have no fear. But I was alarmed by the fact that the great ape was so docile and acquiesced so completely in the treatment. He accepted patiently rice, cereals and food from a huge spoon when Emily De Konza offered them to him, and would lean over gladly to take whatever fruit and vegetables I brought him, always permitting me to touch his hand.

When he began to be bored with just getting well, my optimism returned — this was an indication, surely, that his suffering had ceased. We now gave him things to play with for he had, orang fashion, begun to test out the nuts, bolts and pins which held his cage. Emily provided him with sacks and a long piece of very light hemp rope. This he wove in and out around the bars of his cage in intricate patterns, then took almost as long to untangle it. He wore out several lengths of the rope before this fascinating pastime bored him. As I watched him day after day at his task, I reiterated the thought I had expressed several times in the past: it is too bad that the orang's intelligent mechanical ability cannot be trained for useful activity. Of all the anthropoids, orangs alone seem to have something man could really use if properly handled.

The gaping hole in the laryngeal sac was drawing closer and closer together. It looked now like a great puckering. Dr. Schroeder told me that he felt sure Katjeung would not even bear a disfiguring scar. That morning my report from the hospital, dated January nineteenth, read: "Katjeung: Drainage established; healing, prognosis good."

I asked Dr. Schroeder to write to the Eastern zoo with which we had arranged a very advantageous trade for Katjeung, describing the injury, its probable cause, its present condition, and what the result in the appearance of the ape would be. Soon we had word that someone would be out to look at some other animals and would probably take the ape back, if pleased. This was good news, but we were in a dilemma. We did not wish to move the great ape back into his big cage, now occupied by the two young ones. Neither did we wish to hold him in the heavy shifting cage, for part of the daily

[113]

treatment was moving the big hospital cage out on its rollers into the sunshine. But restless energy — the last characteristic one would associate with the lethargic, slow-moving orang — was beginning to manifest itself. Several times hurry calls had been sent to the maintenance department to come quickly and strengthen some bar or part of the cage. The cage had begun to have a patched-up look; everyone was now on the alert for some sign of weakness. One day Katjeung braced himself and pushed the sliding door off its track so that it could not be moved; he had also bent several of the heavy rods of which the sides of the cage were constructed, and sat slyly waiting for some visitor or keeper to approach so close that he could extend his mighty hand with lightning speed and grasp the unwary one. Discovering this, the caretaker sent for help.

Later in the day, Dr. Schroeder came to me with a sick and worried expression.

"I have just taken Ralph to the doctor," he said. "Katjeung got him."

I learned that, in answer to the hospital's emergency call for someone to repair the cage, Ralph Virden and an assistant had hurried over. By the time they arrived Katjeung had nearly taken out another bar. As Ralph passed between the cage and the wall, Katjeung struck, grabbing his arm and pulling him so close to the cage that his whole body was encircled by the great hairy red arm. Only Virden's strength and agility, coupled with the fact that he was wearing a heavy leather jacket, saved his hand and perhaps his life. As the beast pulled, Ralph allowed the sleeve of the jacket, with its double cuff, to slip farther and farther down over his hand until just as help arrived he pulled himself free. Two fingers

[114]

were horribly torn, a finger bone was broken, and the hand itself was deeply lacerated. For many weeks he was under medical care. This taught everyone to increase his caution. The cage was heavily reinforced, but our problem of holding Katjeung grew greater constantly. It was with relief that we finally consummated the trade and saw the big fellow leave, in his old fourteen-hundred-pound crate, for an Eastern zoo, where a cage strong enough for his confinement awaited him.

During all of Katjeung's time at the hospital, Emily fed him and while she too was alert when dealing with him, he never tried to grab at her. Frequently, also, I visited him, usually with a treat. Not once did he show anything but the most kindly and intent interest in me. He looked back into my eyes steadily with his own slanting small ones. At first they were dull with illness, then brighter and happier. With a deep-throated guttural rumbling through tight lips, he would murmur a friendly greeting and reach over with his lips to take the food I held out.

I doubt if I could ever have come to feel the affection for Katjeung that I have felt for most of my apes, but knowing he would not remain with us long I made such overtures toward friendship as I could in order to add to his health and make his stay with us happy.

The story of a group of apes in any zoo is never written, for gradually each group grows up to reach an age of staid contentment, when they spend the time covered with sacks, lolling in the sun on cold days, or in the shade on warm ones, stirring reluctantly to come to the wire when one calls them, urged on by mild curiosity as to what sort of treatment they may receive or what kind of treat one brings. But always, at about this stage, some new younger group arrives to add life and interest to the exhibit.

So now when Maggie and Mike, having reached the age of maturity, find life easy and slow, we have next door, in the cage where Katjeung used to sit venting his hatred of patient old Mike, a pair of young orangs, Kok-Kok and Goola.

Goola came to us in 1936, as a tiny red-haired creature who spent most of her time en route in Mr. Perkins' arms and who, within a week of her arrival, literally adopted us all as doting parents or willing slaves. "Goola" means sugar, but her name really should be Vanity. She is of all the animals I have ever known the most delighted with her own beauty. She could spend days at a time adorning herself with bits of string and cloth.

Kok-Kok was brought by Karl Koch on the same ship with the great Katjeung. At first we hesitated about putting him in with the bigger Goola, but after they had occupied small cages side by side for some time we turned them together gradually an hour or two each day.

Until I saw Goola with Kok-Kok, I failed to realize how our "little sugar" had grown and how black her cinnamon-brown face had turned. I recall with a smile her spindling limbs, her heavy distended abdomen, the heavy cold from which she suffered and my feeling that we could never raise her. I truly think she is now the ugliest and, I am sure, the naughtiest little ape I have ever seen. She begs from the visitors by wriggling her long hands out through the wire and making ingratiating faces at them. When she sees any of the staff approaching, she quickly withdraws her hand and, pursing her lips, spits at the visitor as though he were the transgressor. But she is as strong as an ape twice her size should be, and is sly and spiteful, making quick grabs or passes at visitors if they are not exceedingly wary.

Kok-Kok, a little younger than Goola, is still at the cunning-child age when he craves constant love and affection. He presses his soft lips against your face in a kiss, and reaches his long arms about your neck to hold you close. He is a little shy with strangers, but if they permit him to make the advances, soon he is clasping them as lovingly as he does those of us he knows the best. As Moore says, "It takes two men and a boy to break him loose." He and Goola romp and play, and he takes a good deal of punishment. Usually he keeps silent, wriggles his loose joints and stout muscles out of her grasp, and seldom retreats when he does get loose. Now and then he gets even with her, as the other day when he carried an old tire aloft in the cage and, watching his chance, dropped it on her as she passed a few feet below him. He is contented just at present to let her bully him, seeming to know that in a few years he will surpass her in size and come into his place as master of the cage.

I feel that surely, between two pairs of adult orangs — Maggie and Mike, Goola and Kok-Kok — we shall eventually have at least one baby orang born. If this should occur during my life at the zoo, I can hold out no promise of leaving it with its mother. As delicately beautiful as I found the baby gibbon, Primo, and as engagingly cunning as I considered baby Georgie, the little chimpanzee born in our zoo, no human heart, least of all mine or that of anyone living in a zoo, could withstand the appeal of a baby orang. It would take more self-control than I have.

When I saw the first living mother orang with her baby at Madame Abreau's in Cuba, I could not believe

[117]

that that great, rotund, coarse-skinned mother could ever have produced such a completely perfect baby. As Madame Abreau and I approached, the little round head turned towards me. The tiny red body was sprawled across the mother's obese body, but as we drew nearer the little arms slipped as the clutching little fingers let go of their strangle hold on the mother's coarse long red hair, and the face, with white lips and white skin encircling the eyes, screwed into an entrancing grin. The baby had recognized Madame Abreau! He was then three months old. A sharp spike of red hair stood erect on the top of the little red head. Suddenly he turned his face downward. Once more the groping fingers reached a little farther to grab the favorite locks of hair on the mother's shoulder and side, and the tannish face snuggled down into the fat rolls under the mother's arms where pendulous breasts hung full of warm nourishment for the babe.

From that second I have wanted to hold and play with and keep close to me a baby orang. I know they are difficult to raise, that they become mean, headstrong and destructive, and that they are mischievous and always into things, but all this is entirely offset by their thousands of cute expressions. No other baby animal has anything like the innocence, the confidence, and the complete dependence upon you and your love as has the baby orang. Your desire to grant them all that they expect, and much, much more, is awakened to an irresistible degree.

During a recent visit to the St. Louis Zoo, I saw a thick-coated mother orang with a baby not yet a week old. She was sitting near the side of her cage and Mr. Vierheller permitted me to go close to the glass of the window. When I gazed upon that toothless little face with its puckered mouth turned toward me, with a

kewpie peak on the round little bullet head and its innocent baby stare, I knew again that a baby orang is something I must really have one day in this, our lovely zoo.

Probably the first of the really complete records of a
young orang was kept at the Philadelphia Zoo where
several were born and where many of Madame Abreau's
finest apes found their final home. According to the
published reports of this zoo, their baby orang was quite
helpless at birth but the mother was so wisely careful of
it that it was able to cling strongly to her body as she
climbed about the cage.

Not until our adopted orangs have lost their baby
teeth have they ever shown any inclination to bite, and
that is easily stopped by a smart little slap on the mouth.
They are dexterous with a spoon at quite an early age,
and much prefer food offered them in that way to sucking from a nipple. All become very friendly with much
less difficulty than our imported young chimpanzees.
Although the chimpanzee may not be very much afraid,
it has a certain caution or lack of confidence in the human race that makes it necessary for each individual to
make a friend of the baby chimp.

But to think of babies in our orang family just now is
to speculate pretty much in the future. We must enjoy
to the utmost the two children we have, especially young
Kok-Kok, with the affectionate kisses which he offers so
freely to everyone after a few days' acquaintance. He
forces his heavy hands through the wire, pulls my face
just as close to his as he can, and his long, soft lips do
the rest. I am trying to teach him to kiss my cheek, but
apparently in his home at the Surabaya zoo lip kisses
were permissible. He is very much disturbed and hurt
when I turn my head away from his ardent caresses.
The other day as I started away from the wire, after

[119]

refusing to accept any more, I heard a sharp little ping of his lips and glanced around just in time to discover that he was preparing to show his displeasure by spitting; if not on me, at least in my general direction. He already knew it was a naughty gesture (which he learned from Goola) because when he saw that he was detected in his contemplated act, he turned quickly and pulled in his pointed lips as though he had no such evil thought in mind.

One of the most amazing metamorphoses in the animal world is the one that changes the entrancing, laughing, pathetic, ever-changing little face surmounting the active, agile, cunning, cuddly little body of the baby orang into the serious, slow-moving, stolid, monstrous ape known since ancient times as "Pongo, Man of the Woods."

PART THREE
PAN: THE HALF-MAN

CHAPTER VIII

Bondo and His Mates

IN COMMON with most persons whom I have known, when I came to the zoo I classed in my mind as apes all of the monkey and baboon tribes of creatures, and naturally I was not able to distinguish between the hundreds of species of smaller primates. And so I find it easy to understand the confusion that prevails among laymen. It was with the idea of giving you a clear picture at least of the four families of great apes that I began this book about them, but as I progress with the stories of these friends of mine I find that that is not what I seem to be doing; rather I am trying to acquaint you with my favorite independent characters. If there accrues sufficient characterization of the different species, as such, to make each family distinct and clearly defined, I shall be happy, indeed. But first I must know that you would recognize Gibby and Blackie and all of the lovely characters among the men who walk on the trees. And surely you would recognize Maggie if you were to meet her in any zoo, for what zoo in the English-speaking world has not had an actual "Maggie" in its collection of apes? Our Maggie without a doubt is the universal — should I say collective? — female orang.

But after I became really acquainted with the differences between monkeys, baboons and apes, I found it pleasant first to segregate them in my mind, as we do in our exhibit, and then to approach each from a widely different angle and derive an additional joy in understanding their true characters. This is an experience I wish you might share. Many successful zoo employees and executives have never done this; perhaps because they came into zoo staffs knowing too much generally about the work and the science upon which it was founded. I had everything to learn about each and every creature; my time was limited and so I progressed slowly in my natural science. But how rapidly, oh how rapidly, I went forward in my personal friendships and acquaintances! That has worked out an intimate knowledge of individuals first, and a growth from the individual to the species and genera. To the student and scientist, this procedure is beginning at the wrong end, nevertheless in my case it has taken me along a most interesting, joyful trail. In almost every case of ape friendship the first creature I have known has taught me the essential facts about the whole of his family tree. In no single instance has this been more definitely true than in the case of the shiny-coated, black-faced chimpanzee to whose family I was introduced, almost the day I came to the zoo, by Bondo and Dinah, at that time the only representatives of the Great Apes in the zoo.

Almost every zoo, circus and animal act, especially as shown in moving pictures, contains trained chimpanzees. This makes the chimpanzee the best known of all the anthropoid apes — so much so that he is by many called by all three names: orang-utan, gorilla, and chimpanzee — or just ape.

Distributed throughout the Western area of tropical Africa, the chimpanzee was perhaps the earliest ape to be identified in his true habitat. He is called by the name *Pan satyrus*, based upon the mythological god of the forests Pan, who was half-man, but implying by the specific name that he is something of a lecherous and comical figure of a man, surrounded, of course, by legend and mystery. Without doubt he appeared thus to those first early explorers who honestly believed the reports by natives that he was originally the child of a human mother sired by a beast. He was called by the common name chimpanzee, which I hope will soon be universally accepted as the specific name. It is a native word, and as such I like it.

Due to his ready adaptation to the ways of captivity and his hardy body, the chimpanzee will always be much more frequently shown in zoos and circuses than any of the other great apes. His training is comparatively easy, for he is naturally imitative and usually is more inquisitive and less sensitive to changing conditions than any of the other apes. He is so comical that most people are attracted to him and seem to overlook his repulsive similarity to man; but not for long. Visitors do not linger at our chimpanzee cage as at the cages of the other great apes. Personally I, too, have found the chimpanzee less appealing than his kith and kin. This feeling may result from the fact that I saw my first chimpanzee dressed in clothes, thus starting a prejudice that has been difficult to overcome. An animal dressed like a man is never funny to me, revealing all the hideous likenesses and pitiful differences between man and beast, and concealing all of the real fineness and nobility found in most wild creatures.

Actually it was more than a year after I came to the zoo before I paid any intelligent or personal attention to the two young chimpanzees, Bondo and Dinah. Dinah remains in my memory as the most unlovely of all the apes I have known, yet it was possible for me to grow

[125]

very fond of her, to spend considerable time around her cage and honestly grieve at her death; and this is the way it was.

Bondo and Dinah had been the property of Dr. Wegeforth's father-in-law, Mr. Ralph Granger, who had purchased them from a dealer for his own pleasure and companionship. He had a fine cage built for them in his back yard and spent, as people usually do, whatever irregular time his fancy prompted him to allot them. He played with them as anyone would with a kitten or pup, without realizing that in addition to fellowship they needed stern discipline and constant control. And so one day when Bondo was out of sorts or particularly boisterous, he became too playful and rough for Mr. Granger. But with courage born largely of inexperience, Mr. Granger continued to go into the cage and romp with them, trying to exercise some control and caution, until one day Bondo jumped on him so viciously that only the timely arrival of help rescued him from injury. Mr. Granger then yielded to Dr. Wegeforth's pleas and decided to put them in the zoo.

When I had arrived at the zoo, Bondo and Dinah were not more than five or six years old and were frequently taken out of their cage for pictures, parties, and the general gratification of a keeper who liked to show off his own intimacy with them. Our monkey group was then very small, so that he had plenty of time to entertain himself and the public. The two young chimpanzees delighted in his attention. He went into the cage with the chimpanzees for each meal and, calling them to a small round table, he would give them their fruit, one piece at a time, making them peel the oranges and bananas and carefully pick up the pieces and put them in his hand or pocket.

Even then, however, Dr. Wegeforth told me he believed the chimpanzees were dangerous and was firmly opposed to handling them with this careless ease, and he had strictly forbidden their being taken out for any purpose. Both were showing signs of sexual maturity, and Dinah, who had one slightly crippled leg, was becoming very erratic and having frequent fits of temper which threw the cage into a turmoil.

I noticed that when I stopped at the cage she would come close to the wire and peer intently but somewhat idiotically into my face and grimace hideously toward me. Among her repulsive habits was smearing excrement on the walls of the cage and returning to eat it surreptitiously, which drove me away many times. Our foreman, Norman Johnson, noticed how she leered at me and spoke of it, but I attached no significance to it until I returned to the zoo following my first vacation. Dinah saw me coming over a small rise of ground and such a shouting and commotion she began! She shrieked and, as she was wont to do, beat upon the wire and floor of the cage with the soles of her feet. It was evident to everyone that she was greeting me affectionately.

From that time on I felt an obligation toward the two chimpanzees and spent more time near their cage. Dinah plucked her hair along her thighs and shoulders so that she always looked ratty and untidy. She also kept her mate carefully plucked in patterns suited to her changing and erratic taste. Bondo was usually patient and good-natured with her, but at rare intervals seemed to feel called upon to assert his masculine superiority. On such occasions he would fly into a wild, inhuman rage, throw himself at the sides of the cage, scream and beat the doors and walls. Then, indeed, was Dinah's joy complete! She would flee, shrieking in pretended terror, to the top of the cage, wildly urging her mate into greater and ever greater frenzy. As soon as he would retire — physically and emotionally exhausted — to his stump or shelf, Dinah, showing all her teeth in a seductive grin, would advance humbly and fawn upon her tempestuous mate, pretending a submission which, if sincere, was quite temporary. But when Dinah had a tantrum it was another story. There was nothing of pretense about it and she was apt to drive Bondo into real seclusion in the top of the cage until she had completely vented her fury. Then, with tender grooming and whatever other cajolery she deemed necessary, she would coax him down.

I had great respect for the forbearance Bondo exhibited toward his erratic mate. Dinah used her feminine charms, if necessary, to keep him in subjection, but usually he was amiable without her blandishments. He permitted her to pull out hair in masses from parts of his body with the result that at no time during Dinah's lifetime did he ever have a completely perfect coat. I have seen him sit and permit her to pull out the long, coarse hairs that were sprinkled over his upper lip and chin without resistance, although he winced and jumped at each extraction.

I have never known a chimpanzee which did not know the indelicate art of spitting and use it to his advantage. When I first knew Bondo and Dinah, I supposed that they had been taught this trick, but it is so universal that it may be an inherited instinct or perhaps it has been copied from older associates either in zoos or the wild. Bondo had many ways of making his skill most effective. He knew that from the top of the cage he could shoot the spray farther into the crowd than from the floor. He would hold a mouthful of water for several minutes with so innocent an expression that the crowd of visitors would be completely disarmed. Suddenly he would leap to the top of the cage and spray the individuals in front of that spot to the great delight of the others watching. It served no purpose to warn visitors back from the cage. Sometimes, to give added force and dramatic effect, Bondo would leap to his table, then to a swinging bar in the center of his cage and, at its widest arc, jump to the top of the wire side of the cage, spewing his lukewarm water over as many persons as he could to shouts of delight from children and from those adults who escaped. These occasions always made visitors rush from near-by parts of the grounds to see what was going on, and it was usually some of the new crowd, pressing close to the wire, that got the next baptism. Most of the erstwhile victims thoroughly enjoyed the sight, forgetting their embarrassment while watching their successors in misery. Also, they realized that it was fresh, clean water, not saliva, and that it quickly dried, usually without ill effect. However, Bondo several times cost us a cleaning bill and a great many apologies.

Much of the time chimpanzees employ spitting to attract attention to themselves and often in the spirit of fun entirely. But occasionally there is a certain maliciousness in the demonstration. Bondo and Dinah used it when they were jealous of the attention that people showed to their cage-mates on either side. Dinah would coax visitors to feed her by dancing, holding out her hands and being as ingratiating and attractive as possible. Often when the visitors obeyed the Do Not Feed signs, in spite of her blandishments, they were deluged with a stream from the vindictive beggar.

My greatest interest in any creature's intelligence is the way he uses his cleverness when uncontrolled to solve his problems of living, or what he does on his own initiative rather than through memory and outside suggestion. I have watched Bondo and Dinah do things which excited my greatest admiration for their individual intelligence, as well as their teamwork or cooperation.

Service men in uniform were at one time admitted to the zoo without charge and consequently visited in large numbers, often because they could afford to do nothing else. Many such, being out only for a good time, drifted into mischief in the zoo. Bondo, as a result of their teasing, didn't like uniforms and frequently flew into a rage if a large group of uniformed men collected around the cage.

One Sunday afternoon quite late, I walked out to the monkey mesa and, hearing boisterous laughter at the chimpanzee cage, I strolled in that direction. Five sailors were hanging over the guard fence which was about three feet out from the cage. They had a galvanized tie-wire which they were poking into the cage. The two chimpanzees were crowded down close to the wire, much interested in what the sailors were doing. When several feet of the wire had passed through the cage, one of the chimps grabbed it. But before Bondo had a firm grasp, the boys snatched it back, slipping it through the chimp's fingers so rapidly that it burned quite sharply. Time after time this happened until the two chimpanzees, convinced that they were at a disadvantage, walked off to a corner, standing on all fours with their heads together as though they had lost interest in the play. The boys kept trying to attract them. Finally they came back once more. The wire was again extended. This time, Bondo, instead of pulling on it, let it lie loosely in his hands. The boys pushed it farther and farther and suddenly Bondo grabbed it and bent it around his hand like

[130]

a loop. He may have seen the loop the boys had in their hands, but I rather believe it was his own idea. Before he could get a firm grip, however, the three boys pulled so hard that the wire cut into Bondo's hand. He had to release it.

Again Bondo turned away with indifference. The boys coaxed a long time before he would reach for it once more. Meanwhile, Dinah had quietly filled her mouth at the drinking fountain and had returned to sit for a few minutes beside her mate, as though greatly interested in the affair. Suddenly she climbed part way to the top of the cage and hung there — about six feet off the ground. Bondo glanced at her and, as well as I knew them, I failed to see anything like a signal pass between them. However, Bondo grabbed the wire unexpectedly and pulled. At the same instant, Dinah sprayed a huge mouthful of water all over the three boys, huddled close together. Taken by surprise, they released their grip and the wire, with its twisted loop, was dragged through their hands by the two chimps working excitedly together. This time it was the boys who suffered chagrin, not only by being spat upon by an inferior, but because the sliding wire burned and the twisted end cut into their flesh as it had into the chimps'.

"Good work, Bondo and Dinah," I silently applauded while the crowd laughed uproariously. The chimps found that the boys, now that they had lost the advantage, did not want to play any more. No matter how many times Bondo poked the wire toward them, the sailors refused to touch it.

For several years Dinah and Bondo were the only representatives of the great apes we had in the zoo. Then Mr. C. R. Holmes of Santa Barbara presented us with a

[131]

mature female who had become too difficult for his private collection of wild-animal pets, and so to Bondo and Dinah we added another. Her name was Violet, but this creature was anything but the modest being her name implied. When she came to us, one of the keepers remarked, in a moment of exasperation, that he was sure I had misunderstood Mr. Holmes; the name must have contained an "n" because of her violent nature.

Since the newcomer was younger and probably could not defend herself, we dared not put Violet into the cage with Dinah. But gradually Dinah had been failing in health; her shriveled leg had become more of an impediment and her scrawny body more and more emaciated and naked. Finally she refused food and, in spite of our efforts, died. The autopsy showed an enormous hairball composed of her own and her mate's hair, so solid and firm that we could not pull it apart. It had filled her stomach so completely that there was no longer room for food. So, with no real ailment, Dinah had starved herself to death. Her passing gave us a clue to feeding which we have since used with good effect. We now add salt in blocks or free to their diet. This keeps the chimpanzees from eating their own salty hair and skin-scales, and, we believe, has lessened greatly the almost universal chimpanzee habit of consuming some of their excrement. Dinah's death left Bondo free from jealous tyranny to accept the handsomer and more normal Violet.

Sometimes I think, as I look back over my chimpanzee friends, that the less said about Violet the better. This may be something a little like jealousy or personal chagrin on my part, for try as I would, I never could make a friend of Violet. She turned readily from her devotion to Mr. Holmes, her first master, to our men keepers, but showed a complete indifference, to speak mildly, to human beings of her own sex. She took, also, the most unreasoning likes and dislikes toward the men who worked around her and never during her whole life at the zoo did she show the real affection for her keeper that most of the anthropoid apes do. Her greatest crush was on Mr. Virden, superintendent of construction, who is generally too busy with his own work to pay much more than casual attention to any individual specimen. But Violet refused to permit him to ignore her. She would rush shrieking to the side of the cage if he approached to direct some repairs or work on her cage or another. She would turn her back to him and push her shoulders close against the wire, coaxing him to rub her back. She was so treacherous that nobody would touch her unless she had her back to the wire, and many times, as I watched her coax Ralph to pet her, I observed that her hands were always safely tucked under her arms, assuring him that she would not suddenly try to grab his fingers and hurt him.

We had hoped that we might have a nice family of children with the magnificent Bondo as father. But year after year passed with our wishes unfulfilled until, finally, when a chance came to exchange both Bondo and Violet with other zoos for specimens more desirable to our own, we did so. I felt no regrets that Violet was shipped across the Pacific Ocean to a home in the Surabaya Zoo in Java. With her disposition, she would be as happy in any zoo as in our own. My only concern was that she be well cared for. Bondo went to another zoo in California where he found an old and well-remembered friend — his first zoo keeper. I understand that at this writing, six years later, he is hale and hearty at the age of twenty at least. Seventeen years of his life have been lived under our observation. After Dinah's death, he grew a most magnificent coat of long, shining black hair, practically untouched with gray when he left us. He was one of the healthiest apes I have ever known. I cannot remember even one slight illness that he had. He threw off colds and other common complaints with ease. He also set a standard which I have had no other chimpanzee equal, not only for good character, but for intelligent, friendly co-operation, and self-control, and as an entertainer.

I am no longer able to understand the confusion that at first existed in my own mind between the chimpanzee and the orang-utan. The chimpanzee is strikingly unlike his red-haired cousin of the forests of Eastern Asia. But the name *Pongo*, meaning a forest genius or fetish, was applied indiscriminately by early naturalists to both chimpanzees and orang-utans. Possibly because no one was familiar with both species of ape, their mutual manlike qualities convinced scientists they were one and the same from different regions. Many names have been applied to the chimpanzee in different localities, such as *Cojas morios*, meaning Man of the Forest. One of the most illustrative and interesting of his descriptive titles is that by which he is known in the native tongue of the Congo, where he is called *"Eujoko"* — a command meaning, in free translation, "Hold your tongue!" This is perhaps the result of vocal combats between the apes and natives in which in volume, at least, the apes left the natives with no better retort. But I am inclined to believe it refers to the chimpanzee's inability to use words in spite of his manlike appearance. The chimpanzee vies with the gibbon rather than the other larger apes in the strength and volume of his voice though not in the quality of its tone.
Strange and exaggerated tales of the habits of wild

chimpanzees drifted back during the early days of exploration; such as chimpanzees returning for medical treatment after they had been cured and released from bondage, or of captive chimpanzees performing housework and such simple tasks as making beds and sweeping. That they might be trained to do such things is true, but the task of directing the performance and following the routine would be more arduous than doing the work itself could be. I have seen trained chimpanzees giving a fair imitation of such performances temporarily, but have never seen one with the mental ability to make the sustained effort which would make them useful or the docility to become a servant, or useful citizen.

Although chimpanzees are essentially ground-dwelling animals, they are strong, active, agile climbers. Their natural gait is on all fours, but they can be taught to walk erect with their long arms dangling or used as a balance. While walking on four feet, the soles of their feet come much more evenly in contact with the floor than do the tightly curled, much longer and typically grasping feet of the orang-utans. They rest their weight on the second joint or closed fist of their hand, never to my observation putting the palm of the hand down flat with fingers extended. I doubt that this is possible.

The toes of the chimpanzee, though long and supple, are short compared to those of the orang-utan and gibbon, are much more manlike toes than theirs. The great toe is much higher on the foot than is that of the orang, and it is broader and heavier, like the human great toe. The thumb is quite small and is placed in the same relative position as that of man, but like the orang's thumb it is rather weak and useless. Chimpanzees pick things up between two fingers. I have never seen them use the thumb when picking up a small object off the floor or from some other flat surface. The last resort, a clever one I admit, is to scrape a grain of corn or single peanut off the shelf into the palm of one hand with the outside of the other. The chimpanzee foot, with its flexible instep, is an excellent grasping and carrying organ. The name of *Quadrumana*, meaning four hands, is aptly applied to the chimpanzee.

Chimpanzee faces shade from a soft, dull black to almost a tan color; some of the faces have light skin covered with big brown freckles. The chin is usually adorned with a scattered growth of short, stiff white hair which they pull out of each other when in affectionate moods. In some chimpanzees, the face below the eyes, spreading from each side of the nostrils, is noticeably lighter in color than the part around the eyes. The eyes are deep-set under overhanging brows. The lips are thin and loose, showing exaggerated canine teeth. The ears are wide and fanlike. While some chimpanzees have thick hair growing over the crown of their heads and down each cheek in front of the ears, others are bald far back over their heads.

The average chimpanzee is smaller than either the orang-utan or gorilla, and weighs not over one hundred and fifty pounds when grown. The arms are much longer than the legs, placing the face in a favorable position for seeing well ahead as the animal advances upon all fours.

The chimpanzee, in spite of his broad back and full chest, has a pinched abdomen and pelvic region, and his legs are loosely attached to his body without the appearance of hips or buttocks. The head, with its round, dome-shaped crown, shows an approach to human relationship that is belied by the chimpanzee's facial features.

Of all the great apes, chimpanzees show the most

changing expressions, and, I am tempted to say, the most personality. With age, they begin to turn gray in different patterns; usually a plentiful sprinkling of white hair is to be noticed all over the body. Many males first have gray backs; others turn gray first on the thighs and later over the back up toward the shoulders.

The wild-life history of the chimpanzee is most incomplete. They are reported generally to be rather gregarious in habits, living in small groups or bands which may easily be founded on the family as established by one adult pair. Apparently they are not monogamous as a band may consist of a male and his consorts. Only in the case of old males do they seem to be found in a solitary condition. The young chimpanzee, being extremely playful, is at the same time fond of young company and seeks it in captivity, which may lead to the natural conclusion that they would do so, also, in the wilds. Nests where chimpanzees may spend more than one night have been reported in the chimpanzee's native territory. These nests are often grouped together and so it is reasonable to suppose that the occupants were joined in some sort of organization, however loose. I have talked at length with J. L. Buck, who has collected chimpanzees for the market for many years. He has told me that the tree nests are occupied by the same band for at least several nights in succession, and it is not unusual to find one fairly large band composed of immature chimpanzees entirely. These are youngsters of both sexes no longer needing parental care, but too young to be establishing their own households. In the zoo, chimpanzees show no tendency to make nests, even if material is provided. They prefer a bed of sacks.

Like the other great apes, the chimpanzee lives upon fruits and vegetables, eating tender growths and raiding the farms of natives in the wild. In zoos, they will accept almost any vegetable, fruit or leaves.

In our zoo, breakfast is given to them before they leave their house in the morning, but they carry most of it out into the cage with them. Each seeks his favorite position for the early-morning duties of urinating and evacuating, and holds his breakfast in hands and feet while this is accomplished. Although not so tidy in their sleeping rooms as the orangs, they do not foul their quarters needlessly.

During the day, they are given light feedings of bananas and usually a bottle of milk. Late in the afternoon, when the doors of their sleeping room are opened, they rush in, chattering and anxious to get out of the cool air and settle down in the warm dim privacy of their adjoining sleeping rooms, connected by barred doors. Their heaviest meal is now provided: carrots, apples, vegetables (including sweet potatoes) in season, and fruits, often some stale bread, cooked rice flavored with steamed prunes and raisins, or with milk and honey and eggs, making a real rice pudding. They love onions either steamed or raw and usually gobble those delicacies down first. They can be taught to drink from cups or bottles and to eat with forks and spoons, but these utensils are usually kept for show. They prefer a nice big pan into which they can sink their thick, extended lips or their long fingers to scoop out the rice, carrots or sweet potatoes.

Living in a zoo is a very tame, safe matter for these creatures. They show their adaptability and their contentment by breeding frequently and living to a ripe old age that is probably seldom equaled in the wild.

CHAPTER IX

Family Life in a Chimpanzee Cage

MY WARMEST friendship with any chimpanzee began in 1930 when, shortly after he had given Violet to us, C. R. Holmes sent us another of his young chimpanzees. People often wonder why men or women who collect private zoos happen to do so in the first place and why, after a certain length of time, they part with the creatures they have collected at such big expense. The answer is easy. The desire to collect wild creatures and the pleasure of owning them is inherent in man. Travelers will see cunning baby animals — and every baby animal is cunning — in some market or native quarters, will purchase them and bring them home. But it is difficult to hire caretakers who are satisfactory with more than one type of animal, and it is hard to keep friends and the general public from being too venturesome with such wild pets. Sooner or later, most private animal collectors find themselves unequal to coping with the task of keeping a few wild animals which insist upon growing up and becoming dangerous to meddlesome people. Hence most private collections eventually find their way into a zoo, or are given to a community in order to form the nucleus of a zoo.

All California zoos have profited greatly by the interest of Mr. Holmes in wild animals and birds. He has

[139]

supplied several zoos with some of their rarest specimens and we ourselves have acquired from him three of our finest chimpanzees, many birds and monkeys, and one elephant.

The second little chimpanzee to arrive was called Tim or, more affectionately, Timmie. He was a short, stocky young male chimpanzee with a very black face, heavy shoulders, and the manners of a Bowery tough. He has enjoyed his reputation for toughness, though I have long been secretly convinced that it is undeserved and that, at heart, he is something of a softy. Tim was wise in the ways of men, having been among them since early infancy, and was ready to give a good account of himself if need arose. We were delighted to have him and put him at once into a big cage between the gorilla cage and the one containing Violet and Bondo. Tim and Violet showed mutual recognition and we thought that when he grew older, we might combine the three into one family.

Tim was cocky for a new arrival, sticking his chin out as though to hide the real terror and homesickness he felt when his trainer left him to start back home. Tim, in spite of all his bravado, looked pretty small and alone in the big cage in which he so suddenly found himself. When his friend had left, he climbed high into the corner and looked out toward the afternoon sun as though wondering what would become of him when daylight was gone. Unfortunately, our experienced primate man was away on vacation and no one had much time to make the little fellow feel especially at home. But the men, lacking experience, expected no trouble getting a tame little "chimp" to bed. So after a while Tim's supper was put inside the house, his bedding arranged and the door opened. But Tim was not hungry, having been

Photo E. H. Boldrick

Tim — Gray and Dignified in Late Maturity

Katie, Who Settled Down into an Excellent Mother

fed heavily on the way to the zoo to keep him quiet, and he did not know the meaning of the activity going on about him. He continued to sit high in the corner, shivering with loneliness. The men called. He looked at them and pouted, refusing to come down. They threatened and coaxed as well as they knew how, but their strange voices meant nothing to Tim. Finally, in his inexperience, one of the men thought force might do. He used a pole to try to force Tim down, with no effect. At last he turned a stream of water on Tim. It made no difference that it was a gentle stream lacking the force to do any damage. Tim was not only terrified, but all of his sense of wrong was aroused. He became furiously angry.

I had been very busy and my good intentions of going out early came to naught when I suddenly realized it was almost dark. I rushed out to see if Tim had been made comfortable for the night. I intended to pet and play with him a little in his sleeping quarters, hoping to make the little newcomer feel at home in that way. Instead, I heard his cries. Rushing to where I could see him I discovered the little chap, dripping wet in the high corner, rebuking his foes with all his might and refusing to budge. You may be sure I added my own rebuke and soon the man had the hose out of sight. I then ordered them all away. Going around the cage until I was directly under the little chap, I began to talk to him, calling him by name and coaxing him quietly and sympathetically.

At the sound of my voice so near, he looked down. I had not yet learned, if indeed I ever will, just how much the proper tone of voice can do for the morale of an animal. Tim stared at me for a second or two and then, sticking out his flexible baby lips as far as he could,

[141]

he began to cry in earnest, the most miserable little homesick wail that I have ever heard. I continued to talk to him. Suddenly he began to climb down the wire until his little face was on a level with my own. His wet little body was pressed close to the wire and I thrust my fingers through the big mesh to smooth his hair. Immediately he seized my fingers in his own, clutching them frantically. I petted and soothed him a few minutes and his grasp relaxed. I called one of the men to come back and asked him to open the door so that I might enter. When I did, Tim flew into my arms, hugging and being hugged. He sobbed and whimpered and told me of his misery in a language no one could fail to interpret. I rubbed and dried him with a big, rough sack and cuddled him close, unmindful of what this did to my clothes. While I was doing this, the man heated a bottle of milk and beat into it two raw eggs. At last Tim permitted me to carry him into the sleeping room and there on a pile of bedding, wrapped in clean dry sacks, he drank his warm milk from the bottle that I held. Gradually, as his body grew warm and comfortable and as his spirits revived, he permitted me to slip out an arm long enough to shut the barred door. I waited until the warm milk and friendly touch had done its work. The little fellow, completely comforted, had cuddled down in sleep. But not until the long, slender fingers holding mine completely relaxed did I withdraw my other hand, walk out and close the door. The man who had used the hose looked pretty much ashamed of himself and that is the last time a stream of water was ever used in our cages except for cleaning and for extreme emergencies, perhaps to save an animal's life.

Tim has, apparently, never forgotten his rescue. For eleven years he has held me in a regard that he has for ew others. In fact, I might go farther and claim that he has at all times treated me as an equal and a pal, which is high testimonial of friendship from an aristocrat like Tim. For Tim without any doubt looks upon himself as a chimpanzee set apart, with a mission to uphold the dignity of his race and maintain its reputation of being overbearing, impudent and hard-boiled. He has always been the dominant figure in the life of his cage. He takes the best of everything and his family can divide his leavings. He flies into the most magnificent tantrums of any chimpanzee I have ever seen. He sits for days like a god in a temple and ignores his family, his keeper and the visitors in the zoo. At such times, even I have been accorded little recognition, although, at the sound of my voice, I have seen his eyes turn toward me hoping that I might hold out some offering he could not resist. At other times he sits with his back against the wire, hoping that I will pet him. He accepts fruit or candy from my hand and has never tried to grab me as he has almost everyone else. He fully realizes that at some time, with no really vicious intent, he may yield to temptation and grab *me*, and that it is for this reason I never relax my vigilance.

For some years Tim occupied a cage adjoining the gorillas, and during this time I made a special effort not to rouse his jealousy toward them unduly. He and Mbongo entered into something of a friendship and actually worked out several types of racing games they seemed to play with mutual delight. Tim was the leader in such play at first, but Mbongo also had ideas and was not easily cheated or made ridiculous. I have wished many times that we could have turned them together. I have never seen chimpanzees play tag and wrestle as gorillas do; it would have been most interesting to see

[143]

the intelligent Tim catching on and developing the new type of play. After watching Mbongo beat his chest and clap his hands, he actually tried to clap his own hands, but the feeble sound produced by his long, thin palms was ridiculous even to him in comparison with the lusty boom of the great gorilla beat. His stamping suffered by the same comparison until he completely discontinued it.

Tim has been very clever about improvising play of a lonely nature. We gave him all sorts of attractions in his cage: balls, swings and an auto tire. The tire he enjoyed immensely. He learned to roll it around very handily and one cold morning he brought out a handful of straw from his bedding and packed the hollow center of the tire full of it. Then he lay down with that protection between his body and the cold floor. He moves the tire about on the floor to follow the patches of sunshine; also, so that his bed will be warm.

Now, Tim resides in a fine cage with high crossbars to swing and climb on. But through all the years that Timmie has been getting old and gray he has never lost his love for a tire. He would not leave the old cage until he had seized his tire and carried it into the cart with him. Immediately he was in the new cage he discovered one advantage. By taking his tire up onto the trapeze he did not have to move to follow the sun. So he laboriously carried it up to the top and balanced it properly on the cross arms over a very tiny square platform. He curls up in it and far from the disturbing crowd of visitors sleeps away the day in peace. Katie, his cagemate, would not think of touching the tire. But the roguish son, Georgie, now watches his every chance and when his father has been particularly overbearing in the matter of choice food rushes up a pole, gives the tire a tremendous push, and grins from ear to ear to see it crashing to the floor. Tim, torn between admiration of his son's astute impudence and his fear of losing the perfect spot, rushes after the tire and lugs it up again.

Of all the chimpanzees I have ever known, perhaps Timmie has been the most proficient spitter. One of my most embarrassing moments occurred when Osa Johnson and a party dropped into the zoo late one evening to see her "black children," the gorillas. They were so engrossed with them that they paid little attention to the chimpanzees in the neighboring cage. Suddenly I saw that one of the chimps was filling his mouth with water. I called to everyone to watch out, but my warning came too late. Osa's mother, Mrs. Leighty, elegantly attired in a black fur coat, was deluged with water Tim had sucked out of the basin. He retired to a high perch, tucked his chin deep into his chest, and became the picture of outraged innocence, while his victim generously laughed away his naughtiness.

As Katie, his mate, grew to maturity under our care, she lost gradually all her cunning baby loveliness and acquired the erratic temperamental qualities of most female chimpanzees. She plucked her own hair and Tim's until they were both unlovely; she was filthy in her personal habits, treacherous in her dealings with her keepers and friends. She flew into fits of futile rage, shrieking wildly and, in fact, was like the normal female of single cages in zoos. Then suddenly she became docile, friendly and ingratiating in her attitude toward us. She fled, not in simulated but in real terror, from Tim when he raged around his domain. She held out her hands pleadingly to her keeper, clinging to him and begging for his attention.

Watching her one day as she sat high in the cage, I

[145]

realized unexpectedly that there was a cause for her changed nature, that within a short while she would surely become a mother. I had learned from others that the female chimpanzee did thus become docile and friendly during pregnancy. I called the attention of her keeper and the head keeper to her condition and we decided to separate Katie and Tim as quickly as possible so that she could have every chance to bring her child up in peace and security. We thought it might be very difficult to bring about this separation. She was really devoted to Tim, but actually, when her cage, which was next to the one occupied by herself and Tim, was ready, she took the keeper's hand and walked as willingly as a baby across the space between the two and entered her new home. Tim was terribly forlorn. He stormed and raged across the few feet separating their cages while she talked and comforted him.

A member of our Zoological Society, who had seen a group of monkeys playing with a cow bell in a Texas zoo, purchased a bell and brought it to our Tim as a gift. This treasure came just at the proper time. Timmie had nearly worn out his big old tire by pushing it around as he wailed his story of abuse to whomever would listen. The big brass cow bell with its clanging noise amused him greatly. He sat and rang it with all his might until we were driven nearly mad. Then he began to try to take it apart. At last, by banging and throwing it, struggling aimlessly with all his strength, he got the clapper out and then he became enamored of that. He lay by the hour with it under his cheek on the floor of his cage. When called to his meals, if he started without it, he would rush back and get it. It was the last object he touched at night and the first thing he had in the morning, for he took it to bed with him.

[146]

Chimpanzee Family — Katie Instructs Her Child, Georgie

Photo E. H. Boldrick

Georgie Poses Alone High in the Cage

Finally he found a new use for it. He would lay it on the floor on the broad side, and, closing his right hand into a fist, he would press it on the top of the bell. Running on his other three legs at full gallop, he would slide the bell under his hand around and around the cage. As he ran he chanted the song of the deserted chimpanzee, calling upon us all to witness his suffering. It was always the same side that was next to the floor, for he would turn it over to see the bright scouring of the cement floor to make sure.

On the morning of February 23, 1938, we found that at some time during the night a baby chimpanzee, "Georgie," had been born. For two days, Katie remained inside her house, her entire attention given to her child. On the third day, we opened the door and Katie jumped out, a tiny, black-haired, pink-faced infant clinging tightly to her breast. Katie had no thought that this son would not be welcome to his father. She climbed right up into the corner close to Tim, as she had been in the habit of doing each morning after the separation. Tim looked at the tiny infant hung low on her abdomen, supported by her bended knees and his own clinging arms and legs, and went into a fit of rage. Katie tried to soothe him by answering him across the narrow alley between the cages. Suddenly Tim dropped to the floor, filled his mouth from the fountain and, leaping upon the wire of the cage again, sprayed the two with water. Finally, seeing that his temper was not making any difference in the situation, he subsided.

The black mite of an ape sprawling across Katie's front, clinging with his strong little mouth to the nipples of her breast, flaunting the tiny flag of snow-white hairs on his little rump in his father's face, remained oblivious of the trouble his arrival had created. Not until he was quite a large baby did he become conscious of his father, and not until he was six months old did we carefully transfer Katie and the baby into the cage with Tim. We stood tense and worried, ready to interfere if Tim got too rough, but Katie was capable of handling the entire situation. She permitted Tim to see the baby, even to touch him and hang on to one of the little legs in a not too gentle manner, but, for the greater part of the time, she kept her own body well between their son and his father, coaxing him to groom her and now and then muttering to him fondly, pulling out a stray hair on his lip or chin, cleaning him and doing all the necessary little childing of a spouse returned home to her mate after an enforced absence. The infant, terrified, looked at the frowning, excited, whining Tim with round-eyed wonder, clinging with mouth and hands more firmly than ever.

For several weeks prior to this move, George had been struggling to get out of his mother's arms. Although not permitting this, Katie had encouraged him to seize the wire of the cage and pull with all his might to free himself, knowing that such exercise made him strong. The introduction into family life put him back several weeks in his freedom, for his mother feared that Tim might be too rough for the tiny fellow. Although we have never seen him really abuse the baby with intent to do him injury, he does even yet handle him in a way that could not be tolerated if Katie were not there to protect him.

By the time the baby was a year old, he was climbing all over the top of the wire cage eighteen feet off the ground. His mother apparently knew from instinct that he would have fewer dangers to face off the ground and, although I have tried to find something about the treatment of young chimpanzees by their parents in the wild, I am able to confirm only that the mothers carry them until they are quite large, fully a year old, and it is even reported that at times they have one young child riding on their back and one infant hanging to their breasts when traveling with a group through the chimpanzee territory of West Africa. I have become privately convinced that monkeys, and especially the great apes, do feel a sense of responsibility toward their helpless young for much longer periods than is the case with other animals.

Georgie passed through the period of infancy, cutting of teeth, learning to walk and weaning with as careful observations as we were able to make with Katie's interference. To my own great chagrin, she refused from the first to permit me to come near him or touch him until he was much more than a year old. She constantly warned him that I was dangerous and that he must avoid me, although she permitted Moore, her beloved caretaker, and Charley Smith, the head keeper, to play with him, examine his mouth and hold him in their arms in her presence. She apparently suspected me of ulterior motives and I was *verboten*. It was a situation I had never met before and I was both hurt and embarrassed by it. She would cover him, head and all, when he was tiny whenever I approached. She was amazingly clever at folding him up between her bended knees brought up to a level, with her chin and her arms, and her body forward, curving it over the little fellow and dropping her head on the opening. No one would have suspected her of harboring an infant so natural was her position.

And when he was nearly two years old, I returned from a month's absence to find that George was weaned

and free. He could come down as closely to me as he
dared and run scampering back to his mother. He was
already learning to reach out and get his share of family
treats. The meal of milk which his family received each
afternoon was now divided into three parts and Georgie
took his turn at drinking from a big quart bottle held
for them one at a time by their devoted keeper. If he
didn't get his regular turn, or if the milk seemed to be
running too freely down his father's big gullet, George
squealed and fought for his rights. As I walked down
the cages with some nuts and candy, the first morning
after my return, Georgie reached through and pushed
my hand to call himself to my attention. With a big
lemon drop stretching out each small cheek, and his eyes
popping with pleasure over the new food, he decided
that I was no longer a dangerous enemy but a friend.
And from that day forth, he has encouraged my friendliness. He had known my car and when, some months ago,
I bought a new one, quite a different model, he recognized me just the same as I drove by. Showing every
tooth in a broad grin, he rushed to the side of the cage,
beating the wire with the futile little fists and heels,
pushing the slender heels through and stretching them
as far out to me as he could. Once in a while I do not
have time to stop and play; then the disappointment in
his face is most pathetic.

One day I lingered so long with the gorillas that he
feared they would get all of the fruit I was distributing.
Hearing a funny little whimper behind me, I turned
and saw George, his rump in the air, his face buried in
his hands on the shelf, crying — really crying. I hastened
to make amends and he was soon all sunshine.

Tim is most jealous of my attention to George. He
has dominated the cage so long that he resents greatly

[150]

any attention the crowd gives except to him. So we, who know his weakness, realize we "must watch our step" and see that Tim is given a generous amount of food and attention before we give any to George. But George is also aware of the situation and understands what we are doing. He waits his turn or slyly slips around where he can receive a bit of the treat without being noticed. At times, though, he rushes in boldly, grabs something and shins up the wire or a convenient pole like lightning. Again when Tim is asleep or sulking, George slips up to us so quietly that he has his mouth crammed with fruit or popcorn before Tim realizes what has happened.

Georgie is never still. He climbs all over the high trapeze bars in his cage with the skill of a veteran. He runs the full length of his cage, forty feet, on an inch-and-a-half steel pipe as fast as his speedy feet can carry him, touching nothing with his hands and moving far too quickly to be really grasping the bar with his capable feet. Again, as he runs, he will suddenly step off almost into thin air, dropping the full length of his body to catch at arm's length and swing at ease with apparently no fear of falling. His first trip across the ten-foot space between two of the upright supports, however, was a venture that taxed his courage and endurance. His hands were so small they could not reach around the pipe. So he hung on one side with the fingers of each hand curling over from the same direction. Suspended at the full length of his arms, he looked toward his mother, who had moved away to the next cross pipe and had left him swinging. He glanced at her, then at his keeper and me, who were watching, but not down at the ground. He slipped one hand very carefully along the pipe until it touched the other. Then he moved the second one just a few inches and pulled the first one up again. His mouth was working and his little legs were beating the air as though he were swimming. But that first gain gave him courage and he slipped the foremost hand even farther along the pipe and inched himself along until he swung near the mother who reached down and pulled him to her.

Within a week, he was moving suspended by his arms on the high pipe because he liked it and, although his little legs still waved wildly in the air, he was really taking one hand off and not just slipping it along the pipe. Finally he was strong and proficient enough to cross one arm over the other as he moved. Then, indeed, was he proud of his aerial skill! From the time he was four or five months old, his mother had been teaching him to grip and cling to the bar by pulling at the little body while he clung to the pipes to free himself from her arms. I have seen her take one hand off finger by finger while he fought to retain his hold and then, as he hung by one arm, she would swing the little body and whirl it halfway round to make him sure and agile.

Not until he was proficient in the top of the cage did she try him on the ground. One day Moore told me she was teaching him to walk and promised to call me when he saw another lesson. When he did, I rushed over to observe the education of a baby chimp. Katie, standing erect on the floor of the cage, was holding George suspended by his arms as far as she could from her body. He was struggling to reach her and holding his feet off the floor, knees bent, the pink soles of his feet curled tightly almost into a fist. The struggle between them was silent. A human infant would have cried aloud, but not the chimpanzee baby. Katie finally took both his hands into one of hers and, reaching down under him, pulled first one foot and then the other down to the cement floor of the cage. George drew them up again, but she persisted until, with his feet dragging, she took a few backward steps. Up went George's little feet again, but Katie was determined. He took a faltering, irregular step or two and the walking lesson was over.

One of the sweetest mother-and-baby pictures in any zoo or among any creatures is that of an infant chimpanzee clinging to his mother, to her leg or perhaps to her shoulder, with one little arm as she moves about the cage or in the wild upon the grassy plain. The little fellow clings closely and walks on his feet dependent upon her and utterly confident in her ability to protect and support him. Then the mother, if she wishes to hurry, reaches around casually and gathers him up to her breast under her body. It is the loving protective gesture of every mother and the trusting dependence of every child.

Georgie celebrated his fourth birthday in February 1942. He still wears his little white flag, his face is still tawny with the color of infancy, but he is becoming a personality known to the zoo visitors who call him by name hoping to see him rush, grinning from ear to ear, to welcome the owner of a voice he knows. He waves as they wave to him and then, with a burst of speed, dashes across the cage, slides down a pole like a fireman, and speeds away to give his friends a show. Now that his parents are old and gray, the family life in the chimpanzee group would be very staid if it were not for the baby chimp.

At each stage of his development, in fact on every day of his life, his keeper and I have assured each other that

[153]

George is cuter and smarter than ever before. Just now, we are convinced that at four he is the cleverest and handsomest baby chimp in the world. This is in spite of the enormous ears that he cannot seem to catch up with no matter how fast he grows.

Today as I stood with Moore watching the gorillas, the delivery truck came by with a bottle of milk of magnesia to be left with him. All of the apes were very curious about it and so Moore took off the cap and permitted them to smell it. Georgie reached eagerly through the wire for a share. Moore walked up to him and showed him the bottle. The little fellow thought it was milk and as it was almost time for his bottle he was sure that Moore was ready to feed him. But Tim, the father, also came up and shoved the baby away and wanted a share of the milk. He is so jealous of George that we always have to give him something whenever the youngster is fed. Moore, thinking he had satisfied the baby's curiosity, started away. Georgie was aghast that his idol should treat him in this cruel and inhuman manner. He stood on his little feet and holding both hands toward Moore, ran the length of the cage, his little lips drawn back from his teeth so that every one showed, and wailed as loudly as his high little soprano voice was able. Moore came back and tried to convince him that he was going after milk, but Georgie was not to be consoled. He had been cheated and was heartbroken. Finally, seeing that he was getting nothing for his wailing, he rushed at his mother, threw himself into her arms as he did when tiny, and cried at the top of his voice — not forgetting to peer under the long hair of her side to see if Moore was returning.

The sequel of the story is that Moore set the feeding hour about half an hour ahead, and all of the chimpanzees had their milk: a quart divided between the parents and a full quart pan for the baby. Down his lips went into the rich milk and he scarcely drew his face out of the pan until the quart was gone, for he knew that on the other side of the partition his father was finishing off his pan in record time. Down to the last drop he drained the full quart. His little stomach became round and hard and his chin dripped with milk. Then he was ready to play. Snatching up his pan he held it over his head trying to catch in his open mouth any drops that fell. When Moore asked for the pan he gave it to him, and when he said, "Come, let us see your stomach," George proudly pushed it up against the bars for us to poke a little. Then he sat down and slid his little legs as far out of the cage as he could for me to grab and play with. He had never been quite so intimate, and I know I have missed a lot because during the past two years I have worked too hard to find the proper amount of time to play with Little George. There is nothing more delightfully childish than the little face puckered up and the long slim arms flailing out in every direction, hoping to do murderous damage to something. At times he pulls out his hair, again he beats himself upon the head and shoulders — indications that Georgie is a regular fellow and will someday be among the most vociferous and erratic of male chimpanzees, which is, I suppose, what every chimpanzee mother looks forward to as a career for her son.

Although after the birth of Georgie Katie had lost that first extreme gentleness that had characterized her early pregnancy, she had never fully regained her erratic and unfriendly attitude. Several times, for short periods, because of her good behavior, we believed that she was about to present us another chimpanzee child to delight

[155]

our visitors, but each time we were doomed to disappointment. However, early in October of 1941 we noticed that Katie was surely about to become a mother. Our cages were filled with apes; we had already divided the orang cage to make room for our suddenly acquired young female gorillas. We contemplated a division of the large gibbon cage or the chimpanzee cage with disfavor, and so we studied the situation, wondering what the effect upon our darling little Georgie would be when Katie would have another child. Would she leave him to Tim's not too understanding and loving care; would she abuse him in her love for the newborn child? Several times lately she had been quite severe with him, particularly in the matter of holding him and sharing her food. But when night came she always kept him in her sleeping compartment and we could not separate them despite our best efforts.

On Saturday morning, the twenty-fifth of October, the new ape keeper, Charley Hulse, who was, by the way, doing an excellent job in spite of his lack of experience with primates, called me to tell me that he was in really serious trouble. On arriving at the zoo he had entered the chimpanzee cage, played a minute with Georgie and looked casually at Katie who sat facing the door, eager as always to get out. So he slid the door open and out she dashed. Only then did he discover that during the night she had given birth to a new baby and that the birth had been so recent that the umbilical cord was still attached to the placenta. He was frightened but did not know what to do as Katie, refusing to return, was moving excitedly around the outer cage and Georgie, his hair all on end with excitement caused by the new creature held in his mother's arms, was clinging to her desperately. Fortunately Hulse had not released Timmie, who was now beating on his door, clamoring for freedom, also greatly excited by the increase in his family.

I had Tim's breakfast put in the end cage, leaving three unoccupied with opened doors between them. Thinking that was the way out Tim rushed into the end cage where his breakfast lay. The door separating it from the adjoining cage was hastily shoved into place and Tim, realizing that he had been outmaneuvered, flew into a raging temper.

It was a simple matter now to clean up the cage farthest from Tim for Katie, fill it with bedding and sacks, lay out a tempting breakfast and a pan of warm milk, and then we opened the door for her. She, too, recognized that Tim and his clamor were safely shut away. So with her newborn baby clinging to her, carrying the umbilical cord in one hand and with the other arm around Georgie, Katie came back into the sleeping room prepared for her. Charley Hulse breathed a sigh of relief and leaving the little family to quiet down by themselves went on about his work in the other cages.

As for me I stayed close, watching to see what she would do with Georgie should he approach and try to touch the new baby. He played with me at the bars, drank a little warm milk and then went back to investigate the new arrival. Katie gently shouldered him away, keeping her arms so closely around the new baby that I could not get more than a glimpse and Georgie could not touch it. It appeared to be a large sprawling sort of child, nearly naked, and when it looked around it seemed as old and mature as Georgie had been at two weeks. Its face was surprisingly black in contrast with Georgie's pink bare skin, a thin patch of hair on its back seemed to be its only natural covering, its head was perfectly bald and its strong clinging arms and legs

[157]

completely without the long shining hair that made Georgie such a little beauty.

Later in the day it was reported to me that the baby was a girl child, and I was forced to admit that nature had run true to form, for female chimpanzees are notoriously homely as compared to their mates. Within a few days we realized that Georgie, at nearly four years, was nursing his mother along with the baby, and that Katie was growing thin and giving her darling son much advantage over the new arrival. So we began a campaign to trap Georgie away from his mother, even calling Moore to the zoo on his first week-end leave, to try to help us separate the two chimps. They had meanwhile all three been turned out into the big cage with Tim and to our great joy Tim was truly interested in the new baby. Katie showed little fear that he might harm it. But the antagonism between father and son which had always been present in a minor degree seemed to grow with the birth of the new baby and Katie's tender protection of George took the form of giving him the care the new baby needed, rushing madly at Tim when he bullied the little George and tucking the new baby under her arm while permitting Georgie to nurse when the little sister needed the food. She was a cross, hot-tempered little creature, afraid of us, and fighting her mother fiercely to get her own way. The need to take Georgie out of the cage grew hourly and every possible trick to separate him from his mother was tried.

Suddenly Byron Moore walked in and said that due to eye defects he was discharged from the navy, and would we want him back? Probably no man was ever more gratefully welcomed into his former job by his employers; and the man he would supersede, Hulse, could return to the animal work he really wanted, and

[158]

Moore's first walk down the row of ape cages was almost a triumphal parade with all but the new gorillas showing their excited pleasure at his return in his working clothes.

At last, after constant effort, Georgie was trapped and taken into an isolation cage inside the service yard of the monkey-cage group. There he received every attention. Moore and "Curly," in charge of the little monkeys, played with him. He was heartbroken, mad, and hated man and I was included in that term. But Georgie was not the stuff that martyrs are made of; he wanted to play and he loved the attention of his keepers and so, day by day, he became, if not completely reconciled to his isolation, at least somewhat happily resigned. But his public refused to be reconciled to his absence and kept demanding that he be put on exhibition so one day we did put him out in a monkey cage where he could see his folks and enjoy the crowd of visitors at close range.

And the little sister grew apace. At five months she was getting some hair. Her mouth filled with teeth and Katie was giving her liberty she had never dreamed of giving the smaller George. She ate food he had never tasted until he was a year old and crawled all over the top of the cage. She still disliked all of us and, screwing up her homely little face, clung to her mother, who had remained as impatient with her disagreeable actions as we could possibly be. When Gracie, as she was unfortunately named, has a real tantrum about anything the mother still tucks her tightly under one arm and, holding her there forcibly, lets her have her tantrum, beating the air, screaming and wailing. This treatment will always remind me of the old-fashioned way of correcting a spoiled child by "letting him cry it out."

CHAPTER X

Chimpanzees Here and There

I AM fond of saying that there are two shows in the zoo and sometimes when I make that observation ·I feel that I might well go on and say "All the world's a stage." And in the zoo, not only the men and women are actors, but many of the creatures within the confines of the cages.

The animals never dream — of this I am very sure — that they, too, are part of the show, for they are eagerly watching the show beyond their cages, and responding to the actors with every gesture and grimace to show that they appreciate the efforts being made to entertain them. And it is a sad, dull world inside the cages on rainy days when no visitors are about. Visitors, on the other hand, are sometimes quite conscious that they are putting on a show and enjoy the response they get from people watching and listening even more than they do the response from the creatures on exhibition.

And for employees of the zoo and regular visitors, those who see and recognize the show on both stages occupied at once, there is the greatest measure of enjoyment of all. The two sets of actors, the two stages, and the mutual reactions present a picture of animal and human life of so similar a pattern as to be scarcely believable. This is the show I personally like very much.

[160]

I do not care as much for trained-animal acts as I should perhaps. The things that animals do when left alone are so much more cunning and smart, and I cannot say too often that never does an anthropoid ape become so pitifully short of being noble, attractive and interesting as when dressed in clothes and imitating the actions, feelings and even passions of men. Certainly at no other time do their hideous, pitiful human likenesses stand out so clearly. My feeling is not prompted by any belief that training and acting makes them unhappy, for no one could possibly look upon the large group of six to nine trained chimpanzees at the St. Louis Zoo, while they are putting on their show under the excitement of the cheering crowd, while they are being trained, or when just sitting around on exhibition in their fine home, and fail to see how important they feel and what fun they have during the performance. Their program consists of dances, rides, solo performances, musical numbers, and winds up in a wild tandem pony race. The chimpanzees are so eager and excited that no one could possibly doubt their happiness and the true spirit of rivalry that exists among them. Their routine is excellent. They know it and require so little direction that you almost forget that it is a man-taught and controlled affair. The beauty of this performance is that the men who train them are the chimps' own keepers who care for them in their quarters where they are on exhibit and live. It is evident to anyone who understands their nature that the devotion between the men and animals is mutual. The funny, extemporaneous tricks introduced by the chimps, the men tell me, are different each day and are not punished; for that is, as Mr. Vierheller has discovered, one of the chief charms of his acts. And so as I enjoyed the act along with the chimps themselves, I

[161]

found I could almost forget my aversion to animals dressed in imitation of human beings; only when I would see some chimp sitting back awaiting his turn would the feeling come to life sharply. Much as I love the apes at other times, I cannot bear to touch one with clothes on, a shrinking that has survived from my little girlhood when once I unintentionally picked up a kitten dressed in my sister's doll clothes and became violently ill.

During my first Eastern zoo trip, after becoming head of the zoo staff, I, with a group of other park executives, made a quick trip to Havana and there, because of our real interest in her remarkable collection, the zoo executives in the group had the pleasure of visiting Madame Rosalie Abreau. Madame Abreau was a Frenchwoman who had lived much of her latter years in Havana where her husband had large agricultural interests. Surfeited with the social and political life both of Europe and Cuba, she had developed instead an intense, almost fanatical interest in monkeys and apes. This had made her famous. Her situation was ideal, her success phenomenal. She was one of the first persons, if not indeed the first, to raise chimpanzees and orang-utans in captivity. I had long been fascinated by reading of her family groups, her grandmothers and their daughters and grandchildren living happily there. Madame Abreau's life centered about these creatures, her income was largely spent in supporting and purchasing new ones, and all of the territory and garden immediately adjacent to her home was filled with cages containing them. She had, when I saw her collections, nearly half a hundred chimpanzees and orangs. The chimpanzees were all taken into her magnificent castle at night lest some enemy, imaginary or real, break in and injure them outside. She employed native servants to care for them, but she herself did much of even the hardest work. I will never get over the shock of sitting in her magnificent salon and watching through the dim light while the huge black attendant walked slowly up the beautiful marble stairs with a half-grown chimpanzee sitting on his shoulder and leading another by the hand. Later, Madame Abreau told me that those particular ones shared her own bedroom. To her each was a precious friend, dearer almost than any human being. She had recently purchased two new little ones and they had arrived just before our party appeared. In her engrossment, Madame Abreau had scant time to greet her human guests, who fortunately could understand and gladly overlook any shortcoming in our reception. The little chimps had arrived in a large crate in charge of a loud-voiced, excitable man who claimed to be able to do anything with them. Each had a little suit of clothes and the man, holding the suits in his hands, was shrieking at the babies, beating the crate and ordering them to come out and dress themselves, as he had promised Madame Abreau they could do. He grabbed the suits and shoes and held them as far in the crate as he could extend his arms, all the time giving voluble orders to the attendants.

Finally the two excited, confused youngsters were forced out of the box, which stood at the end of a long bench or table. There the man, instead of calming them and permitting them to become a little accustomed to the surroundings and bright light, immediately began trying to make them dress. Suddenly one of the little fellows turned to the spot I had attained, by edging closer and closer to the table, and with a sob he rushed into my arms, followed by the other. They clung on each side

[163]

of me. Then Madame Abreau seemed to see me for the first time. She had previously been in correspondence with me and I had profited by her advice about my young orangs. She had repeatedly invited me to visit her in Cuba, but she had apparently not realized that I was among the visitors. Now she rushed to me and put her arms about my shoulders where the baby chimps had buried their little faces, and exclaimed, "Oh, you are Mrs. Benchley; you are a good woman, the little fellows always know!" Somehow I imagined that she would not for long try to keep these little creatures acting and dressing like human beings, for as much as she did humanize her apes and monkeys, even to the extent of sharing her devout religious fervor with them, I saw no evidence of her caring for artificial acts.

After that visit, I had many interesting letters and alluring invitations from Madame Abreau, and one of her letters, written shortly before her death, informed me that she would like to have me take her whole collection under my care if circumstances would make it possible. In almost every letter, she recalled how the tiny chimps had turned to me in their frightened loneliness.

During that same trip, I spent some time in Washington, D. C., and there, in another private collection, met Toto. He was out in a lovely private zoo belonging to Mr. and Mrs. Victor Evans. Because he was greatly interested in all zoos, Mr. Evans usually had a large group of animals freshly imported, which he cared for in what he called Acclimatization Park. The snow was deep on the ground and many of his specimens were indoors in comfortably heated houses. In one such he had a group of little chimpanzees. When we entered, they were sitting at a little table eating a supper consisting of bowls of cereal. Immediately, the littlest one put down his spoon, came over the table toward me, and then stopped suddenly when he realized that I was not Mrs. Evans, his beloved owner. But Toto had no fear of strangers and his hesitation was only for a second.

Mr. Evans was quite concerned about him because the keeper had told him that Toto was developing a cold. Toto tucked his little face under my chin and I was really alarmed at the dry, hot face and lips. But being unused to animals in heated enclosures, I hoped that my fears were groundless. He clung to me for a few minutes and then, reaching up, tried to unfasten the collar of my coat. Failing, he reached for my hat, but the attendant took him out of my arms and put him down on the floor. There he forgot all else, even his cold, in untying Mr. Evans' shoes and removing the strings from the holes all the way down. As soon as he finished, he tried to lace them up again. This process amused him greatly, but every few seconds he would stop and, putting his little hands around back of the heel, try to lift Mr. Evans' foot and remove the shoe. Failing, he would go back to the lacing again. Suddenly, however, when he tried to remove the shoe, Mr. Evans relaxed and permitted him to lift the foot and off came the shoe. Then Toto immediately turned his attention to the other, forgetting the one he had wanted so much. Mrs. Evans told me later that Toto would take off every article of their wearing apparel if they would permit him to, never being satisfied until he completely undressed them. He could even, though he was so tiny, both dress and undress himself except for lacing and properly tying his shoes. I learned, soon after I reached home, that Toto was very ill and had been brought into the city proper to have the best possible care during a severe attack of pneumonia, from which fortunately he recovered.

A few years later, Mr. Evans' collection was divided because of his death, and Toto was the only animal retained by Mrs. Evans. But dearly as she loved him, circumstances prevented her keeping him with her, and as he was growing up and becoming difficult for strangers, she offered him to us at an extremely low price. Knowing that Captain Allan Hancock was interested in a really good tame chimpanzee, I told him about Toto and so the little fellow came out to Santa Maria, California, to live in another fine private zoo. He had grown unbelievably in spite of the pneumonia that he had had more than once and which had taken toll of his health. He was still very tame for a chimpanzee his height and size. He had many tricks, and some cunning suits of clothes. These he would put on and take off, even to the shoes and socks, suspenders and hat, with the greatest delight. He did, however, much prefer to undress human beings and was very persistent in untying and removing people's shoes. He would be perfectly happy as long as you stood still and permitted him to wind your laces in and out in the most intricate way. Twice I have cut the strings out of my Oxfords rather than to attempt to untangle the snarl into which Toto wove them. He rode his bicycle about the Hancock ranch up at Santa Maria and did his funny little stunts for the benefit of the guests or just because he loved to show off. He grew into that lanky, somewhat unattractive age which in apes is comparable to adolescence in boys and girls, and I noticed the first time I saw him after his arrival that when a person tried to control him he was capable of behaving very badly and of trying to bite. He was, in fact, one of those tamed rather than trained creatures which had been brought up in quite the modern belief of complete self-expression. So after some time, Captain Hancock felt that Toto had better come to live in the zoo.

Here with us, he entered into cage life with little relish for it. He cared nothing for any other chimpanzee. He wanted to associate with the staff exclusively, and so he had some lonely times. Every day he dressed himself up in his suits of clothes, exercised on his bicycle and did his little tricks for the pleasure of zoo visitors. Our veterinarian suspected when he first came in that Captain Hancock had been correct in thinking that he was not sturdy, and examined him for tuberculosis and other organic diseases. There seemed to be no particular thing wrong with him, but he did not like anything really good for him to eat. He was subject to colds and frequently showed evidence of sinus infection. But he was lovable and exceedingly smart. He had obviously, during the times that Mrs. Evans had been compelled to board him out, contracted bad habits of eating and living. During his second winter here, he succumbed to a very severe cold. His little suit hung in the monkey house a long time, and his bicycle, too, for there was no one to use it. Finally, it went into the Christmas box at one of the charity agencies in the hope that some child might benefit by it.

As we wished to keep our ape collection more strictly on the scientific level, we decided that we were not interested in trained chimpanzees. In fact, with Henry Newmeyer's death, even the funny little orang-utan acts which had grown up so naturally because Maggie was such a good comedian were discontinued. And so one evening, when a Mr. Haessler of Hollywood called me to say that he had two male chimpanzees well trained and famous for the comic shorts that had been made of them in Hollywood, and that he wanted to give them to the zoo, I told him that we were in no position to accept or exhibit them. We were conducting a large building program, our cages were crowded and already we had two good male chimpanzees and only one female. Mr. Haessler had filmed apes and had photographed some of the work with great apes being carried on by Dr. Hooton of Harvard, and thus he had become interested in these intelligent animals. He had subsequently obtained two young ones, trained them to wear clothes, box, play games, and had not only used them for moving pictures in regular studios, but had made comics of them, as I have said. They had been exceedingly well trained and apparently were very intelligent and affectionate, but now they were becoming sexually adult, enormously strong and could no longer safely be used for commercial work, and it was becoming difficult to confine them properly.

This, however, was not the end of Mr. Haessler's trained chimpanzees, for while being used with several others in what he felt would probably be their last picture, all of the chimps came down with severe colds which rapidly developed into pneumonia, and in spite of the skill of the veterinarian called to care for them, several died, among them one belonging to Mr. Haessler. Again he called me and finally asked if we would accept his fine big male "Shorty" if he could obtain a female for a mate. This was an offer that we could scarcely refuse. So one day there arrived a female chimpanzee from Warren Buck of Camden, New Jersey, labeled SUSIE. Susie was nearly grown and showed some evidence of maturity, although young. She was suffering from a very heavy cold and had a poor appetite. But she seemed sound and no more highstrung and erratic than most female chimpanzees. News of her arrival was duly conveyed to Mr. Haessler, who agreed with us that Shorty should not come down until Susie had been cured of her cold and we thought she was in good physical condition.

Susie had been in America only a few weeks when we received her. She seemed to have more than just a cold and we had difficulty in getting her to take the food and medicines she needed. She was not unfriendly, and although she preferred to receive her attentions from the men on the staff, she did within a few days permit me to pet and handle her through bars and wire screen. When the evidence of her cold had cleared up, we notified Mr. Haessler, and he said that Shorty would be right down. We decided to keep them both at the hospital in the big cages until they had become accustomed to each other, and to us.

Late one Sunday afternoon, Shorty arrived in a closed coupé with only a collar and chain to control him. The young man driving the car was unaccompanied and he walked with a crutch, having one foot in a cast because of a broken bone from which he had not completely recovered. Instead of driving through the zoo as I should ordinarily have done, I took him to the hospital along a back road, for I could not jeopardize visitors in the park who might, if we had to stop any place, excite Shorty. The boy said he had experienced considerable difficulty once or twice on the way down and had realized that Shorty should have been better confined, but that he had always ridden with him in this free way and considered it safe. A clever little book about Shorty, autographed for me by the author, Mr. Haessler, had been badly chewed up in one of Shorty's tantrums on the way down. The canine teeth had penetrated well into the middle of the text in some places and there were other evidences of his tantrums in the car. I felt sure that the young man was glad to complete the final task of leading him into the big cage near but not adjoining that confining Susie. At the same time, he was truly attached to Shorty and hated to leave him. He told us about his diet, his character and his tricks with much pride. He looked favorably upon Susie and I think would have put them right together if we had considered it the proper way of dealing with them.

Susie rushed to the corner of her cage nearest to Shorty and screamed at him in pretended fear or rage. I have never been satisfied with my interpretation of this female chimpanzee habit. Shorty was too engrossed for a few minutes in the new human beings he was encountering to pay any attention to her. She was temporarily just another chimp with whom he might be forced to share a scene in a picture on the morrow.

I took him an assortment of fruit and he came part way down from the top of the cage and held out his hand as though to take it but, suddenly changing his mind, made a grab at me, trying to snatch my hand instead of the fruit. But I was too old at chimpanzee tricks to be caught that way. So I carried the fruit on and gave some of it to Susie. When he saw that he began to dance, clapping his hands and patting his feet down hard on the cement floor. Wishing to be friendly with him, I immediately responded and gave him more than his share.

Thus began my acquaintance with one of the smartest and at the same time most impossible chimpanzees I have ever known. Shorty had any number of tricks. He jumped up and down on the floor of the cage, beating his feet against the cement until it seemed as though

[170]

he would break the bones. He would climb to the top
of the cage, let go and drop to the floor twelve feet
below with a thud that sounded as though he must have
broken every bone in his body. He patted his hands
and smiled ingratiatingly at you and when you approached in a friendly manner would spit at you such
quantities of saliva that you were completely sprayed
with sticky froth. He watched his every chance to grab
at a keeper and he threatened Susie across the twelve feet
of empty cage dividing them so that she alternately
cowered in fear or tried to make friends by whimpering
lovingly and making sex displays for him. As he became
better acquainted with us, however, he became more
quiet and we learned better how to speak to him and
control him. Within a month we moved Susie into
the cage next to his and they began to make friends
through the wire. He seemed most interested in her
and acted as though he would be happy to play with
her and she had apparently lost any fear of him, even in
his tantrums, by the end of the first week of this controlled contact.

Then one day we opened the sliding door between
the two cages and permitted Susie to enter Shorty's
domain. She sidled up to him a little coyly and a little
timidly, too. For one second he acted as though he
would strike at her but, changing his mind, he touched
her gently and they began the familiar grooming which
is considered a good omen. Most of us left, but the caretaker at the hospital was warned to keep a close watch.
Suddenly Susie gave a sharp little cry. Immediately
Shorty grabbed her roughly. He pushed her to the floor,
where she cowered trying to protect herself. Standing
above her, he brought down both fists, beating on her
hips with such force that the boy on duty thought he

was breaking her back. He shouted at Shorty and tried to attract his attention, but Shorty kept right on beating, biting and punishing her until help arrived and Shorty was chased to the top of the cage. Susie, not so much injured as frightened and excited, was slipped into the cage next door.

Then, indeed, did Shorty fly into a rage! He beat himself and punished his cage while Susie took stock of her bruises and scratches and whimpered over the sad experience. For two days she stayed away from the wire, while Shorty continued to try to convince her of his friendly interest in her. Finally they spent most of their time touching, grooming and wheedling each other through the obstructions between the two cages. Frequently, however, Shorty, unable to reach her, would beat himself against the wire, screaming and spitting and then going back to get what sympathy he could from the only creature who understood his ways. He also worked at the walls and sliding doors between the two cages, and one day he pulled so hard that he bent the rod that controlled the sliding door and nearly opened it. That day, we took Susie into her first cage, leaving one intervening between the two. In the morning we found that Shorty, using his same method on the rod, had forced his way through both cages and joined her. There was evidence that he had been both rough to her and kind, but that morning he was on good behavior, as though he knew he could be forcibly removed at the first sign of meanness. This unhappy life continued. We were forced to separate them many times, and Susie began to learn the signs of the storm and either distract his attention from the fit of imaginary temper or cajole him by her attentions. Meanwhile, we were becoming increasingly convinced that the two could never make a public exhibition. Shorty was too ugly at times, had too many offensive habits in addition to his spitting, which was the worst I ever saw in a chimpanzee, and so reluctantly I wrote to Mr. Haessler, then in the East, that either he or we must find another home for the two of them. Susie was a nice animal and, physically, Shorty was perfection; but even in his smart, funny play, as well as in his fits of unreasoning hatred, he convinced me more strongly than ever that trained or man-wise chimpanzees did not fit in either with our installations or our purposes. The two were eventually sent to Florida, where in McKee's Jungle Garden we hope they will give a good account of themselves.

Perhaps when forced to answer the question as to which of the great apes appeals to me the least, and I answer truthfully that I care less for chimpanzees, my answer may not be completely true; for since my first introduction to apes I have had to recognize the fact that chimpanzees do especially like me and perhaps more than any other ape respond to me and obey my wishes. Beginning with our own old Dinah, I have never failed to strike a responsive chord in any chimpanzee I have met, except Violet. I find in dealers' quarters some of the most adorable babies which hold out their little hands in ways I cannot resist, and usually, in spite of warning, sooner or later I become involved and must often, dirty and vile-smelling, be rescued, usually to the disgust of the caretaker. In zoos, the chimpanzees always turn to me more readily than do the other apes, and so if I do have any feeling of indifference toward them, happily I know it is well concealed.

A year ago, at a request from Surabaya, Java, for a pair of young chimps, I filed the order with Warren

Buck, who annually brings in a nice tame group. When two lovely, fat, shining black babies, just about the size of our own little Georgie, arrived, I surrendered to their charms immediately. The little white flags on their tiny rumps were still snowy; their round, fat stomachs were always crowded against the wire to be tickled. I was firmly resolved not to permit myself to love them, but after they had lived with us five months, while I watched Emily De Konza, technician at the hospital, who had fed and cared for them, take them one by each hand and lead them into the box, give them each a final hug and banana, and turn quickly and silently away, I realized I was feeling pretty badly, too. And later, when I got the news that the boat had, due to war conditions, been much delayed and held up at Batavia and Singapore for days and days before going back to touch at Surabaya, I kept from Emily the news that, in consequence of this cruel delay, the little female had died of heat prostration and so had never reached her destination.

After many interesting experiences with individual chimpanzees, I have come to the conclusion that perhaps it is some tone of my voice that attracts them and gives them confidence in me. I may be wrong. One of many convincing instances occurred when I visited the zoo on my last trip to Boston. Hearing a chimpanzee making what I call his unhappy noises, I turned, as did everyone else in the primate house, and walked over to his cage. I could not get very close, but up on a shelf partially screened from the public there sat a fine big male chimp, his hair on end, his shoulders hunched up and his back to the crowd. A man standing near spoke to a companion as though he were one of the frequent regular zoo visitors that every zoo man recognizes. So I turned to him with the question, "Do you know his name?"

"Yes, it is Tommie," the man answered, a little surprised.

So I spoke to Tommie, saying his name over and over, and after one or two repetitions of the name spoken quietly and with confidence that Tommie would respond, Tommie did look around. He did not locate me at first and so hopped down off his shelf and came toward the front of the cage, still making his unhappy "*Wooo-hoooo*." I continued to talk to him and he finally located my voice. Then, indeed, was response instantaneous. He stuck out his quivering lips as far as he could and told me in his most pathetic way that he was not happy; that he was lonely, or perhaps his favorite keeper was on vacation. At any rate, I kept talking in spite of the fact that we had an audience, which is always embarrassing. Tommie realized that he was being understood and loved. Quietly he moved about and picked up some scraps from his breakfast, scattered about on the clean bed of shavings. It was not very much, but all he had, and extending his hand toward me with his offering, he looked intently and contentedly into my face, once again entirely satisfied with his lot. The crowd stood spellbound by the scene they had witnessed and perhaps not completely understood, for I heard one woman say, "Oh, he knows her." Not in just the way you meant it, lady, but in a bigger, broader sense of knowing I think that Tommie did.

PART FOUR

THE HAIRY MAN

CHAPTER XI

The Quest of Gorillas

EVEN though I imagine my interest in and understanding of gorillas is more than normal, I cannot really deceive myself in this regard, for no creature, even among the great apes, has so completely captured the fancy of scientists, travelers and laymen generally as the great beast commonly called our "next of kin" by the white man, and the "hairy man" by the black inhabitants of his native jungle.

Proof of the intensity of this interest lies in the efforts man has made to become better acquainted with the gorilla. Since the first white man learned that in the dense forests of tropical Africa and high on the sides of the mountains of the Congo there did really live one of these creatures like unto himself but greater in stature, more difficult and wary to trap or even see, and more dangerous to pursue than any of the other manlike apes, he has sought to find that creature and bring him back to live with him.

The name gorilla appeared in literature as early as the fifth century before the birth of Christ when Hanno of Carthage, in describing his journey down the West Coast of Africa, used the word to describe wild men, saying: "In the recess [of the coast] was an island having a lake and in this there was another island full of wild men. But much the greater part were women having hairy bodies whom the interpreters called gorillas. . . . But pursuing them, we were not able to take the men. . . . We took three women who bit and tore those who caught them and would not follow. We were obliged to kill them and took their skins off, which skins were brought back to Carthage." And according to Pliny, the two skins were found in the temple of Juno at the time of the invasion and sack of Carthage. But now most authorities doubt that the creature known as the gorilla to science was referred to in this article.

Possibly the first real mention of the modern scientific gorilla by name occurred in 1625, and from then on interest and knowledge grew until, in the early part of the nineteenth century, the gorilla was well established in science and his pursuit by laymen began in earnest. Even by the most ignorant and fearful savage, the gorilla was recognized as something much more manlike in his appearance than the chimpanzee. Being so secretive in his living, so retiring in his habitation, the gorilla was thought to hold something hideously supernatural and mysterious in his nature. The names applied to him differed among the tribes and sometimes confused explorers. As I follow the black brute through the written records, I find many names such as *njinas*, of the West Coast tribes, *ngi*, as he is frequently called, *ingena*, and finally the Swahili version, *ingagi*.

Being what is termed an "armchair naturalist," first through stupidity and choice, but later through the necessity of staying on a job, I have single-handed and alone chased these creatures through the pages of literature, and sometimes I wonder if those men I have looked upon with secret envy have had any greater satisfaction out of being led by natives on *safaris* to the land of these great apes, even to glimpse them through the mists and foliage of the jungle, or to stand holding their breath in the vicinity of a gorilla band — only to discover that they had stolen away in perfect silence — than I have had at stumbling upon a trace of them in books when I was not expecting to. In fact, as I have sought books about the great apes among piles and shelves of second-hand volumes, the discovery of such a treasure as *Adventures and Explorations in Tropical Africa* by Paul du Chaillu, even though he has been greatly discredited of late years, or some free translation or pamphlet referring to gorillas even briefly, is enough to make me happy for a week. And each time I explore such sources for gorilla lore, I enter upon an adventure filled with excitement and hope and confidence that this time I will come upon a trace of the gorilla which I believe at least approaches what I would find in a real jungle.

One of my most recent discoveries came unexpectedly as I was assisting my sister to prepare a piece of property she had just acquired for tenants. In a typical California back shed, a combination of attic, storeroom, cellar and garage, I came upon a Civil War army chest. Opening it, I found it contained what was apparently the entire library of the former owners. One of the books was the autobiography of the great showman, P. T. Barnum. It didn't matter to me so much that it was a first edition autographed and containing a facsimile of the preface in the author's own handwriting. I squatted among the debris and trash I had been moving and with trembling fingers turned the pages rapidly to those chapters of which I had heard. I found them in the very end of the book, entitled "The Land of the Gorilla," "The Battle of the Giants" and "King of the Jungle." There I discovered Barnum's gorilla. And what a gorilla! One who

[181]

went out of his way to wrestle with and conquer croco-
diles, refusing to step aside as others of his band had
done. He met a leopard face to face and, having bitten
the big cat's neck nearly through, lifted the carcass by
the left front leg and tossed him through the trees for
fifty feet, then turned to face an unknown enemy, the
rifle in the hands of the white hunter. Great hunters
were finally sent by Barnum to obtain a specimen for
"The Greatest Show" because, as he naively remarks,
"One has never crossed the Atlantic." They finally did
succeed in capturing a child gorilla by the cruel ex-
pedient of shooting first the father and then the mother.
But unfortunately the little creature, described as being
about two years old and untamable, failed to reach the
destination intended for it.

But I turn gladly from Barnum's jungle pages to the
pages of du Chaillu, for it is with him — discredited or
not — that we make our first journeys into the "Land of
the Gorilla" (which words must head some chapter in
every book on the dark continent). And it is from the
drawings, pictures, skins and skeletons which he brought
to America that, for many, the gorilla began to emerge
from the darkness and ignorance that had surrounded
him and became not a beast that was a little more than
the chimpanzee and much less than a man but a remarkable creature having his own stature, character and
name. And instead of the definitely chimpanzeelike
drawings of former literature about gorillas, a truly
recognizable gorilla head and body emerged. The favorite gorilla painting and taxidermist's mounting even
today continues to be the huge male standing stretched
to the last possible inch of height, his enormous arms
raised to beat upon the hairless chest with clenched
fists, or hanging loosely to his sides in the most human

position possible. But strange and unnatural as this posture appears to me, it is a fine advance over that terrible drawing found in both the Barnum and du Chaillu books and the natural histories which have fixed themselves in the memory of literally thousands of readers. There we usually see the crushed and crumpled body of a helpless native lying at the feet of the giant beast. In its hands is the gun it has wrenched from the grasp of its victim — bent into a crescent or smashed by the strong teeth and jaws into a flat steel bar — while facing the beast stands a valiant hunter, covering him with his rifle, bravely defying death, hoping he may yet save the native. Glistening teeth and dripping jaws of a murderous beast are poised against the powder and lead. The outcome of the picture can be of little doubt.

One of my brief but interesting excursions into gorilla lore brought me into contact with a West Coast gorilla which was a composite of the traditions, observations and mysticism of the blacks and those whites who, cut off from contacts with the past, finally seem to take much of the natives' philosophy and belief as their own. In this book, called *The Great African Mysteries*, I find delightful bits about the heart of Africa, its legends and its rarities. From the chapter on monkeys I can never forget one sentence which stands out clearly always when I think of gorillas, for it says: "They do not amuse us — nobody can laugh at a gorilla"; adding that they inspire terror in the wild and curiosity in captivity. This gorilla has all the habits attributed to gorillas from ancient time, even to the carrying off of the village belles. It is obvious that our narrator believes it, for he knows that they can distinguish between sexes. He describes a giant gorilla, white and hoary with age, that terrorized a colony until he was brought to earth by a white hunter.

Aside from the first sentence, one other made a lasting impression as I followed this gorilla: "Many native tribes well known to the white men never class a gorilla among the animals, but speak of him always with superstitious respect as the 'hairy man.'" Of all the creatures that dwell in the forest, our author pays the gorilla the greatest respect for his courage and ability as a fighter.

But for one thing, I might have turned from my pursuit of the gorilla through the trails of literature. This is a strangely consistent thing. In every account, no matter how ruthlessly and with what determination the hunter sought his prey and slew him, there lurks in the telling of the tale a strange feeling of regret, almost of shame, at having accomplished his purpose; and always there is the implication of the strong fascination the beast has held for the man. And usually, in so many plain words, the hunter says that it is only his eagerness to assist in building up knowledge of the beast or the necessity to save a human life that has prompted the killing. Each claims that at the last minute, when he has come face to face with the gorilla, he has felt the greatest reluctance to destroy a creature which, after days or hours of hunting, in which it has been near him, seeing him without being visible, hearing him while moving soundlessly itself, watching and knowing that it was being sought, has finally been forced to meet its pursuer when cornered and has stood erect so like a man that it has become almost impossible to destroy it in cold blood. Its death has left the hunter feeling like a murderer.

I have been told by others who have lived in the gorilla country, for I pursue this subject avidly through conversation as well as books, that natives fight gorillas as they would a human enemy, in open warfare, and to defend their homes and crops from their marauding just as they must from that of other hostile and thieving tribes.

With possibly one authentic exception, I can find no instance of the beast seeking the man to destroy him; pursuit and attack has always been on the part of the man. Although it has been conscious of man's proximity, the gorilla has not taken the mean advantage it might have had.

Harry Raven of the American Museum tells how, in pursuing gorillas unseen because of the density of the African forest, the great male mountain gorilla would charge a few steps screaming and then stop suddenly to slip off in another direction so silently that he could track him only with the aid of Pigmy hunters who could follow the indistinct trail. Three or four times the great beast would charge, each time following the same tactics; and finally being pressed too close and knowing that he could not elude his pursuers, would come on to stand erect "like a man" and receive a second bullet which ended his life instantly. There was a fascinating tale, indeed, of the difficulties of the chase, the discovery of the nests, in one instance nine in one group built from broken saplings pulled toward and pushed under the gorillas as they sat, gathering whatever growth might be within reach. If insufficient material was at hand to suit his taste in beds, the gorilla would strip leaves and small branches from bamboo and shrubs at greater distance from the bed to use as padding. But the temporary character of these nests gave further proof of the nomadic nature of their builders. One of the instances that made my spine tingle was the finding of a place where one of the giants of the jungle had been sitting while he fed on the thick young growth near him. The damp chewed stems which had been stripped of leaves and bark still showed the tooth marks of the beast and the Pigmies knew he had been there but a few minutes before. Touching the ground where he had sat, Mr. Raven found it still warm with the heat of the great body and he knew that just beyond the screen of shrubbery the beasts must be watching him. In utter silence his party sat listening and watching for long periods, and then heard the grunting sounds of gorillas on three sides of them, by which they keep their individual positions known to the group by the signal they all understood.

There is a group of such fascinating tales by others who have sought and found the hairy man in his native jungles, each with such graphic and incomplete glimpses as this, and so uniform is the story of their ability to hide and elude their enemies, and so lacking is each in anything that would indicate the gorilla could be the charging, defying, threatening beast of the early explorers, that when I read these late accounts I feel as though I had discovered another and very different gorilla, and this time something very close and intimate, even though from the explorers I catch only glimpses. For this gorilla I am indeed very grateful.

Hunting gorillas through the jungles is, I am convinced, a nerve-wracking experience, for I learn in the pages I have read in my own wanderings that many of the trails are low tunnels through which man must travel in the manner of a beast, stooping almost to his hands and knees. And man with his accouterments and equipment is a clumsy creature; he thunders through the jungles, while not even the trembling of a leaf betrays the hunted. Hiding has been the gorilla's business; it has been his only means of saving himself and his children, and so for generations he has crept into the darkest dripping vastness of the heated tropical jungle away from danger, never seeking it. I am glad that having tracked, overtaken and finally destroyed the hairy men, there is nothing to indicate that the feeling is one of elation at the death of a fellow creature; only a natural one of satisfaction that an obligation to science has been met. I know I should turn in loathing from the written or spoken word of one who described the killing of an ape, especially a gorilla, with the satisfaction and triumph of a sporting achievement.

Finally well preserved and measured specimens of gorillas emerged from the wilderness and, at long last, some live specimens, bringing more complete knowledge. Interest grew rather than lessened, for already man had formulated that theory of his origin which had resulted in much controversy and his relationship with the lower orders was becoming a matter of moment. The search for a missing link was to assume scientific importance (not remain just a funny catch phrase) if the theory of evolution was to be adequately sustained. Skeletons of gorillas were carefully studied, weights and measurements of organs made and the startling likeness and differences between man and gorilla brought into prominence.

One day, in pursuing my interesting adventure through gorilla lore instead of gorilla jungles, I came upon a choice bit of scientific writing in the archives of one of our museums. This article on the anatomy of a gorilla, by Richard Owen, contained a surprising paragraph upon how a gorilla might be changed into a man and enumerated the changes that would have to be made in his teeth, nervous system and brain. The sentence, however, that made me pause for thought and which I jotted down in my notebook was: "In the nervous system, the steps in transmutation would be to abrogate the law of the early arrest of the brain's growth and cause it to proceed, especially in the cerebral part, with the general growth and development of the frame, though in a slower ratio." I have many times sat upon a corner abutment of the foundation of our great gorilla cage and watched our two mountain gorillas — which, by the way, I "captured" after a long pursuit — and permitted my mind to play with that thought. As their black faces have come very close to my own and their deep hazel eyes look curiously and affectionately into my eyes, I have wondered what would happen if, in the case of some captive gorilla, that could be done. But more deeply I have pondered upon what it was that happened or did not happen on that long road of time which permitted the brain of one creature to continue in its development and to advance to apparently unlimited fields of mental power while the brain of another, whose body grew in stature and brute strength far beyond that of man, stopped at the very gates of childhood. There it remained without desire or need of speech, without further mental development, a giant in stature, an infant in mind, forced by this weakness to turn back into the safety and darkness of the jungle.

During the past fifteen years more and more frequently gorillas have found their way into the collections of wild animals housed in European and American zoos. When, finally, I saw my first gorilla in the flesh and had him reach out and touch my hand, then sit beside me, I felt that the greatest milestone along the long road that reached from me to the wild gorillas of the jungles had been safely reached. But the end of my quest was not in sight, for I waited longingly and not very hopefully for the time to come when I too might

[188]

say with those other zoo directors, met in conventions or some such gatherings, "Oh well, our gorillas . . ." And then the chance to obtain the Johnson gorillas came, so suddenly that we were as surprised as anybody. The story of that purchase has been told too many times to need repeating. But even with the coming of these great black hairy men into our lives my gorilla quest was not ended, for until someone spends much more time in the gorilla country than has yet been possible, until someone has followed one group of the black beasts, keeping them under constant and intelligent observation, until gorilla life as revealed in the wild is duplicated by family grouping in the zoo and gorillas have been born in captivity, there will still be much to be learned. And as I have written these words that possibility seems as remote as did the possession of a live gorilla in my early life at the zoo.

But did I say in this tale or elsewhere that the story of the zoo is never written? If I have not, I should do it before I write further. If I did say it, I should repeat once again. In fact, I personally would like to shout it to the world from the housetops. The story of a zoo is never complete, for always at the most unexpected moments great things happen. I had no thought that the possibility of obtaining a female gorilla would present itself in the near future. Yet, just now, when difficulties in shipping are greater than they have ever been before, when demands upon our private sources are greater than they have ever been, there suddenly came the chance for our zoo to obtain two female gorillas.

I had never seriously contemplated obtaining one female gorilla, for that would mean either that one of two males must be left alone, which I could not have endured, or at best I should have had to part with one

[189]

and that would have been unthinkable to me. But here were two young female gorillas available at once; young ones, it is true, but that was not serious, for Mbongo and Ngagi were very young in their maturity. Two at once we needed, and they were available. This is how it was.

One of the men who owns what we in California call, for want of a better term, a "lion farm," was sitting in my office while we two indulged in the usual line of professional gossip, when suddenly he asked, "Did you hear that Trefflich is bringing in a big group of gorillas?" "No, for goodness' sake when?" "Well, I heard that he has been expected ever since April." Now this man often takes care of the West Coast shipments of Trefflich and I felt that this was more than rumor. So I immediately wrote to Trefflich and several other friends in New York. The first I asked if he had any such shipment and if so to let me know if there were any females; the others I asked for any news they had. But in every case I met with no reply, and so I was fast putting this information into my little pigeonhole marked *Unfounded Rumors* after all.

But on Sunday morning, September 7, 1941, as I walked into my office, my secretary took down the phone as she said, "New York is calling, just a minute, I will get them for you." And then it came — "Hello Mrs. Benchley, this is Trefflich." How excited his voice sounded as he went on, "I just landed eight gorillas Friday and I have two nice big females. Do you want them?" Did I! And so with both of us talking at once I finally obtained the information that he thought they were mountain gorillas, that each weighed around a hundred pounds, that they were healthy and surely females and that they were being quoted to me at $9000 f.o.b. from New York, and that Mr. Vierheller of St. Louis, who was sure I wanted them, had made him call me. And so I was getting the first chance at them. You may be sure that I blessed the director of the fine St. Louis Zoo for that friendly gesture! Our own zoo is so far away from the big shipping centers and the dealers of the Atlantic Coast that many times the very rare things are snapped up before we even receive our price lists. So the important question I asked Mr. Trefflich, after all, was "How long will you hold them for me?" and when he said until Tuesday I felt once again, as before, that this was the month when the lucky goddess of gorillas was shining her favors upon our zoo, for it was in September, just ten years ago, that Martin Johnson sent me that wire YOU CAN HAVE OUR GORILLAS FOR $15,000, and Dr. Harry went out after the money. This time it was quite different and more responsibility lay directly upon me. Dr. Harry had just gone away forever, and I could not even share with him this great moment of responsibility and joy. My first thought was "Dr. Schroeder can tell me everything I need to know," and so before I did anything else I dispatched a fast wire to him in New York saying: GO TO TREFFLICH'S — EXAMINE TWO POSSIBLE FEMALE GORILLAS, DETERMINE SEX, SPECIES, CONDITION, AGE. WIRE FULL PARTICULARS TOMORROW.

Then I reached for the telephone and called Mr. W. C. Crandall, the new President of our society, getting him out of bed, as I learned later, but I should have had no hesitancy about that, for you don't have gorillas offered to you every day. I knew he would be as enthusiastic as I. He listened to the story, and on one subject we both agreed. We could not afford them unless we could obtain the money as a donation. We were both equally sure

[191]

that we could not afford not to buy them. And so we thought of some of our greatest benefactors, who were anxious to see the work that their friend Dr. Harry had so nearly completed carried out as he would wish it. Both Mr. Crandall and I felt that on this important occasion the backing of the Board should be very definite, and so he willingly gave up his Sunday to go with me in our efforts to obtain the money. Their cordial reception left us little room to doubt that they knew we had come abegging and they made it so easy to tell our story. We were backed up by years of discouraging correspondence carried on by both Dr. Wegeforth and me with the authorities in control of the Belgian Congo, protectors of the Parc National Albert, the great gorilla preserve. This correspondence had been aided, and favorable action on the permit to capture two female gorillas had been urged, by most of the scientific organizations in the United States, but the answers had been always curt refusals even to admit our unique claim to consideration. Being assured that this would have been the desire of our late founder, the gracious patrons promised to consider the gift if Dr. Schroeder's report was favorable.

You can only imagine how excited I was, how anxious and how happy if you, too, had hoped for such a thing as female gorillas through a decade as I had done; if you had met with the discouragements with which I had, and if you longed to know the life story of the gorilla as much as I had. Our two magnificent gorillas are now in the prime of their early maturity and promise to go on for a long period. They are apparently satisfied with each other's company and conditions, but nevertheless they live an incomplete life.

Like our original efforts to obtain the Martin Johnson gorillas, this, too, was a story with a happy ending.

The young females are here and now the whole zoo staff is hoping that the old words "They lived happily ever after" will be written as a finis to their story.

These two are youngsters, caught in the highlands of French Equatorial Africa under permit from the Free French Government. They are certainly not mountain gorillas. This is a matter of little concern, for the differences as indicated in live specimens are so little that the scientific names of several captive gorillas are matters of dispute. There can be little if any doubt that the slight racial difference will make no difference in their ultimate mating — providing they are acceptable to each other. That would have been the big advantage of having two pairs. We could have changed our family relations if they had not been harmonious as first planned.

Our original intention, as worked out by Dr. Wegeforth, with the help of many scientists and explorers who had watched and studied these creatures in the wild, was to keep one pair on exhibit in a large, open, barless grotto while the other pair would be put into a colony of breeding apes which we have long been planning to build in a very favorably located area on a sunny slope just west of the quarantine station at the hospital. This plot has been carefully saved for this purpose. Several times other uses have been suggested, but Dr. Harry refused to permit anything to encroach on his "Ape Colony." There, isolated especially from contagion and disturbance, the best chances of raising and studying young apes are offered.

The two young females were darlings, not so aggressive in their stalking as Mbongo and Ngagi were, much more tired from their long, hard trip and the small crates in which they had been shipped. The smaller one had a slight cold and felt very forlorn as she was released from

[193]

the sleeping room of the cage in which they were quartered. But Kenya, the older one, looked down from the crossbar of the trapeze to which she had, as soon as freed, climbed, and saw the little black girl from her own homeland. She did just what I wanted to do myself; she moved directly to the little thing and in perfect silence she touched her shoulder with her chin in the familiar gorilla gesture I saw for the first time just ten years ago, when Ngagi walked up close to Mbongo and touching him with his chin, grunted deep in his throat. And Kivu, the smaller gorilla, turned with perfect confidence and held out her arms. Kenya put both arms lightly and comfortingly around the small refugee who thus sat shielded from the crowd of interested spectators.

I wish very much that I could tell you that they accepted us with the equanimity and quickness that the other two gorillas did. But these had had a more difficult time in the long trek to the Western world than our first ones did, and they knew none of us. Even Mr. Trefflich, who brought them out from New York himself, had been seen by them first just one week before. No kind black faces had come all the way with them. There had been no sweet-voiced Osa Johnson to talk gorilla talk with them on the long trip. It had been business, and nobody had gained their confidence.

When I sat very close to the wire of the cage and coaxed the baby of the two close, she boldly strutted up and, pulling down the corners of her mouth, scowled at me as though to put me in my place once and forever. But, "Young lady," I thought to myself, "I have been snubbed by a bigger gorilla than you will ever be. I shall not be so easily rebuffed as you think. I shall persist in my efforts and one of these days you will come

Kenya, New Female Lowland Gorilla,
Is Showing Off for the Crowd

The Yawn of a Giant Gorilla Is
Prodigious, but Mbongo Is Sleepy

The End of a Wrestling Bout

to see me and raise your chin and grunt your little friendly greeting, grunt and wonder what I have for you; or I have learned nothing about gorillas in these last ten years."

And now a new era in our gorilla story was just beginning. I knew the pattern well; first a long period of anxiety rather than pleasure, then always that watchful care, for nothing can throw you into such a complete panic as a gorilla suddenly ill.

But now Charley Smith, wise and sensible, is not here any more; both he and Dr. Harry suddenly left us this summer. Byron Moore, my steady, dependable and greatly loved keeper of the anthropoid apes, had been recently called into the forces of Uncle Sam, and early last spring Dr. Schroeder left us at an urgent call from Lederle Laboratory for his services, so there were only new faces on the primate mesa. I was the only one here who had gone through ten years or even as much as two years of our gorilla study. I was the only one who had watched with them through their stomach upsets and their colds, their injuries and their physical developments; through their changes of food and especially those days when they were teaching us all we know about the lore of the gorilla and while they were learning the queer and doubtful ways of their queer white brothers. And I found that I was feeling very much as I did one night in October 1931, when I had just received two other gorillas that I had been looking forward to possessing so much.

They, too, had just arrived and suddenly I was overwhelmed with the responsibility that had fallen upon my shoulders, my responsibility to science, to the animals, and above all to those who had made their coming financially possible. I hoped that I might faithfully fulfill a part of this obligation and determined to do it carefully and honestly and so I began that night to write in a gorilla diary or notebook. In it I set down those things that I observed whether or not I understood them, whether or not my conclusions were valuable. The keeping of this record was, I knew, an obligation I could not shirk. But the earlier record of those other two showed them to be strangely different from these. Captured by people engaged primarily in scientific, not commercial, animal importation, they had arrived in this country in perfect physical and mental condition. These two little ones cringed from every motion made toward them; their appetites were very erratic, and the presence of a heavy infestation of parasites was shown by the first stool examinations.

Experience with animals, especially primates, has proven that the best cure for such a condition is to build the animal up to the point where it can of its own increasing vigorous physical strength overcome the parasites. This was our hope and at first both young gorillas, especially the younger, Kivu, responded quickly to their happier and cleaner living conditions. But with almost no warning she broke out in skin lesions, which indicated that something was not quite right, her appetite began to decline and only oranges seemed attractive to her.

Every sort of food in every sort of way, cooked and raw, warm and cold, was offered to her. She ate a little every day, developed a small but irritating sort of cough, and showed some slight signs of cold. She who had played and beat upon her small chest crept away from Kenya's invitation to romp and avoided us whenever possible. Gradually she succumbed to the growing number of parasites, which could not be reached. The autopsy performed after her death showed that the heavy infestation had been just below the stomach and that it had penetrated into the lungs, causing abscesses and death.

Then indeed did we have a problem on our hands, for a lonely little gorilla is not easily made contented with her lot. Kenya had gradually been growing fat and aggressive. Her response to each of her keepers, for Moore had, fortunately for us, returned to our staff, was somewhat restricted, and she had steadily refused even to notice me or my own feeble attempts to make her my friend. Then Moore had a happy thought. "Let's put Georgie in Kivu's sleeping room and see how they get along." So Georgie was carried over and put in the cage with the barred door closed between him and possible rough treatment by the older, larger Kenya.

The ape children looked through the bars at each other and as Kenya moved close George sprang forward and with the same rough-and-tumble tactics he employs with his zoo friends, including myself, he thrust his arms through the bars, punched her soundly and retreated before the slow Kenya had gathered herself to resist the attack. Georgie sat off and looked at the patient black face with the bright brown eyes steadily fixed on him. Finally, appearing to decide she was a harmless and supine creature who would bear with him, he came forward and suddenly their arms went around each other through the bars. Mutual friendship blossomed with that first embrace.

And so the queer two were turned out into the open cage, separated by about three feet from Georgie's parental home. And how Katie did scream when she saw him! By her demonstration she excited little Georgie. For a while they reached toward each other through the open space between, loudly denouncing the cruelty that kept them separated. Kenya, amazed apparently by such an unseemly outburst, tried to comfort George, which brought down unmistakable invectives from his mother upon her head. Finally Georgie, apparently having decided that his tantrum was getting him no place with Moore or me, turned quickly and bounced across the poles at Kenya, and she grabbed him in the first interchange of child's play he had ever enjoyed. The play has grown, the companionship is happy and Kenya is growing fat, shiny-coated and active in a way unlike any gorilla under the sun. Now Georgie is not always the leader in play, for she has learned all his tricks, but to us the most important lesson he has taught her, in probably one fourth the time we could have accomplished it, is that we are her friends. Moore climbs up into the sleeping cage and tumbles George about on his bed at night and Kenya demands that she, too, be rolled and spanked playfully. When George and I are by turns punching and petting through the bars, Kenya comes demanding her share and permits me to pet her as intimately as I do my little native-born chimpanzee.

She has taken full charge of the sleeping sacks which our older gorillas spurned and which both she and Kivu had refused to touch, and with one draped about her already paunchy form, she races madly after her playmate until they are both exhausted; then she takes him into her arms, wraps him up with her, and sits on the shelf in excellent imitation of mother and child in the cage next door.

And so temporarily the first difficulty of the young gorilla is overcome, the sharpness of the first real tragedy softened by the happy condition now prevailing, and realizing that I cannot possibly find much time to spend with this young gorilla, as I did with the first two, when the zoo was so much smaller and my own time so much less restricted, I turn again to that earlier day and glance through the pages of my gorilla book, hoping that the daily note will be of benefit to those who will have the real task of raising this funny little black girl, and hoping that the lucky successor will receive the same compensation that I have had through the years.

CHAPTER XII

Johnson's Black Babies

NIGHT letter to R. J. Virden: —

SEPTEMBER TWENTY–NINTH [1931]   SAN DIEGO CALIF.
R. J. VIRDEN
C/O BRONX ZOO   NEW YORK
ELEVEN THOUSAND DOLLARS WIRED TO YOUR ACCOUNT
CHASE NATIONAL BANK BY FIRST NATIONAL BANK OF SAN
DIEGO TO BE PAID UPON PROPER IDENTIFICATION STOP
SUGGEST MITCHELL IF AVAILABLE STOP PAY THIS TO JOHN–
SON UPON RECEIVING TWO GORILLAS PROPERLY CRATED
STOP GET CERTIFICATE OF GOOD CONDITION SURE FOR IN–
SURANCE COMPANY STOP FRED FERGUSON NEA SERVICE
HANDLING STORY FOR SCRIPPS STOP IT CAN BREAK THE
DAY YOU LEAVE WE WILL HAVE PRESS DISPATCHES IN SUN
STOP BE CAREFUL OF CHICAGO TRANSFER DO NOT ALLOW
APES RISKED UNNECESSARILY FOR PUBLICITY

              SIGNED: BELLE J. BENCHLEY

OCTOBER FIRST   NEW YORK
MRS. B. J. BENCHLEY
SAN DIEGO ZOO   SAN DIEGO CALIF.
LEAVING THREE P.M. TODAY ALL OK WIRE FROM CHICAGO

              SIGNED: R. J. VIRDEN

OCTOBER SECOND   CHICAGO
MRS. B. J. BENCHLEY
SAN DIEGO ZOO   SAN DIEGO CALIF.

LEAVING CHICAGO TEN THIRTY—FIVE P.M. ARRIVE SAN
DIEGO TWELVE THIRTY MONDAY ANIMALS OK

SIGNED: R. J. VIRDEN

OCTOBER FIFTH
MARTIN JOHNSON
VANDERBILT HOTEL
NEW YORK N. Y.

ARRIVED TODAY WITH GORILLAS IN EXCELLENT SHAPE
STOOD TRIP WONDERFULLY WELL

SIGNED: R. J. VIRDEN

OCTOBER SIXTH   NEW YORK
R. J. VIRDEN   C/O BELLE J. BENCHLEY
SAN DIEGO ZOO

CONGRATULATIONS ON SAFE ARRIVAL OF GORILLAS

SIGNED: MARTIN JOHNSON

I can still feel the excited curls of tense anxiety that
ran up and down my spine as I sat helplessly waiting for
the fruition of one of the greatest episodes in my life to
be fulfilled. From the writing of my first timid letter to
Martin Johnson, selling him my zoo as a future permanent home for the two great gorillas he had captured in
the mountains of the Belgian Congo, until I received
from Ralph that last wire before he arrived home with
them saying: —

[201   ]

OCTOBER FOURTH   ALBUQUERQUE N. MEXICO

MRS. B. J. BENCHLEY

SAN DIEGO ZOO   SAN DIEGO CALIF.

EVERYTHING RIDING FINE IN LA. SEVEN TEN TOMORROW
MORNING

SIGNED: R. J. VIRDEN

years seemed to have passed over my head. Most of
my story remains untold except for those who can read
between the lines. And that night I could not sleep, for
I had been secretly unable to believe that this approaching event could be true. And so, sitting up in bed, I
made some notes of what I had been studying and finding out about gorillas since that first letter to Martin
Johnson, and at the end of the notes I wrote: —

October 4, 1931. I am going to keep a daily record of
my observations and studies of these two gorillas, for I
realize not only the responsibility I have assumed toward
them and the Johnsons, but toward science. And until
such a time as we can arrange to have a better observer
on our staff, I will do my best to keep some sort of
record. It will not be deeply scientific; it may not be
valuable, but it will be accurate and honest.

October 5th: I did not get down to the train to see the
gorillas arrive. I had to be here at the office to answer
phones about their coming and to see that the photographers, the reporters, the Chamber of Commerce and
the other important people were greeted and kept happy
until the apes arrived. When they arrived, the big crate
which looked entirely too fragile and worn-out to me
to be trusted with the safety of such large apes was set
down on the ground. I found myself thinking that the
safari just ending for these children of the jungle had
been a long one indeed.

*   *   *

[202]

I digress from my diary: That *safari* had started in a small opening in the deep jungles on Mount Kivu when, with their hands and feet tied together, they had been lifted on a stout pole to the shoulders of the Swahili natives to be borne out of the jungle to the camp of the Johnsons. There they were put into a cage built on the body of a truck and finally carried across the plains of Eastern Africa to the home of their captors in Nairobi. But this had not been the end, for soon once more they were started on their way and they probably agreed with the statement of their captors that it was in the land of civilization that danger lurked, as they made the long, difficult trip from the heart of Africa to the land the Johnsons called home. It must have kept these two black children in a state of nervous excitement and fear, even though by this time they had become accustomed to their captors who had been kind to them and to the black-faced natives who made the *safari* with them as their caretakers.

When at last they came to rest, the gorillas found themselves in a cage surrounded by excited, gaping throngs of pale-faced people, jabbering and gesticulating, pointing and staring at these two. And always there was the flash of the exploding lights in their faces associated with the black box of a camera. And more crowds as the days went by. Hot, sticky summer days, no room for playing the running games of the jungle. No leafy, dripping shade, and no elders to interrupt their play with the drumming signal which meant to scamper into the nearest lane leading to the deep, hidden recesses of their dark security. But how they loathed those staring faces, those pointing fingers. Ingagi apparently had found the way of defense against that constant irritation. He sat, his baby face frozen into a glare of unseeing hatred, his heavy brows pulled down deep over his yellow hazel

[203]

eyes, his young lips drawn into a hard, drooping line. Congo, the younger, sat near him and, from time to time, reached over to touch the bigger fellow anxiously. "Why don't we play a little?" "*Mugh, mugh*," the guttural monosyllable warned him. "Remember your training," it said. "Hide your body if you can, your desires always, and your interest in these creatures. Secure yourself by hiding what you are feeling deep in your soul. Hide," said the grunting voice of the older gorilla, more steeped in the lore of the black beast who had preserved himself and his kind by his ability to control and conceal himself and restrict his needs to what he found in the land he had chosen.

Endurance of the surroundings in this first American cage was made easier for the jungle children by their mutual companionship. Alone either would probably have sickened and died of sheer nostalgia. Then, too, their captors, who were now their friends, came daily to see and sit with them, to bring them food and comfort and what happiness they could and to encourage them to hope for better days.

But the *safari* was not over, for a day came when once more they entered the great crate which had been their home so long. It was comforting to them in its secluded familiarity. Its close walls had protected them from staring eyes and they settled down with plenty of food and grunts of content. Again the hands of men lifted them and carried them to a waiting truck. Then they were pushed into the close confines of a huge, dark room and for seven days they rumbled and joggled along, never stopping except with a jerk. They were fed when they could be, given milk and water to drink, and so on day after day with no understanding of the reason of this movement or where it was leading.

After a longer stop than all the others, they were
again surrounded by white-faced, noisy talkers, lifted
and shoved out of the security of the baggage car and
onto a truck, a contrivance they recognized at once,
and were whirled away in a land of fresh, damp air and
bright sunshine unlike that of their shady jungle. The
hands of man once more entered the affair and the huge
crate, worn and weakened by the long journey, was
lifted for the last time to be set down on the dry, brown
earth beside a low swinging gate. White faces stooped
low to peer into the darkness of their traveling crate
where the two black babies, clinging to each other for
what comfort the touch gave them, pressed far back into
the darkest recesses of the home they knew so well. Suddenly the door of their crate opened. They knew it was
the signal for them to come out and slowly, one behind
the other, they walked into the brilliant sunlight of a
new land, into a big, roomy cage. It was October 5, 1931.
Congo and Ingagi were home. The long *safari* was
ended.

October 5th [and back to my notes]: Ralph Virden
said the gorillas gave him no trouble on the way. Their
appetites were good, everyone had been most co-operative. We had no trouble getting them out of the crate.
They are unbelievably black. Their hair is long, looks
coarse; their faces look like velvet. They have hips and
heels! One is a little larger than the other. We do not
know which is male or female. Their names are Congo
and Ingagi. We weighed them in the crate and then
weighed the crate. Their combined weight is 269
pounds. They do not look at any of us. But they are not
afraid. If they know we are here, they do not show it.
They went in and out of their sleeping room, which we

[205]

left open, several times. We put food in there and they went in and took it, selecting what they wanted to eat with a good deal of caution. But they have good appetites. It will be interesting to work out a good diet for them.

I feel very lucky to have two gorillas under my constant supervision. Nobody else in the world has the chance to spend as much time with two gorillas . . . (I hope they are a true pair) as I have.

Every few minutes all afternoon, I have rushed excitedly out to see what They are doing. As the crowd who came to catch a glimpse gradually dispersed, They grew more content. They have done some exploring. They have eaten most of the food we have offered and They have played a little.

4 P.M.: It is getting dark and cool. Congo is lying on his belly across a big eucalyptus stump, his arms and legs are dangling relaxed. He looks very young and innocent and a little homesick. Some way, they seem very childishly dear to me.

October 6. I wish I could record in these notes the many different impressions people seem to get from these gorillas. It will be sufficiently difficult, however, to record even my own impressions and keep them distinct from facts that I observe. Some way, already the facts of what I have seen this day are strangely mixed up with what I know are impressions and interpretations of facts and actions. I wonder if I could possibly be exaggerating the peculiar closeness I seem to have for them. This morning I arrived at the zoo an hour earlier than usual and went straight to their cage. But Henry, who lives in the grounds, was there before me and, because they were awake and eager to be up, he had released them. I brought some Tokay grapes for them, but they ignored me and my offering. They are enjoying the freedom of their cage and are by turns exploring it a little more definitely than they did yesterday. They seem perfectly at home, and yet their actions indicate restraint and caution. Here I go interpreting their actions. I believe they are kings of pantomime, so clear and so clever that even an ignoramus like myself can understand them. They walk constantly on all fours. They rest the weight of their fat, round bodies upon the second joints of their fingers and the flat foot. Their backs sway a little, their shoulders are elevated. There is something dignified and military in their bearing, these strange, hairy men who walk on all fours. Again I am impressed with their power of withdrawal from their surroundings. For just as yesterday they looked naturally at the crowd without appearing to see the people, they look past me and even Henry. They had eaten everything Henry put in their rooms last night. We are feeding them Dryco, the powdered milk the Johnsons used, with a formula for feeding that Martin sent out to me. This calls for a few drops of viosterol every day, fruit, vegetables and milk. I hope with our out-of-door life, we can do away with artificial vitamins and drugs. They like salt very much. The smaller one's stool seems too loose. It may be excitement or change of water.

October 7th: I felt very much elated today. Congo, the smaller gorilla, came to the wire today and took grapes from my fingers with his. It was very cunning to see him take them back and show them to Ingagi both times. The older gorilla appears to be more shy, but investigated whatever Congo was eating after he carried the food away from the side of the cage. They take things very definitely between the ends of their first finger and thumb. I held on to the grapes as much

[207]

as I could to get a good look at his hand. The skin of the fingers is jet black. The hair grows to the first joint, the thumb is short but sturdy and they use it just as we do ours in picking things up and holding. I have seen orang-utans pick up grapes between the ends of their fingers or curl their fingers around them, but not definitely between finger and thumb as Congo does. Chimpanzees are very apt to pick up small things with the backs of their fingers between the first and second joints, but never use their thumb in the gorilla fashion.

While I stood near the cage with the grapes, Congo ran rapidly at me as though he would hit the cage head on, then suddenly turned and struck the wire a glancing blow with his right shoulder and ran on, circling back to Ingagi, who gave a queer, startled grunt and bristled ready to defend Congo if necessary.

October 10th: As each day is very much like the others, I can see no reason for making daily notes, except when something different warrants it. Today I am jotting things down that may prove valuable after a while. I notice certain characteristic attitudes or postures of the gorillas.

For instance, they sit on low cement blocks around the eucalyptus stumps in their borrowed cage. Their backs are very erect, their knees are bent and a little apart and their feet are flat on the floor in front of them. They lie on their backs in the little corner shelves with their heads hanging over the edge and their legs at right angles to their bodies, their heels against the wire of the cage above them. Both lie on their fat bellies over the stumps with four limbs dangling. But more often than anything else, they lie on the floor, their knees and elbows supporting them. Their heads rest in the palms of their hands or the folded backs and their heavy abdomens rest on the floor between elbows and knees. They always do this after eating.

October 18th: The gorillas have been very active the last few days, running around and around the stumps, chasing each other like boys playing tag. They wrestle and box a good deal too. It is all very good-natured and they seem very happy. Henry thinks they know him very definitely. He said Ingagi got quite excited this afternoon when he came out of the gate from the monkey yard with their pans of milk. This gate is close to their cage — just across the road. We are rushing their new cage because the Johnsons will be here the ninth of November and we want the gorillas in it.

October 20th: I was out watching the gorillas this afternoon when Henry came out of the service yard. Both of them showed excitement and I know they thought he was going to feed them. They watched him go on past to the chimpanzee cage and were plainly disappointed when he did not stop. I am going to be out tonight when he feeds them. He says they know their food pan and run round and round the cage trying to get into the door of their sleeping room. We put straw in for their bedding about three each afternoon, then we drop the doors so they cannot go in until night.

October 23rd: I saw Ingagi drinking today. I thought at first that he drank as a gibbon does by putting his hand in the water and licking the water off the hairs. But he lifted quite a lot of water into his cupped palm and then held it high above his head to pour it into his open mouth. He spilled some and it splashed down over his fat stomach. They beat their chests and I have taken motion pictures of them running around boxing and slugging each

[209]

other and eating. They pay no attention to me, that is, serious attention, but Congo charged toward me again. [After ten years of knowing Congo intimately, I would have interpreted that as play.]

October 24th: We were getting some pictures preparing for publicity about the new cage and the Johnsons' coming and all, and Frank Preciado, the photographer from the Union, wanted to go into the cage. Henry went in with him and took a broom so that if one or the other of the gorillas rushed Frank, he could hold them back. Although these gorillas are only babies, weighing not more than 130 pounds or so, they are almost as big as a full-grown chimpanzee and every bit as heavy. Frank took several pictures and then Congo, the smaller, suddenly made a rush, swinging in as he passed Frank, hitting him with his shoulder just as he strikes at me through the wire. It sent Frank and his camera sprawling. Henry, who is so alert and quick, failed to stop the rush, but the little gorilla ran right on and Ingagi grunted crossly or fiercely, ready to step in if need be, but he never moved from his tracks. Frank didn't get his picture, but neither gorilla tried to carry the matter further. I talked it over with Dr. Wegeforth and we have decided never to go into the cage unless some real emergency arises. [*Note:* September, 1941 — It never has and we have followed that determination always.]

November 1st: Ralph has certainly been rushing the new cage. It is fine and I wish it had more time to dry before they have to go in. The two sleeping rooms are of solid concrete. The cage is made of especially woven wire, number-four gauge, and the steel structure is of eight-inch I-beams. It is reinforced strongly everywhere. Because the gorillas love to play in the water, we are giving them a big enough pool for them both to get in at once. [I should like to see them try it now, ten years later.] We are going to suspend a two-inch rope from the ceiling. They pay no attention to the hoops and chains in the orang-utan cage they are now in. However, Henry hung a rope down from a beam and both swing on it constantly. Mother has given me a big oak tree from her Lakeside ranch and that is solidly set in concrete, braced with stout wire at the top. They do not climb on the wire netting, but probably will on trees.

November 8th: For two days we have had electric and gas heaters going in the cage to make sure it is dry. Today the gorillas were put in. It is amazing how easily they went into their old shipping crate and were moved over here. Tomorrow the Johnsons will be here. I am very anxious to meet them. I hope Martin approves the cage. His letters seem friendly, but I know he has very definite ideas.

November 9th, 10th: I was too busy to write anything in the diary of Congo and Ingagi last night. It was too late after the lecture. "Congorilla" is a wonderful picture. The thing still seems unbelievable. That they should have captured two gorillas this size at once and that we should have them here at our zoo, probably one of the poorest zoos, financially I mean, in the world. The gorillas recognized the Johnsons without a doubt. The first time I ever heard them really make a noise or saw them much excited. Ingagi pretends not to like them, but hung back wanting to be noticed and feeling a bit disgruntled, I would say. They opened the door and Osa Johnson stepped into the opening just for a minute and gave Congo a banana. The first words Martin Johnson said to me before he even said "How do you do?" were: "You know I don't really like zoos. I never want to bring animals into captivity." How many times during the day after that he turned to me and said: "This is the most perfect zoo and the most humane in the world. I am glad my gorillas are here." He and Osa called them their "black children" and I have learned everything I could from them about the gorillas in the wild, as well as these two since they were captured. Martin told us that when they carried them down off the mountain, he thought the troop was following but he never saw them. As soon as they got them in the crate, they released their hands and feet which had been tied together and offered them plantains and each took one and began to eat immediately. That night they heard gorillas around their camp, especially around the truck where the two little ones were. They whined and talked, but did no damage.

I have had much correspondence from people interested in gorillas all over the world. I am hoping some of the scientific institutions can arrange to study them, and several have made tentative suggestions about such studies. One man suggested we change the name of the smaller gorilla before any studies were made as the famous Burbridge gorilla was called Congo and the two by the same name might lead to confusion. That is the gorilla upon which Dr. Robert Yerkes made a series of studies in 1927, 1928, and 1929. So I talked to the Johnsons and said I had thought of changing his name to something that sounded like Congo and wondered if they had suggestions. As they did not, we decided to call him Mbongo, which is the last syllable of the mountain range in which they were captured. He answers to that as well as he did to Congo. Both of the gorillas knew their names when they arrived. I noticed that Martin Johnson did not pronounce the first I in Ingagi and he said the natives slurred their vowels and so now we say Ngagi as the Swahili do.

November 17th: Both gorillas love their new cage and climb the oak tree a lot. One of the horizontal limbs, which is not very big, is their favorite place and they "skin the cat" from it at times. Both sit in it together. It sways downward sharply with their weight and I fear it will break when the sap is gone and it becomes brittle. I can surely think of lots of things to worry about with two gorillas.

November 20th: Henry sent word for me to come out quick. I did, thinking something had happened, and there was Ngagi, body bent at the hips so his head hung down as low as his feet. He was beating his chest at Henry who was tickled to pieces because it was the first time Ngagi had acted friendly toward him especially. Both of the gorillas go up the tree carrying the rope and swing down from a high limb or climb up the rope and, swinging over to the tree, hold the rope until they are ready to swing down again.

November 21st: Mbongo is ill. Acts like a person with a bilious headache. Holds his head, rubs his eyes and shuts them tight against the light. I worry about roughage because he refuses to eat green things and the way they divide up their meals, Ngagi gets all of the coarse food. Gave Mbongo a dose of milk of magnesia in his milk and he took it. Ngagi is worried too and tries to get him to come out and play. That will be a big advantage about having two; they will stimulate mutual activity.

November 25th: After four anxious days, Mbongo seems all right again. Gave him several doses of magnesia and cut out bananas and sweet potatoes, giving him mostly oranges. This morning he is chasing Ngagi all over the cage; they are swinging up and down the ropes like sailors. They go part way up and then, holding the rope in one hand and bracing their feet against it between the great toe and the other toes, they lean out almost at right angles and beat their chests with one hand. Both of them go up one rope and wrestle and struggle to push the other off until it takes your breath away. I suppose that is the way they play on vines in the jungle. Remember there is no such thing as a cement floor in the jungles my hearties! They climb trees like fat boys. Mbongo hangs and drops from a limb eight feet off the ground, making his drop about two feet, but he is terribly proud of that stunt.

November 27th: I have been much interested in the casual way in which gorillas defecate and urinate. Chimpanzees and orang-utans usually rush to the top of the cage in the morning and evacuate the first thing when they are out of their sleeping room. Not so the gorillas. They usually stop and stand still during urination, but walk about or play as they evacuate their bowels, reminding one of hoofed animals rather than any of the primates I have seen. They are exceedingly clean about their hands and food and carefully pick any foreign matter off their coats, scraping their fingers in the sand if they are sticky or dirty, but they never appear to wash themselves. When I went out late this afternoon, I saw that each gorilla was up in a corner of the high cage staring toward the east. Suddenly the gate to the monkey yard opened. They thought it was Henry and became much excited, but when it was someone else, they sat back and resumed their staring. Suddenly the gate opened and the very tip of Henry's food cart appeared. Down they came and started running and chasing about, much excited, ready for dinner and bed and

[214]

Henry. As they passed the closed door, they banged hard on it with an open hand. First one and then the other stood and beat it rapidly. Don't know how long they have known where they can look for Henry at five o'clock. The gate is at least three hundred feet away from the new cage.

December 4th: Mbongo has another of his headaches. Dr. Whiting has been giving him mineral oil. I think I will put them on cow's milk and see what it does. This one is not bad, but they worry me. Martin Johnson said they had not noticed these symptoms when the two were with them. Mr. 'Johnson included in his letter further description of the food of wild gorillas, especially mountain gorillas. He wrote: "Gorillas feed on the coarse rather bitter celery which is found in open places throughout their region, the young sprouts of bamboo and a plant we thought was lobelia. They eat wild cane and young corn stalks." Johnson emphasized in the letter that the climatic conditions here in temperature range are comparable to those where these gorillas are found because of the high altitude, but it is much more damp there. Martin said the gorillas could sleep out of doors now [this in November] if it were not for the danger of their being molested.

December 6th: I tried the gorillas on honey. Both refused it as though they did not like it, which is just the way they treat sugar. Recently, I have noticed Mbongo looking at my clothes. The other day as I stood against the wire of the cage, he took a piece of my dress in his fingers, pulled it through the wire and smelled it. They like prunes which I give them each day. They hold a prune between finger and thumb and eat the meat off the seed, which they drop. Neither gorillas nor chimpanzees apparently eat or know nuts. The orang-utans

[215]

crack every seed between their teeth and eat the meats. I think the gorillas would eat every minute all day long, if we permitted them to. Apparently they eat as they wander and play, having no set feeding time, never permitting their stomachs to become empty. We have given them food in large quantities, placing it on the shelves in their sleeping room and leaving the door of the room open. They go back into the room frequently and bring out articles of food every little while. After they eat they are lazy, lying around for an hour, and when they wake up they go right in after another lunch.

I am trying definitely to make friends with them. I can see little result except that they recognize me and come to the side of the cage and take food out of my hands. Ngagi has been doing that ever since the Johnsons were here. Until that time, he would accept nothing we offered unless he took it away from Mbongo. He is definitely the boss (dominant I presume is the word). I can see no way to determine the sex. Johnsons think that "Congo" is the female. My impression is that unless they are the same sex, which I fear is the case, Ngagi is the female.

December 18th: It has been raining and the gorillas have been out every day. They have more pep than at any time since they arrived, chasing each other around and around with almost hysterical joy at the rain. The wetter their hair gets, the happier they seem. Today I saw Ngagi walk erect for the first time, except when he was standing at the door or holding onto the rope or beating his chest as he ran forward. He stood erect so that the water fell directly on his face. He opened his big, red mouth wide so the rain would get in it. Suddenly he clasped his hands behind his back and, as he stood thus, his back was very much swayed at the waist.

Then stepping with his right foot first he walked around the cage nearly three times, slowly, really walking and with even steps, his feet almost straight ahead, with steps almost as long as a person would take. This was no orang-utan's shuffle. His hands clung tightly together and he looked like a dignified, very short-legged, massive-shouldered black-skinned man — something rugged and primitive. They are both apparently right-handed.

December 23rd: Today there was a very large crowd around the gorilla cage and they climbed around on the wire a good deal. They are learning to be more agile and sure on it than they were at first. I stayed around, gloating at what the crowds were saying about them. Suddenly they both went into the house and we could hear them scuffling and boxing in there. They stamped loudly on the floor as they seem to do when they are happy and playful. After wrestling a few minutes, Mbongo came out, as though winded, and sat down over in the corner. After about a minute, Ngagi came to the door and stamped and grunted. Mbongo got up, went straight to the door and the instant he was inside, the wrestling began and went on very strenuously for a few minutes. Suddenly it stopped and the smaller gorilla came out again. They repeated this over and over again at such regular intervals that one of the visitors took out his watch and kept time for them. The "rounds" of play lasted approximately three minutes and the rest periods for about half that time. One of the men said, "Who says Darwin was wrong? That's where prize fighters came from." The "fight" went on for eleven rounds while we timed it. Must have been a draw.

December 26th: Took Mbongo and Ngagi some whole oranges today. They were freshly picked from Mother's trees, the rind was oily and they smelled good. Mbongo climbed up to the lowest branch of the tree and sticking his short, powerful thumb in the stem end, peeled a little of the skin off, picking chunks of the oily, thick skin off with his fingers in a very childish manner. When he had it less than half peeled, he took a bite out of the top and ate the rest out of the rind. Ngagi took his orange up into a corner of the cage, and facing the corner, spread his feet across the corner, standing on the angle irons. Then he dropped his head down between his feet so his back and shoulders were against the wire of the corner. He bit off part of the skin and ate the whole orange out of the skin, allowing the juice to drop on the shelf below. Ngagi keeps much cleaner than Mbongo, who doesn't mind a little orange juice running over his chest. Ngagi often beats his chest at me from this queer position in which he seems to take great pride.

January 1st, 1932: Both gorillas seem in perfect health. They love cold, wet mornings and beat on the door of their sleeping room to get out when they hear us coming. I go in early some mornings while both of them are still asleep. Mbongo hates to wake up and rubs his eyes, yawns prodigiously — never quite appreciated that term before — stretches and turns over. Is this a sex indication? Since they have begun to feel at home in the cage, they do not seem to snuggle so close together at night. They build up good mounds of hay. Ngagi is often lying on his back with his hips and heels against the wall, his short legs at right angles to his body. They talk to Henry now when he brings their supper and they grunt and sort of croon or whinny to me mornings. It is entirely friendly and gentle. I feel as though they were beginning to be fond of me, but they do not talk to me or each other if anyone but Henry or Luke is with them.

Mbongo Clowns, but Finally Weighs in at 6o2 Pounds

Ngagi Eats Popcorn from My Fingers

January 6th: I drove out to Chula Vista to the celery fields this morning when I came to work. Wanted some unbleached celery and finally found a seed farm where I got some. I carried it nice and fresh, with dirt on the roots, to the gorilla cage. I had not given them a treat for several days and they expected something special. Ngagi took a big bunch and went to his favorite eating place. He began tearing right into the heart of the bunch, and when he found it was celery all the way through, he threw it away in disgust and glared at me. Finally he stood up and tramped the celery into the floor, showing me plainly in what contempt he held my offering. The bookkeeper standing beside me also interpreted the dirty look, saying: "I don't think the gorilla is pleased about something." I was pointedly ignored by Ngagi for the rest of the day. He is an artist at ignoring.

January 15th: Mbongo poured out his pan of milk today instead of drinking it. Henry said he never saw anything look quite so impertinent. Then he carried the pan out into the exhibition cage. They banged it around a little, but did not damage it seriously or destroy it altogether as the chimpanzees and orang-utans do their pans periodically. Apparently our gorillas are not going to be destructive. They have never broken anything nor tried to open a door or undo a lock. Ngagi took the pan, which made Mbongo really angry for the first time. He went after the bigger gorilla in dead earnest. They wrestled in serious combat for the first time. Mbongo was angry, and opening his mouth over the shoulder of Ngagi, he bit hard into the hide. Ngagi persisted for a minute, then gave in, dropping the pan and putting his hand to the left shoulder as though it were hurt. The fight was over.

January 23rd, 1932: The gorillas really enjoy and re-

[219]

spond to a crowd of children. Both rouse up and become active as soon as a school group comes. They run about doing all sorts of stunts they do at no other time. They are especially active on the ropes, sliding and pushing each other. They never seem to look at the children, but when the children move on, they lose interest in play. Ngagi has touched my hand when I hold it still. The other day he deliberately pressed the end of his finger hard into my palm instead of taking a raisin off of it. But when I tried to close my fingers around his, he rushed away, and drawing down his exceedingly heavy brows, scowled the rest of the time I remained at the cage.

Mr. Virden put an old tire casing in the cage. Mbongo was not interested at all. Ngagi carried it around then threw it away. Then he walked over and bit chunks out of the rubber. Finally he stood it up on edge like a hoop, but instead of rolling it as the chimpanzees do, he put his hand on the top of the circle and pressed it right down to the rim below with little effort. It was the first example I had seen of their enormous strength. Ngagi held the opposite rims of the tire pressed close together for a second and then suddenly moved away at arm's length, withdrew his hand quickly from the rebound and walked away, completely indifferent to the tire. Neither of them paid any further attention to it for a week and we removed it from the cage.

They care nothing about foreign things. They like their ropes, the tree, they play in the sand, sifting it through their fingers and piling it up around them. They hate a truck and always stop to watch it, and sometimes run aggressively toward it, scowling and grunting in a threatening way.

They know my car, and when I drive around back of

their house they will follow around and then dash into the open door and be waiting at the bars of their sleeping room for me to come in.

Instead of bringing their food all the way out into the exhibition cage, they sometimes pile their bananas up beside them and each leans out of the door of one of the sleeping rooms, resting his weight on his elbows and looking out while they eat. Sometimes they seem to bring their food up into their mouths to masticate it over again.

January 30th: I have been interested in their use of their hands and feet. I cannot reconcile myself to calling them quadrumanous, for these do not carry, hold or grasp things in their feet. They do clutch the rope between their great toe and the group of three which are webbed together next to it. Their instep is firm, solid and unflexible. They walk on the flat foot. They use only their hands for carrying, holding, picking up, and although they walk on their bent fingers, they do not use them as they do their feet. They are certainly bipeds, although they walk on all fours.

Their social behavior, as far as I have observed it to date — the end of the fourth month — contains nothing that I would call grooming or "flea picking." They often touch each other with a gesture of what I interpret as affection. They sit still beside each other and one or the other may put his hand upon a limb or the body of the other. But they do not really groom each other and, when they itch, they scratch, really scratch without the pawing, digging motion or parting of hair as other primates do. They move their fingers back and forth in a typically human scratching motion.

We are still puzzled by their sex. I can see no difference in them and there is none of the sex interest in each other or themselves which characterizes other apes and monkeys.

February 1st: I have been having correspondence with the National Zoo and Dr. Harold C. Bingham of Yale regarding studies involving the use of our gorillas. We have invited Dr. Bingham to come here from Washington, where he now is making a study of little Okero, the small gorilla the Johnsons gave to the Smithsonian Institution, and the lowland gorilla, 'Ngi, they purchased from J. L. Buck of Camden, New Jersey, a couple of years ago. I saw 'Ngi in Washington and he did not look very well, but he was closed up in a steamy, warm glass-enclosed room because it was winter. We have made it very clear to Dr. Bingham, however, that our first consideration is the mental and physical well-being of the gorillas and that we will not do anything that appears to upset or disturb them fundamentally.

February 4th: I gave them fresh pineapple today which is now abundant in the market. I just cut one into quarters and they ate every bit of the fruit out of the rind and then scraped and dug at the rind. They also pulled out the leaves and ate them much as we do artichokes. Finally Ngagi ate even the outside rind of his. Mbongo did not have as good a coat as Ngagi when they came in. Martin Johnson told me one time he was practically naked, having shed all his hair. Now he looks fine, and from a distance you can scarcely tell them apart. But their faces look very different to those of us who know them. Mbongo plays racing games with the young male chimpanzee next door, but Ngagi never pays any attention to either of them at such times. Timmie has taught Mbongo several tricks about racing but gets very angry when Mbongo uses them. Their course is the length of the cage and back twenty feet. Tim gallops and tries to beat by turning before he gets to the corner. Mbongo let him get away with cheating and then one day, when Tim was playing fair, Mbongo turned short of the goal and beat him badly. Tim refused to "play."

Running gaits of the gorillas have been very interesting. They have almost as many gaits as a horse. They chase after each other at times with a regular pace, both feet on the one side going forward at the same time. Again they gallop, bringing their feet forward between their arms at the same time. This is their fastest-looking gait, although the pace covers the ground so rapidly and easily, they could keep it up indefinitely, I am sure. It is very silent and smooth. At times, when they gallop and are full of play, they pat their feet down so hard you can hear it from a long distance. They also have sort of a jog trot that is jerky and fast and awkward.

Henry comes very early to let them out as soon as the sun is up. They are stirring long before the other apes and he thinks it irritating to them to have to stay in too long after they are awake. I think we are all spoiling them, but it is fun.

March 18th: I have been away from the zoo quite ill for more than two weeks. The first day I was able to be out of doors, Dr. Harry came over and took me for a ride and got me as far as the gorilla cage in the zoo. At first Ngagi did not recognize me in the Doctor's car, but when he saw that it was really I, he rushed to the side of the cage. Then both of the gorillas began running around beating their chests and really putting on a show for me as they do for a crowd of children.

Dr. Bingham had arrived late the day before and was sitting on a bench near the fence. Naturally I did not

[223]

know it was he, but getting up from the bench as the gorillas increased their activity, he walked over to the car and said: "You must be Mrs. Benchley. The actions of the gorillas have left no introduction necessary. I am Harold Bingham." I surely was glad that he happened to see their reaction to me and to interpret it just as I had.

March 20th: I returned to work today. I took my black boys a pineapple, but they refused to come to the bars with Mr. Virden and Dr. Bingham standing so close to me. Ngagi made a little by-play of a friendly nature when I stretched my whole arm into the cage between the bars so he could reach the fruit. Dr. Bingham is planning a series of simple experiments and Mr. Virden is preparing the equipment. Dr. Bingham as assistant to Dr. Robert Yerkes has been doing some of the experimental work on chimpanzees, with slot boxes and other such arrangements, in the department of psychology at Yale. He has written them up in most interesting and valuable pamphlets. Many of these experiments he will not be able to carry out as our animals are on exhibit, which means that they have the diverting influence of a crowd around all of the time and that they cannot be segregated or shut up for long periods. Dr. Bingham is watching them closely for evidences of characteristic social behavior.

I know he is greatly impressed by these two gorgeous black beasts. I know that they should be used for scientific observations, but — and perhaps it is just a little jealousy on my part — tonight as I jot down these observations, I feel as though I had lost something; my own intimate closeness with the Johnsons' Black Babies is being shared. Tomorrow their perfectly natural relationship with me is ended, at least temporarily, for day

[224]

after tomorrow the first experiment will be tried or test be given, and we will hope to have gained a little light on the mental processes of a child gorilla. And day after tomorrow is March twenty-second. I am eager, yet loath, for it to come.

CHAPTER XIII

The Mind and Heart of a Gorilla

WITH the arrival of Dr. Bingham I began to have a new
and quite different interest in the two gorillas. Up to
this time they had been just two black hairy children
with whose physical welfare I was much concerned,
and about whom I had been eager to learn everything
that would contribute to the perfection of their life
in captivity and my own success and pleasure in caring
for them. During the five and a half months I had known
them, I had not realized that my pride in them and my
happiness in associating with them was quite so personal.
Now I realize that I had unknowingly become a little
jealous lest others fail really to appreciate and admire
them as I did.

Dr. Bingham had worked extensively in the department of psychology at Yale with chimpanzees, and had
recently made a trip into the mountain-gorilla country.
He had obtained as much insight into the natural life
of gorillas in the wild as possible. This has always been
almost a superhuman task, owing to the wild and extensive territory through which the comparatively few
mountain gorillas wander; to the difficulties of getting
through the dense undergrowth; to the handicaps of
either rain and mist or the humid heat, and to the deep
shade which makes it possible for these jet-black fellows
to melt into the obscurity of their background.

[226]

He many times told me, during our brief association, how dissatisfied he had been with his observations, and how many of his conclusions, based upon evidences along the wild trails left by the gorillas, were being either confirmed or contradicted by the observations he was now making upon our own two. He told me of the deep ruts around stumps and fallen logs which he now recognized as tracks of young gorillas at play, chasing each other in their delightfully human game of tag. He told me of the shallow rather untidy noonday nests of these nomadic wild men. He was sure that they had rested there amid the litter of food they had carried to a comfortable resting spot, consuming and digesting their morning meal. As I have watched Ngagi and Mbongo after finishing their mid-morning meal, I have formed a somewhat more vivid picture of these noonday nests, for I see the troop of gorillas separated into pairs or small groups of congenial friends, enjoying together what is the most intimate and personal habit they have. I can picture our two lying there, as they have done here in a corner of their cage, regurgitating and remasticating their food, not once but several times, ejecting skins, seeds or stems they have swallowed. I have seen their hands moving in a strange, somewhat circulatory fashion beneath their mouths, ready to catch the food if it should pass their lips. This was their happiest, most confidential time which they shared with none but each other. For just as at the beginning of their life here, during these moments they would withdraw completely into the past and become all the world to each other, excluding not only their beloved master, Byron Moore, but even me, their acknowledged favorite among all their human relatives. I learned not to intrude, so would sit quietly near, and I would frequently hear them grunt softly

[227]

and satisfyingly to each other as feeding and resting gorillas are said to do in the wild.

Dr. Bingham told me that none of the hardships and illness that he suffered in his exploration had made him lose any of his keen desire to solve the mystery of the gorilla. His first-hand accounts of mother-and-baby nests, and the nests of the half-grown ones now and then, in the heavy hammocks of the vines in the trees gave me the opportunity to go back of written words and ask him many things I really wanted to know. And our two, as they wrestled, boxed, played tag, chased each other around and around, rested, slept and ate, gave him the chance to people with living creatures the empty, silent gorilla trails he had followed through the jungles.

And so, although his time was short and the opportunity offered for experimental work very precious, there was so much to be gained by observing their behavior and activities that hours were spent by us both in this interesting way, and in such hours I learned how to interpret their actions and to watch to see if they were right- or left-handed, if they ran around the stump clockwise or not, and which was dominant in certain phases of their lives; and how much emphasis to put on seemingly unimportant things.

In addition to the lore of the wild gorilla and the background of our two which I learned from him I watched his work with them in his tests and learned something of its meaning and significance as I never could have from books. Strange to say, it was from the seemingly artificial study and my very superficial part in it that there evolved for me the real heart and mind of the gorilla. I speak with no intention of being anything but very serious and sincere when I speak of the hearts and minds and characters of these great silent creatures as they were revealed to me during their life here at the zoo. Their power and their dependence upon us, their childish simplicity and their arrogance, their friendly reception of us and their assumed complete indifference toward us were recognized and talked about whenever we who cared for them were standing about the cage.

Dr. Bingham's visit strengthened my resolve to permit these creatures to grow and live with as little interference as compatible with safety and to remain as far as they could wild children of nature, for as I watched him work and saw these two with a new angle of vision I became convinced that the most valuable contribution we in the San Diego Zoo could make to science would be to have these two live out a natural span of life, which was then figured at forty-five or fifty years. Failing in this objective, our ability to permit them to live as naturally as possible for so long as either or both of them might survive would still furnish much valuable material to add to the meager gorilla lore then existing. The most valuable factor was the gorilla companionship of a congenial nature, really self-selected, for these two were playing together when captured, and their mutual attachment and accord in the way of life has never been questioned. In this plan of dealing with these and all future gorillas the zoo might acquire I hope my successors will be of the same conviction and remain as unhampered by interference as I have been.

With the coming of the gorillas into my life I had been greatly stimulated in my previous somewhat casual study of the work of such men as Yerkes, Köhler and Hooton on mental measurements of apes and experimental psychology dealing with them. It was something much simplified along the lines that he and others had

[229]

used with chimpanzees that Dr. Bingham planned to use in his study of the gorillas. I was greatly impressed by his gentle approach to them and his slow procedure in trying to win their confidence. At the same time I was amazed at their quick acceptance of him into that small circle of intimates. This he generally attributed to their complete contentment in their surroundings and their confidence in us and our treatment.

My own work prevented my constant observation of the study, but I spent every possible minute with Dr. Bingham, watching for the things he was expecting and trying silently to interpret them for myself, falling far short of correct deductions, and drawing far too definite conclusions in the way of amateurs. The account of his work has never been published, and so far as he was concerned was entirely inconclusive. But I am now boldly undertaking to describe some of his work that I witnessed and in which I participated as assistant observer, and I am trying to set down my own opinions and the continuing result of those observations as they have formed such opinions through the last ten years. These opinions are neither scientific nor psychologically valuable, nor are they so far as I know anything like those which Dr. Bingham might have formed. They are, as radio announcers are so fond of reporting at the end of a talk on controversial subjects, "the views of the speaker and the station is not responsible for them." Without doubt, this subject is highly controversial.

On the morning when we planned to make our first test we opened the door of the sleeping room so the gorillas might enter to receive their lunch. Then we dropped the doors behind them, locking them in, contrary to our usual custom. While they were shut inside we suspended a banana on a stout cord from the top of the gorilla cage at a height above their reach and also, we believed, too far from any of the sides of the cage for them to reach it. Our first task having been set, we opened the door and the gorillas, their curiosity aroused by their confinement and the sound of a man on top of their cage, hurried out. They looked about to see what had happened or what we had done to their home during their confinement. Today, as I read over my diary, I find myself smiling at the title of the page, "The Trial of the Suspended Banana," in my best Sherlock Holmes manner. My observation was that Ngagi did not see the banana as he came out of the room, but that Mbongo saw it instantly and having spied it, sized up the situation at once and started up the wire wall nearest to the banana in the first attempt to reach the dangling lure. I felt sure that it was not until having attained a height parallel with the banana that Mbongo reached for it; that Ngagi saw the bait and realized that Mbongo was about to win the prize. Ngagi started toward the banana, stopped suddenly, seeing it was beyond his reach from the floor, and hurried to the rope and climbed rapidly until he too was at the height of the banana beyond Mbongo's finger tips. Contrary to my expectations Ngagi did not try to swing for the banana but paused to watch Mbongo's second attempt which he made by changing his position and his hold on the wire of the cage, hoping thus to increase his reach. But the smaller gorilla failed again and at once gave up the attempt and climbed down the wire as though planning to start at another angle. On seeing this Ngagi slid down the rope, dashed to the exact spot where Mbongo had been and which was, by actual measurement made later in the day, nearest to the suspended fruit. Mbongo changed places with his cage-mate, hurrying frantically

[231]

to the rope, and climbed excitedly. Ngagi, as though fearing that Mbongo might beat him via the rope, climbed hastily and, before he was quite high enough, reached once in an abortive attempt to snatch the fruit. He climbed a few inches higher and his considerably longer arm enabled him to snatch the prize from Mbongo, who was apparently planning to swing within reach.

I was interested that Ngagi touched the string just above the fruit but instead of trying to break the string, slid his hand down to the banana and broke off the small stem of the fruit itself, holding the prize firmly in his hand, thus avoiding any chance of losing it.

There remains one very definite, still unanswered, question in my mind. Why did not Ngagi swing for the fruit? Was he sure he could reach just that much farther than Mbongo? Or did he figure that Mbongo should have taken a bigger chance and, stretching farther away from the wire, gain the prize?

The strongest impression that still remains in my mind was of the speed and precision with which Mbongo saw and sized up the situation and chose the easiest and most direct method of obtaining what he saw. Neither of the gorillas wasted time nor effort on the matter as I have since seen other apes do, nor did they interfere with each other's opportunities. Was it a mutual understanding which resulted in two simultaneous and simple approaches to the same problem?

Our second trial with a suspended lure was made a trifle more difficult by the way in which the banana was hung, for neither gorilla could possibly reach it from the side of the cage. Mbongo was always the first to see, the first to try and most often led the way to using new equipment or playthings. I had noticed that every time they came out of their sleeping rooms they looked at the ceiling or glanced hurriedly around, expecting another treat. Mbongo, seeing the second banana in the suspended position, rushed to the closest side of the cage and began climbing up. He did not stop when he reached the height of the banana but hurried on clear to the ceiling and up over the top, obviously intending to pull up the fruit on the string to within reach of his hand. The banana was also out of reach of the rope but Ngagi, as though seeing he would have sufficient time, ran to the rope, climbed to the proper height and swung widely. Holding the rope with his right hand, with his left he reached not for the fruit but the string above and, slipping his hand down just as before, he again broke the fruit which he was grasping too tight for any chance of losing it. He won by an uncomfortably small margin and Mbongo good-naturedly climbed down. I found later that Dr. Bingham had also been surprised by their instant procedure to the direct solution of this very simple problem.

This sort of problem, however, concerned two things familiar to them in their wild life: first, the fruit suspended as though growing from something too high off the ground for them to reach even by stretching up. I can readily imagine that many times each had looked at a bunch of plantains or other fruit and calculated the best and quickest way of securing it for himself before other members of the band or the other of the pair obtained it. Such a problem presented only slightly artificial conditions. For more than a year they had not had to seek their food, but had everything brought and handed to them, in sufficient quantity for both, with no effort necessary on their part. But competition among the troop and between each other was close in the background of their memory and their old methods might have returned promptly to their aid.

The next type of problem was to suspend a banana on a rope several inches beyond their reach outside the wire of the cage. One end of the rope was tied to the wire side of their cage. From this point it was stretched somewhat loosely toward the guard fence, slanting away from the side of the cage very gradually. Where the rope passed one of the huge upright I-beams, it was perhaps ten inches from the cage; where it passed the corner five feet beyond, it was at least twenty inches away. But it was easily within reach of the stubby fingers for the first foot of the distance, and the slack as well as the elasticity of the white-cotton rope gave them plenty of play. A banana was tied three or four feet from the near end of the rope and beyond the I-beam it hung about twelve inches from the wire. Then the gorillas were released, and again I was amazed at the speed with which they discovered and approached the task. First Mbongo walked to the knot and tried to pull the rope toward him while Ngagi stared at the banana from the closest spot, drawing down his brows and scowling as though perturbed at the sight of fruit beyond his reach. Suddenly, as the rope gave to Mbongo's manipulations, the banana swayed slightly toward Ngagi. He followed the rope with his eyes to Mbongo's hand and immediately walked to where Mbongo was feverishly manipulating the rope, pulling it gradually by holding it with the fingers of one hand extended through the mesh while he crossed the other hand over and secured hold just beyond with the second hand. Hand over hand he worked it cleverly until he came to the heavy eight-inch beam. This was the crucial spot and the widest space he had to cross his hands, being eight inches instead of

[234]

two or three. The rope was more taut here and slipped, out of his fingers. Without discouragement he hurried back to the knotted end and began over again. Ngagi interfered this time and again the rope slipped. Several attempts were made. I did not record the number of failures, but suddenly Ngagi seemed discouraged and showed signs of temper, thrusting at the string and striking the wire near where I stood. Mbongo, however, had again turned to begin at the beginning again and with slower, steadier movements, as though he would profit by his errors, and with no interference succeeded in holding the string with his left hand close to the beam while he released his right, crossed his arms and barely caught the rope to the left of the side beam. This brought a hasty solution of the problem and the banana, broken and bruised, was pulled through the wire and gobbled up.

The last in the series of rope-and-lure problems was that of a banana suspended from a rope which ran through three pulleys in such a way that the rope, running inside of the cage, had to be pushed backward rather than pulled toward the gorilla to enable him to obtain the fruit. Whenever Dr. Bingham and Mr. Virden and Henry would work about the cage where the gorillas could not observe them, the apes appeared excited as though certain that something was being planned for their entertainment. Both of the gorillas always showed intense excitement and curiosity until they discovered what had been done. On this occasion, while the boards supporting the rope were put in place, the door to the unused sleeping room, usually open, was closed. The gorillas had entertained themselves by pounding on it and racing about, playing their favorite tag, until the apparatus was in place and tested. Then the door was opened and in they rushed. A suspended banana was an old story to them now and as though they realized it was theirs for the taking, they immediately went to work. Ngagi took the lead this time immediately upon entering the room and seeing the fruit. His eyes moved rapidly along the rope from the banana to where it touched the bars of the sleeping room. He moved directly to that spot and, reaching through the bars, grasped the rope, pulling it slightly toward him. But as he did this I noticed that his eyes were not on the rope but on the fruit itself. He saw that as he pulled the rope the fruit moved away. He took his hand clear off the rope and then cautiously reached farther through the bars and grasping the rope moved it both ways, still watching the fruit constantly. As he moved his hand away the fruit drew toward him. There was not another false movement but, apparently with perfect confidence that he knew what he was doing, he slipped his hand along the rope back toward the cage and then pushed the rope through the pulley away from him as far as he could reach. Releasing the rope the gorilla drew his hand toward him and repeated his pushing until the banana was within his reach and then he pulled it off the rope and had his reward for his cleverness.

There were many handicaps to the interesting work Dr. Bingham was attempting, chief among them our entire out-of-door arrangement, the constant intrusion of the public which distracted both the observer and the observed, and the lack of large inside quarters where the gorillas might be given problems which would necessitate the use of piled-up boxes and other equipment. Also, we were all reluctant to separate them and work with one at a time, for their complete dependence and constant need for each other was immediately evident to everyone around them.

Dr. Bingham, however, decided that he might be able to use what he called slot boxes in a short series of experiments which could be done fairly well under the circumstances. These boxes were five feet long, six inches square and closed at one end. In one side, directly in the center, a slot was cut approximately two feet long and just wide enough for the gorilla to slip his big fingers in and move them back and forth for the length of the slot without scraping. He could not withdraw his fingers unless they were open nor could he put the fingers of both hands in at the same time. On an adjoining side two similar slots, one near each end of the side, were cut. The ends of the single slot overlapped these and it was possible for the gorilla, reaching through these slots, to touch his fingers together or to hold between his hands an object he was moving through the box. This slot box was wired tightly to the wire at one end of the cage in a horizontal position, the side containing the single slot being at the top, the side with the two slots facing toward the inside of the cage. Into the closed end of this box Dr. Bingham introduced an orange and an apple. The box had been installed after the gorillas had been put to bed, and as repairs or changes in the cage were frequently done at like periods the gorillas were not made more curious than usual. They do apparently have a perfect sense of whence sounds come, and remember where to look for changes that have been made. The fruit was put into the box early in the morning so as not to delay their release. When Ngagi came out he did not even glance in that direction, but Mbongo did, started to walk past it to his favorite corner, turned suddenly, approached the box and peered into the slot, immediately detecting the fruit. He tried and succeeded in reaching it through the slot nearest the closed end, and as he rolled it up well into the area of the slot, tried to pull it through several times. Dr. Bingham was timing and watching carefully. As the activity and excitement of the gorilla increased in intensity it attracted the attention of Ngagi. Ngagi came over and shoving in also tried to remove the fruit by digging his fingers into it and pulling it hard against the side of the box. For several minutes he tried, then walked away to the farthest end of the cage with an appearance of complete indifference. Mbongo, who moved aside, sat still a few seconds and, becoming convinced that Ngagi was through, returned to the task. He moved this time with greater caution, slowly shoving the fruit along to a spot where he could see it through the top slot. At this point he held the fruit between the fingers of his right hand in the upper slot and his left hand in the side slot. He tried several times to manipulate it in some way to get it through the slots. I thought once he had quit and again that he had lost the fruit, but suddenly poking the big fingers of his left hand down into the top slot, he slid it along easily. His right hand was ready at the third slot, and the fruit moved out in the matter of a surprisingly few minutes; actually within twenty-five minutes from the time they had emerged from their sleeping quarters the slot box was empty. The first piece of fruit rolled out on the ground. Ngagi, who had been observing it more carefully than I realized, came across quickly and took it and ate it. Mbongo was apparently much more absorbed in the solution than the food and was already starting to remove the second piece. This time Ngagi held out his great palm and the apple rolled into it.

Mbongo (left) and Ngagi (right) at Slot Boxes

Ngagi Always Stood at the Left, Mbongo at the Right, Side of the Box.
Their Methods Differed. Mbongo Always Finished First

Ngagi (right) and Mbongo (left) in Youth

The attitude of the two gorillas was very different. Mbongo wanted to get the fruit out, Ngagi wanted to eat it, and so both were happy. As Dr. Bingham continued his observational studies of the gorillas he continued his friendly association with them until they appeared to know they were playing a game with him and look forward more and more not only to his presence but to the diversion he furnished them. In the course of his work he made the solution of the slot-box problem more difficult by gradually raising the open end so that the bottom of the box sloped sharply, making an incline down which the fruit would roll unless the big fingers held it until hands could be shifted.

For several days the problem of getting out the fruit was solved by Mbongo alone and so far as we could see, Ngagi only approached the open end of the box to hold his hand under and catch the fruit. Then one morning he grunted his bossy grunt and Mbongo moved away. Ngagi solved the puzzle as rapidly as Mbongo had been doing, showing for the first time some of the extreme excitement and eagerness that had been plain in Mbongo at first. Mbongo had gradually been working back into his usually phlegmatic attitude but this time he showed resentment at being shoved away and so another box which we had used with orangs and chimps for purposes of comparison was set up so that both gorillas might have a box.

During the latter part of Dr. Bingham's stay, the slot boxes were in rather constant use, although sometimes he let several days elapse without placing the lures in them, but they were not at any time removed from the gorilla cage. Often I carefully watched the two leave their sleeping rooms in the mornings to see if they looked at the boxes. They never approached them or showed any curiosity concerning them unless they were baited. If they did look it was too rapid to see. Apparently, however, their eyes took in at a glance whether or not they were baited for, if fruit had been placed in them, each proceeded directly to his own acknowledged box with a show of eagerness and worked rapidly until it was empty.

It was during these mornings I realized what a wide field of vision can apparently be taken in at a glance by a gorilla. They can turn their eyes until the cornea is nearly hidden by the socket on either side, and apparently see perfectly from this angle.

After the first few trials they proceeded systematically, using first the left and then the right hand with precisely the same movement each day, holding the fruit against the incline of the box with little effort or inconvenience until the boxes were perpendicular. For another six or seven months the boxes remained in this position and the gorillas looked forward with evident pleasure to the fun of emptying them at irregular intervals. Always they worked in silent but excited haste, as though vying with each other in performing the delightful task.

Ngagi, the taller, had an advantage in the matter of the upright boxes but he never surpassed Mbongo in speed or skill, as the smaller gorilla worked with such smooth easy movements. In the many times that I saw them work with the slanting and perpendicular boxes, I failed to see either of them drop a piece of fruit, lose his temper at a slip, or try in any way to break or tear the boxes loose from their fastenings. During the few trials which we gave the chimpanzees simply for comparison under similar circumstances, they, although they did finally remove the fruit, were not so steady or methodical in their procedure, less patient and seemed to fail entirely to solve the problem or make a systematic plan of procedure from day to day. The orang-utans, with the same box, pulled and pried it away from its moorings, bit at the openings, ripping off splinters, attempting persistently to reach the fruit from the open end, and finally mashed the oranges and apples to bits and scraped them out through the slots, which, because of their slender fingers, gave them much more chance for such work than the gorillas had. In neither of these cases, however, did we pursue the study to any length, nor were my own observations anything except entirely casual and inconclusive.

One of the outstanding results, and in my own opinion by all means the happiest, of the tests and studies made by Dr. Bingham, was to increase the friendly relationship already existing between us and the gorillas. They seemed to connect these delightful games with us as human beings and to feel grateful for the entertainment we had offered. It also seemed to create more interest in such mechanical things as their hoop swings, their seats and other contrivances which we had given them but they had heretofore scorned. Frequently now the gorillas would pull themselves up into the hoops. When squatting on his heels and holding the chain upon which the hoop is suspended, Mbongo could just sit within the circumference of the hoop without bending his head. It was even then a trifle short for Ngagi. His crest crowded it a little. These hoops are thirty inches in diameter. I also think these trials overcame to a small extent their fear of such things as sprays and tools.

Perhaps I tread upon dangerous ground in comparing the procedure of the three apes, the chimpanzee, the orang, and the gorilla, when offered the same task, under the same conditions, and with the same general background, especially because of housing, handling and previous training, but I am stepping boldly forth, once more assuming full responsibility for my own interpretation of what I saw.

The gorillas had one disadvantage. One of the orangutans had been a trained movie actor, and both of the chimpanzees had been petted and tamed and while babies had been treated intimately by human beings. All of our members of these two species had been in captivity four or five years or more. The two gorillas must have been about four years old when captured and had been too large at that time to handle or treat familiarly. They had been in captivity less than two years when these studies were made. The gorillas exhibited neither the excitement nor rivalry toward each other that was evident among the apes in the other cages. This was not because the dominant Ngagi took advantage of the other for usually the problems were first solved by the meek Mbongo with no interference. The chimpanzees proceeded to work at once with apparently no particular method in mind and the desire for the fruit the only object. During the two or three successive days we baited their box they did not materially decrease the time consumed in the solution or proceed along a particular pattern of behavior in obtaining the fruit unless they did become more adept at breaking it into pieces which they could fish through the slot. With chimpanzees used in such experimental work in laboratories properly equipped for careful scientific observation I have no experience, but in the meager experiments upon our two I could detect no interest displayed in the problem as an abstract thing, in other words, the solution

[242]

for the problem's sake. The orangs damaged the box so excessively that we had to coax them into the sleeping room and remove it before it was broken to pieces to become a dangerous weapon with which to punish each other or a tool for prying loose the wire. One end was torn completely away from the cage and part of one side broken in two when rescued. They did use a stick we had carelessly tossed in each cage when preparing the test, as a fishing instrument.

Even from the first trial it seemed to me that Mbongo had studied the entire problem and had some procedure definitely in mind. When he approached the box the second time after Ngagi had crowded him out to make a trial after Mbongo's first failure, he sat down and moved with steady caution in removing the fruit. The second day there was no doubt in my mind that he knew precisely what he was doing from the first move; the only delay was caused by his awkward thick fingers. The first solution by Ngagi, which came several days after Mbongo's success, and the rapidity with which he removed each piece of fruit convinced me that he had watched and evaluated the younger gorilla's every move.

During the solution of their problems, one of the outstanding contrasts was the degree of concentration applied to the work. The gorillas seemed to consider it a strictly private affair in which they could expect no help from the outside, and apparently they wished none.

Repeatedly our chimpanzees stopped working and came near us as though expecting help or encouragement. They lost heart and quit, then returned perhaps to another attack, but not once would I say that they appeared to begin at one definite point and proceed along a line of action to solution or failure.

The orangs used their technical skill to remove the

box; their strength to destroy it; but at no time did they solve the problem of removing the fruit either whole or piecemeal. Although they alone tried to use the rod, they used it first as a lever, then finding it useless, tried it as a fishing tool without success.

If the chimpanzees and gorillas noticed the rod it had no significance in connection with their test.

Years after the experiments had been discontinued I was reminded of my conviction regarding their solution of the problem and my feeling of its having been studied out before it was begun by an interesting episode in their lives. Because of a slight illness, Mbongo was left shut in the house. From the very beginning of their lives here the gorillas were terrified if left shut in their house alone during the daytime. He fretted and stormed and was most unhappy. Ngagi, outside, hearing him, was equally unhappy and finally walked directly to the sheet-metal door — a piece of heavy steel that slips up and down in a groove and drops into a piece of channel iron at the bottom that is too deep for them to get any leverage under the door itself — and pressing the great cupped palms of his hands against the iron surface until he had sufficient suction, raised the heavy door with perfect ease. Then, releasing one hand, he held it under the door while the younger gorilla bounded out. Suddenly Ngagi removed both hands, letting the sliding panel fall of its own weight. As it is balanced by a counter weight the fall was not too rapid for safety, but the amazing part of the affair was that for more than seven years they had lived in the cage with the doors operated in the identical manner and, although they had romped around and beat upon them, had kneeled on the floor and peered out through a tiny hole to see what was going on inside their cage at times, we

[244]

had never dreamed that either could open the door. But when the need arose, the response was instantaneous.

This success, however, worried us for we knew that either the door must now be padlocked as in the case of the orangs and chimpanzees or there could be no safety for a man working inside the cage. Each day for two or three days Ngagi opened the three doors, going out or into the sleeping quarters at will. Then Moore, without saying anything to us, greased the doors on both sides so that the gorilla's hands slipped and would produce no good suction. After trying each door thoroughly, he walked away, sat down, gazing into space, and so far as we know he has refused to be made a fool of again. But for safety's sake we did contrive a brace which would prevent his opening the doors.

This again was the solution of a problem accomplished without a false movement, but with the same precision with which he slipped the fruit, piece by piece, through the slots. For nearly a year we left the slot boxes in their final vertical position. From time to time their keeper or I would bait them. If they were empty, neither ever approached or examined the boxes. The solution became so matter-of-fact and uniform that they were not disturbed by photographers, flashlights or any outside influence like school classes. They took their places at the boxes which were wired to upright steel beams ten feet apart, Mbongo to the west and Ngagi to the east. Each had his preferred box. Mbongo stood very close and always moved more smoothly to the solution, beginning with his left hand in the lowest slot, then using his right through the center; again the left hand lifted the fruit through the open end into the waiting right hand. Ngagi moved first with his right hand, which always made the final taking of the fruit with his left hand. But he always transferred it to his right hand before eating it. He often braced his foot against the wire and stretched because he stood farther away from the box. The shortest timing we made was exactly four seconds from the time the gorilla reached the box until the apple was in his hand. This was clocked on Mbongo a few days after the boxes had been placed in the vertical position, some time after Dr. Bingham had returned to New Haven.

We regretted that there was no one on our staff qualified to continue such studies, and no one in our vicinity sufficiently interested with liberty to work along the same lines.

The work of Dr. Bingham convinced us that we were dealing with creatures which we could accustom to certain artificial requirements with a good deal of ease. We had been much interested in weighing them, and had proposed several plans. The simplest had been to rig a heavy spring scales on a stout arm above the roof of the cage and suspend from it a rope sufficiently strong for weighing them. Accommodatingly they climbed it, and finding the spring arrangement to their liking, bounced up and down to their own delight and our discomfiture. In fact, so great was their delight in this new arrangement, which added zest to swinging on ropes, that they nearly fought over the chance to bounce and practically ruined the scales in the first few days.

Our new plan consisted in introducing the entire platform of our warehouse scales through an opening in the safety-cage door. I stood within to work the weights and entice the gorillas onto the scales with fruit and biscuits.

When Ralph Virden finally contrived a better plan for weighing them, I wondered if there was any way we could convey to the gorillas just what we required of them. The first venture was a success; each was weighed several times so that we could be sure of our accuracy. The gorillas realized instantly that they were rewarded with a choice bit of food only when they sat directly on the scales, their hands off the wire door in front of them, and no part of their bodies touching anything except the scales. Never from the first have we had any difficulty nor any doubt that the gorillas knew just what was expected of them. Twice we were frustrated, once by our own stupidity in not realizing that Ngagi had so far outgrown the original scales that he could not possibly sit on them without additional room. After he tried to hunch his body to smaller space and finally squatted on his haunches, we agreed when Smitty, our head keeper, said, "To weigh a bigger gorilla you have to have a bigger scale" and gave him his reward for trying. And once Mbongo tired us out with his clowning and playing off to a crowd of moving-picture men who were there for a newsreel, and we left him unweighed, much to his apparent discomfiture.

One other interesting experiment convinced me that the gorillas were not stupid about mechanical things, merely indifferent. This experiment was tried as a matter of physical health, not to test mental aptitude. We dreaded our long dry summers for these children of the mountain mists and planned to give them as much dampness as they seemed to want. Again Ralph Virden's ingenuity made possible for them an overhead shower with a spring attachment that they could turn on by pulling a light string. This string, attached to a small chain, released a fine, even spray over a circle about five feet in diameter on the floor of the cage as long as the gorillas pulled the string and held it open.

After our experiments with the bananas on ropes and

strings they were always eager to see what we were doing to their cage, or for their entertainment, and as much of the mechanical part of the shower had been installed while they were out in the cage, they had watched the work with the greatest interest. As soon as the shower was ready and the light rope dropped down into the cage, Ngagi went to it and took hold. Nothing happened because the water had not yet been turned into the pipe. We had feared that they did not like the looks of the bright gadget above the cage and would refuse to touch the twine, and so we also had a lure, which proved unnecessary, ready to tie to it if it became necessary. The next day we again dropped the slender rope through the wire and Mbongo snatched it as he walked by, but did not stop really to grasp or pull it. Ngagi, having handled it freely the day before, walked over and stood up, holding the rope, and leaned his weight upon it. The unexpected shower appeared to startle him and he released his hold on the rope instantly, walked just beyond the damp circle and sat down sedately and studied the contrivance thoughtfully. Beginning at the end of the string where his hand had been, he followed it with his eyes to the top of the cage and the bright metal shower bulb from which a few drops were still falling. Suddenly Mbongo, whom we had all forgotten to watch, walked over to the rope and deliberately pulled. When the water struck his back and shoulders he gave an audible gasp and ran to the edge of the circle, retaining his hold on the rope but not pulling it. In a few seconds, still holding the cord, he climbed upon the nearest log and, sitting there, alternately pulled the shower open and let it close, extending his hand far out to feel the water coming down. Supporting all of his weight on the little rope and chain,

[248]

he swung through the shower, dropping the cord on the other side of the circle of "rain." There he sat, reaching out first with one hand and then with the other "to see if it were raining." He seemed bewildered by the fact that it had so abruptly stopped but just when I was convinced he had not realized how he had produced the delightful shower he reached out and, catching the rope, turned it off and on again at will, always reaching with the free hand into the spray as though to convince himself it was real. Finally he let go of the shower pull as though tired of the novelty.

Ngagi, who meanwhile had been watching this activity, walked over to the north end of the cage near the corner where the pipe had been installed and climbed up the side across the top of the cage and tried to reach the pipe or shower through the meshes of the wire. I have never been able to put any reasonable interpretation on this attempt, but failing in whatever plan he had he took hold of the pull near the top of the cage and, letting it slide through his fingers, finally took the end of the cord in his mouth and carried it over to the higher shelf in the northeast corner where he sat, pulling and relaxing on the string to turn the shower off and on at will just as Mbongo had done. Mbongo sat watching this as though his interest had been rekindled and when Ngagi dropped the rope he also took it again and pulled it on and off until he too was satisfied that he had solved the problem.

Although they frequently played with the shower the two gorillas did not use it as much as we had anticipated. Mbongo loved to run past and jerk it so hard that he frequently broke the chain or even the shower, and much of the time it did not work. One day we had just repaired the apparatus and Ngagi, being annoyed by the man working on the top of the cage, had done his share of annoying. As soon as the man left he climbed up and hanging by all fours under the shower, peered seriously into it as though to see what had been done. Mbongo, with such a devil-may-care manner as only he could assume, started from the opposite side of the cage, rushed on all fours across the forty feet and grabbing the string as he passed turned the full force of the shower suddenly into Ngagi's face. We laughed because it was funny, but I was terribly frightened for a second because the sudden dash of water directly in his face almost made Ngagi lose hold on the wire and he might have fallen to the sand-covered concrete, eighteen feet below. Nothing could convince Henry Newmeyer, then in charge of the great apes, that Mbongo had not played the trick intentionally. If he did, that was endowing the gorilla with a sense of humor that I seriously doubt he possesses, although I freely admit that he clowns for the crowd and loves to be laughed at.

The gorillas were filled with childish curiosity and as they gained confidence in us investigated everything we did for them; but they have never lost their immense caution about approaching new things and new situations. They would smell anything new in the way of food before tasting it; try out everything, as does the elephant, before trusting their weight to it, and were easily upset by sudden unknown noises or sights, especially of other animals. When we were training, or rather conditioning, our camels for picture work by long daily walks through the zoo, the gorillas alone of all the animals showed real fear as the camels were led in a row past their cage. They appeared to have concern not only for themselves, but for those of us they like and would protect. Several times they warned me that a

[250]

hostile gibbon in the next cage was trying to grab me, and when I touched something of which they were afraid, their concern for me was as plain as though they had spoken in words. They resented very much any attention given to other animals; their jealousy toward each other was no greater than their jealousy toward anything that distracted our attention from themselves.

These two gorillas had a very strong sense of protectiveness and ownership for anything that was theirs or a part of their equipment. Once we closed the door between two sections of their cage while we did some repair work and moved out a big stump. Ngagi dashed at the partition, grunting angrily as the men moved his log out of the way. I knew by experience that it would be disastrous to try to remove a bit of food that they wanted from the cage or even to move it into a more convenient position if they were present, for they would resent such liberties angrily.

Once, when I was using a public-address system near the gorilla cage in talking to a college class, one of the professors came up and, without speaking to me, reached out and took the mouthpiece from my hand to address the students. Up to that minute I was the only person who had ever used it near the gorillas, and to Ngagi that was my machine. He rushed angrily at the side of the cage, which startled the professor into handing the mouthpiece back lest the gorilla take the cage apart and walk out. Ngagi, his purpose accomplished, turned peacefully away. During the past spring I had a most amazing experience, showing their protective attitude toward anything they associate with themselves. Mr. and Mrs. Holger Jensen, sculptors, were engaged in modeling the gorillas. This time it was a bust of Ngagi. Both gorillas were greatly intrigued with the light-gray monster growing under the skillful hands. They looked it over the first thing in the morning and actually would sit so still in their absorption that they almost seemed to pose at times for their busts. Mr. and Mrs. Jensen had become a part of their official family and instead of resenting close scrutiny, as they so frequently do, they seemed to like and respond to it. During the absence of the Jensens the model was covered and Moore would wet it down as is required. The gorillas watched the work, watched Moore sprinkle it, and stood by while he carefully uncovered it for me to see. But one day I had a distinguished visitor taking moving pictures of the great apes and me, and when we got down to the gorilla cage he saw the enormous bust with its crest and jaws revealed under the swathing cloth. He walked directly to it and laying his hand on the cover said, "Is this a carving or is it being modeled?" Before I could answer, Ngagi charged, hitting the wire near the bust with all his might, muttering angrily, every hair on his great arms erect. I did not blame the man for being scared and withdrawing his hand from any contact with the modeled gorilla. I did not agree with the man who was sure that Ngagi knew the bust was of himself, but he knew to whom it belonged and was determined to protect it for the owner — when the Jensens carried the huge plaster models out for finishing touches before they were to be cast, the gorillas showed complete indifference to the act.

The next morning Moore, who had seen the rush, asked the same question: "I wonder if Ngagi knows that is himself. He watches so closely and is getting so he doesn't even want me to touch it." Of course he knew it was something closely associated with him and Mbongo, and felt the necessity of protecting it against the touch of any stranger. Mr. and Mrs. Jensen greatly enjoyed

and seemed to understand the sensitive nature of the
gorillas, the shyness and reserve of them. They also appreciated that the interest of the gorillas in their work
and the co-operation they received from them was a
distinct compliment and tried to justify it. They formed,
with no suggestion from any of us, the same opinion of
the two great beasts and their characters that we held.

To sum up the mind and character of a gorilla as
revealed by my own purely personal study of our two,
I should say they were sufficiently intelligent to learn to
employ simple mechanical things but were not essentially
interested. They had excellent memories and they sized
up a situation understandingly and rapidly before they
even attempted a solution. They were impatient with
futile effort, apparently lazy, and perhaps easily discouraged. They were inclined to follow the line of least
resistance, although they were not cowardly. They were
very much more creatures of routine, perhaps much
better organized as individuals, than any other of the
apes in our collection. They did not recognize a stick
or rod either as a tool but feared such things as a weapon
and would cower back at a slight gesture. They were
much more alert to sights and sounds than their apparent
self-absorption would indicate. Their sight, hearing and
scent were all very acute. I nearly said their hands and
fingers were awkward and still since I have seen them use
their thumb and forefinger to pick up a grain of wheat,
half a peanut, or a piece of straw as deftly and quickly as
a child, I cannot say that those great blunt fingers were
either awkward or insensitive.

They frequently have stopped short of accomplishment because of lack of desire. Perhaps I can better ex-
plain this feeling by saying that strong as their cage is
I have often looked at it and wondered how long it

would resist if either gorilla or both should decide to walk out or take it apart. I do not know, but there has been nothing to indicate any wish to get out. That cage is their security; they obviously feel at home there. They have had food, shade, water, bedding, security, companionship, variety of interests, room for play and exercise, and protection from predatory beasts — all that they sought and received of the jungle.

CHAPTER XIV

Drums and Voices

COMMUNICATION between animals is quite evident, and sometimes I think almost as definitely understood between them as is human speech by men. It is perhaps, after all, not a very great stretch of imagination to jump from the simple language of savages, almost entirely lacking in vowels, to the varied tones and significant inflections of many animal voices. Some of these, like the daily song of the gibbon, are stereotyped and always the same. What they express is rather general, with not much significance. But that same gibbon mother whose ringing tones have filled the morning air can utter soft little notes to her baby which plainly tell her child how much she loves it, coaxes it to her arms to be cuddled and warmed, warns it of danger and chides it when it is too bold or disobedient.

The shrill screaming voice of an adult chimpanzee trying to incite cage-mates into a noisy agitation, or by shrill screaming to prevent an attack upon herself and offspring, can suddenly become soft and wheedling, intended to disarm you and coax you into doing something you do not wish to do, or giving her a favor you wish to withhold. And the sound of a tiny orang crying from loneliness or anger, or the thin sharp-voiced whinings or whimperings of a baby chimpanzee, are the nearest thing in the world to the vocal sounds made by a human infant. And so when people ask me, as they often do, "Can gorillas communicate?" it would not be entirely accurate to reply in the negative.

One of the early means of communication, one still common among primitive people when they wish to converse over long distances, is the native drum. The vibrations of the tom-toms, especially those hewn and hollowed from whole trees and beaten only by the open hand, can be heard for miles. The messages are caught and relayed for even greater distances on out into the jungles, telling by their cadences as plainly as words to all who listen what events are taking place, that travelers are on the march and danger threatening, and I have read that the report of the death of the great white queen, Victoria, was carried by the drums far ahead of the wires and mail, and that the blacks living in the most isolated areas knew long before the whites had received the news brought by carriers and wire that the queen was dead. This is a well authenticated instance of speaking with the drums.

It is not strange, when birds have signaled each other and called their mates through the forests by drumming with their bills, or imitating drums and bells with their voices, that we find among our "hairy men" of ancient and modern times the use of this simple method of communication. Drumming is a part of their daily life and whether the drumming of the gorillas preceded or was copied from the drum of the savage, its use by both is undisputed. Unlike the savage, the gorilla has not produced his drum but used what nature provided for him, and his drums are the trunks of trees and fallen logs, and his own great broad chest. In captivity he has used the walls of his house and the floor of his cage and in both wild and captive life he has thus expressed his feelings and communicated with his kind to his own satisfaction.

Like most people whose acquaintance with gorilla and savage is a thing of books, pictures, and word of mouth, I had understood that the drumming of the gorilla indicated passion, presaged an attack, and was a sound greatly to be dreaded. Now my interpretations of the drumming are founded only upon my own observations of our two captive mountain gorillas. I do not claim it is the whole picture, or the only accurate account, of this fascinating habit, for here, after all, they were not faced with the same situations as arise in wild life. Our two were, as I have said, both males, which at once makes any picture of their social behavior a one-sided affair. They had, when captured, grown well into childhood and must have been to a certain extent independent and self-sustaining members of their large troop of wild mountain gorillas. And so their actions, at least during the very early part of their life with us, were brought from that wild life and must have to a certain extent reflected the social picture of the group. Fortunately, also, they had not been spoiled by too much handling and restriction after capture but had been treated with the dignity that their importance warranted, which would make it appear that my observations, beginning thus early and continuing over so long a period as ten years and during so many hours of each day, should be comparatively comprehensive and reliable ones.

Although there were great personal differences between these two, a wide similarity of pattern existed, and basing my observation on these I am compelled to differ positively with many reports and conclusions which have

[257]

been made in the wild or upon the study of one captive specimen. For in many ways in which the behavior of our two and their reactions were identical, they differed greatly from general opinions, and so it is with drumming.

Ngagi and Mbongo had been in the zoo only a few hours when the smaller gorilla, which had been pursuing the larger about an old, rough eucalyptus stump in their temporary cage, suddenly caught his quarry and after a rough-and-tumble, good-natured wrestling match he stood very erect and sway-backed upon his funny short legs and raising his arms at right angles to his body, at the level of his armpits, he danced a few steps up and down and beat a rapid tat-tat-tat upon his then hairy chest. It was so rapid that I failed to see the actual beating but so loud and resonant that I was startled and looked to see if the wrestlers had been struggling in earnest instead of in fun as I had thought. But the drooping, half-open lips, the dancing clumsy body, and the altogether calm acceptance of the challenge by the older gorilla left no room for doubt that the message had been friendly. The first story the drum had told was not of anger or fear but good-natured play.

This first experience with chest beating increased an interest which had already been roused by the tales of a friend, now a businessman of San Diego, who formerly had spent many years in the heart of Africa and who had presented me with a real tom-tom hewed from the trunk of a tree and covered with zebra rawhide. Possession of this drum and his description of tom-toms had interested me in reading all I could find of the real significance of African drums which send their messages rolling out, not in dots and dashes of a telegraph code, but with a rolling, rising and falling volume of sound which, to the initiated, speaks almost with words. I have been told that long after all other impressions of Africa have completely faded, the sound of the drums lingers in the mind, clearly, mysteriously and at times even dangerously and frighteningly.

And just as the human drums have carried their messages of joy and sorrow and kept the black men in touch with each other, so do the hairy men seem to use their beating to keep the troop close together, to warn and call and carry the messages, good or bad, off through the deep underbrush so dense that even members of a band feeding in a small area are out of sight and touch with each other.

Several days passed after ours arrived before I actually got a good chance to watch a gorilla beat upon his breast. Although I have now seen it hundreds of times, it is always exciting and I still watch for it and try to interpret it with as great an interest as though my association with my captive gorillas were not one of years. I have never seen our gorillas beat upon their chests or any object with closed fists, but rather with a loosely opened hand, fingers spread apart and slightly bent or curled, for they cannot open flat. Just as we can increase the strength and volume of the tone when clapping our hands by cupping the palms, so does the gorilla's huge, hollow palm add to the depth and resonance of the drum when a gorilla beats upon any surface, especially his own great chest. But like the hollow drum of the native, it carries far, seeming to gather volume as it spreads even when he uses his unbelievably rapid beat.

I have tried holding my fingers pressed tightly together, slightly curved, to gain something of that resonance as I have beat upon my chest, but neither I nor the hundreds I have watched try to imitate a gorilla could reproduce even in a weak way the depth of tone, the fullness of sound or the rapid, even rhythm of gorilla drums. But in the literature to which I have had access I have found no corroboration of my observation of the open hand except in the magnificent volume in which Dr. Robert Yerkes collects material from all known authorities on the manlike apes. There he quotes Otto Hermes, writing in 1892, as saying gorillas beat with the open hand, but adds that this is contrary to his own and all other observations. Carl Akeley's magnificent males in each of his museum groups stand stretched erect, hands clenched in a tight fist resting on their hairless chests at the end of a downward beat. But the enlargements from movies of the famous female gorilla "Congo" taken over a period of several years all show a blurring of her extended fingers, which were stretched wide open as she beat rapidly upon her breast or other objects. I may perhaps misinterpret the word fist. I speak of it as a hand with the fingers tightly closed. Now and then I have seen either Ngagi or Mbongo strike with the side of his closed fist upon the door of his house as he runs past it, but it is one quick blow. He would never stop to beat a real tattoo as when signaling his desire for entrance.

I have seen our gorillas beat upon any smooth surface near them. I have seen them, especially when younger, lie at opposite corners of their cage and clap their hands in almost perfect rhythm, whether keeping together or alternating the beat. Again by elevating their short legs as they lay flat on their broad backs they would pat the soles of their feet with the big hands, then pat their breasts, and produce something almost like two drums. At such times they seemed not so much to respond to each other as to imitate the sounds the other made. At first I thought it was something that they had brought with them from the jungle, but if it was, the significance to them was entirely gone, and with maturity this childish response to each other ceased and we heard little beating except upon the doors and shelves and their chests.

When they were younger and would beat their hands together, they assumed all sorts of positions. Ngagi, the more shy in many ways, seemed to find self-expression thus and especially liked to lie on the shelves with his hips against the wire, his legs perpendicular and his arms hanging over his head while clapping his broad hands. Again he would climb to the top of the cage and standing upon the great angle irons meeting there across the corner, he would drop his big torso down into the triangle between his legs and the cage and his great head hanging upside down, his mouth loosely open, he would beat upon his chest or clap his hands rapidly and loudly in our direction. At such times his face would assume almost as roguish a look as Mbongo was capable of and he would, as Henry Newmeyer, their first keeper, said, dare us to copy his stunt. At first this stance gave us great anxiety lest his foot might slip off the narrow smooth steel bar and he might drop to the shelf below, but he would stand firm and steady in the awkward position until he was ready to come down or we had ceased to be impressed. Mbongo often tried to dislodge him and once, standing on the shelf below, he reached up to beat upon Ngagi's chest, but never did he imitate the older gorilla's special act.

It is always when gorillas are running and playing that we can expect to hear the loudest and most rapid drumming. Although sometimes they do beat briefly when sitting still, they seldom stand still when they beat upon

[261]

their chests. Instead they dance up and down or run forward with rapid steps, or hang by one arm from a swinging hoop. The movement of the beat is so rapid that it can be caught only with a cinema camera and too often they are running away from the photographer. There is always something sudden and unexpected in the beat. The gorilla seems never to premeditate it and makes no preparation. Often when I thought Mbongo's mood presaged a little chest beating I have tried to prepare the cameraman or observer, but always Mbongo either failed me entirely or beat rapidly and stopped before I could utter the warning or the man could take it in. And always it was when he was playful. But when he got tired of the glaring reflectors which blot out the heavy wire and deep shadows of the cage for the photographers, he walked off and went to sleep, or the two of them would charge rapidly toward the camera or the man holding the reflectors. There was no mistaking that they meant business, but they stopped always short of touching the wire, although once Mbongo reached out and took an expensive lens off a too slowly retreating camera. It had been thrust through the mesh in the wire for a better picture; but there was no warning, no beating and no sound except a deep grunt from Ngagi. Having taken the camera apart, Mbongo didn't even look at the lens — just dropped it on the ground and walked away.

Mbongo, who was the better-natured and more spontaneously playful, beat his chest much more frequently than the dignified Ngagi, just as he was usually the one to originate the games of tag and wrestling bouts. Part of their organized play consisted of racing and a sort of King-on-the-Castle game in which one would mount the big rough eucalyptus stump while the other would swing from a corner shelf and try to pull or push his playmate off the stronghold he had chosen. Over and over again, especially if the king were not dislodged, he would stand up as the other swung back to the shelf and beat rapidly, triumphantly, upon his chest and usually being the challenger, Mbongo sounded the challenge of the drum much more frequently than Ngagi.

When either one had to be confined within the house for any purpose, the other tried to call him out by rapid drumming. This drumming, both on chest and objects, was unmistakably a call to come and play. When they were younger their early-morning exercise was quite strenuous. As soon as they left their beds each attended to evacuating his bowels, and each seemed to respect the other's right to take care of this daily necessity. Then one or the other would, with that sudden swift rush of which they remained capable in spite of weight, tear past his friend and as he neared him, swerve his body just sufficiently either to bump him with the near shoulder or to tweak a bit of hair off an arm or leg, and then as he reached the end of his rush, the aggressor would rise and with the rapid beat of a snare drum defy his playmate to stand his ground or come on and pit his strength against him. It was such good-natured fun that it always aroused much enthusiasm even among human beholders.

Many times beating with the feet accompanies this hand drumming on the chest. Mbongo would stand up on the wide triangular shelves in the corner and stamp up and down, pounding his heels alternately hard and fast in almost the same rhythm as when producing with his hands. I have not seen Ngagi stand on the shelves; he has always been too large to do it comfortably and he shuns anything spectacular in public, but when he is in his sleeping quarters he will often stand erect and

[263]

drum with his feet on the floor. This good-natured drumming is produced in several rhythms, very fast and very slow, and then again in an uneven broken patter made by dancing on the feet, first bringing down one foot with a resounding thump and then the other, with the hands either alternately or in unison filling in the lighter rapid beats upon the chest.

Drumming with the feet, however, is not confined to standing still. One of the most expressive beats is that which the animal produces while running on all fours. Their rhythms are as diverse and numerous as their gaits. They are all, however, created by striking the floor or ground with the flat, heavy, broad foot. They pat defiantly and loudly with both feet at once when running at a gallop; suddenly changing to a canter, they alternate the beat. It always pleased us when they chased each other with the heavy pat of big feet, for we knew again there was no anger or impatience in that run, but just excited, good-natured racing and play.

Charley Smith was a natural trainer of animals and before being employed at our zoo had produced a really remarkable act of chimpanzees combined with monkeys and baboons. He was most eager to train the gorillas when he first came and thought our plan of their growing naturally "just the bunk." He took care of the apes during his first year here at the zoo and very soon became fully converted to our theory of gorilla care. But he tried many simple things with them which we permitted, as we felt he added to their happiness. He was big enough, too, not to try to undermine their affection and trust in me and never did any of the things I had used effectively. One of the things he coaxed the gorillas to do was to change their gaits at the beat of his own feet on the ground. Hunching himself into a strange resemblance to a great ape of no particular species, screwing up his comical, heavily lined face into what he fondly imagined was a mask of ferocity, he would beat his chest and race back and forth on the long side of the cage, stamping his feet hard upon the bare ground. Soon Mbongo, who had already learned to race with Tim, the chimp in the cage next door, took up the challenge, and after a few weeks Mbongo would also change his pace at the change of beat of "Smitty's." I think this was brought about, however, first by the man's imitation of the hard beat of both feet on the ground as he ran with the younger gorilla, changing when the gorilla did. Ngagi never entered into this play but held aloof as he had when Mbongo and Tim raced each other. Smith always believed that Ngagi did not play because he was too dignified, but after watching him look at the two I was sure it was because he was too shy or self-conscious.

The two gorillas when young frequently sat in a very childish manner upon the floor of the cage, spreading their short heavy legs widely apart so that they might, by bowing, beat upon the floor of the cage between with a steady, solemn beat. Up, down, up, down, they bowed, with each broad hand patting the floor in unison or alternately, an obvious salaam to the god of their well-being. Especially when the sand on the floor of the cage was saturated by the rain did they love to pat it with their flat hands. At such times after a few salaams they might move their hands back close to their bodies and by rapid and not too gentle beating with the open palm bring a show of water to the surface. This phenomenon was quite what they expected, apparently, for they would always stoop far over, extending their mobile lips, and sip up a few drops of the muddy-looking water, which they let run out at once. I have seen them prepare

[265]

an area around their drinking fountain for this ceremony by scooping out great hollow handfuls of the water until the sand around the pool was saturated and then sit facing each other, beating rapidly or slowly as their mood was, enjoying the sharp smack of the hand on the wet sand, and always sipping the water thus brought to the surface.

And on rainy days, too, the beating upon the dripping chests was almost continuous. Ngagi, who must, I claimed, have worshiped some pagan god of the waters, was never so happy, so active, and so noisy as on a very rainy day. He even yet will walk about the cage, his face held up so that the fullest force of the rain strikes directly upon it. And always while he thus walks, his hands are clasped tightly behind his back, but from time to time the exuberance of his feelings is too strong for his control and the great hands swing around and sound the booming tattoo of his native drum. The sound seems always so much more resonant when hands and chest are thoroughly moistened with the rain. During the long dry summers Mbongo was, even in his maturity, apt to stoop over the still water of his pool and perhaps seeing his own good-natured reflection feel called upon to salute the broad black friendly face and so he would beat loudly upon his chest, then without waiting for an answering beat, stoop and beat the surface of the pool or scoop up handfuls of the water and splash and beat his chest with the fluid, seeming undisturbed that his action discomposed the gorilla to whom he was sending the challenge.

And while they were still small children I have seen them beat or pat upon each other's back, which resounded almost as loudly as the chest, or pat the soles of each other's feet, and more rarely sitting facing each

[266]

other as do children playing Jack Be Nimble or Bean Porridge Hot, they would pat the palms of their own hands together, then holding their hands out, slap the extended palm of the other's huge hands in humanly childish play. This game would last sometimes for several minutes, although there was never any real sequence or finish to it. Smitty used to say that it usually ended with Ngagi slapping "Little Mbongo" hard, but I never saw a rough ending in the numerous times I watched them at it. I have seen them bend forward with their long arms easily and touch hands when the soles of their feet were almost touching, legs straight, either spread or close together. Thus was the greater length of the arm a distinct advantage in the primitive game which we can all remember having played sometime. But there was always a loud smacking pat that made me sure that it was the noise of the beating they loved rather than the contact itself.

But it is not always a happy story I have learned from the drums, for now and then, especially when they were younger, it seemed a little pathetic, that story the drums told. Sometimes as they beat they stopped suddenly and seemed to listen as though expecting an answer from some other youthful member of their band who might be feasting on tender shoots just beyond their sight, and often, as though disappointed, the youngster might stand and beat again and run off around the log, for surely just beyond he might find someone to join him in his play, someone he had lost. But the intervals between these solemn drummings became so long that eventually we ceased to observe such periods at all and we realized with gratitude that the world of our two gorillas was now encompassed only by each other, we few whom they had accepted, the familiar setting of their cage, and to some substantial degree the crowds of changing visitors securely restrained beyond the boundaries of their guarded home.

But to return to the story of the drums, they beat out now more often than any other message the story of their lazy, happy contentment. Too languid to move or stand, too happy for complete silence, they would sit and slowly but with some emphasis beat upon their breasts, from which the once thick baby hair had completely disappeared. They would strike the walls of the house, the shelves and floor of their cage, and the great flattened wooden ball that has replaced the huge logs which they had learned to move about too freely. Those logs had long been shiny and worn with the constant pat of the great hands with moist sticky palms, and in the center of their sheet-metal doors there is always a patch where the shining silver paint is worn off where the great hands beat their tattoo. Huge and heavy as they were, the giant gorillas would stir into action late every afternoon and tearing about on all fours with speed almost unbelievable would give each other the old "bum's rush" and bump each other with their shoulders in good-natured rivalry. They would stand erect now and then to issue the old challenge of the jungle, or running at full speed pause, one after the other, to beat loudly upon the resounding metal doors — the notice to their greatly beloved keeper to hasten for night was due in the jungle, where it is twilight all day and then suddenly dark, that it was time to fill the huge stomachs with much food to last until morning, and to retire to enjoy the companionship of each other in the silence of their familiar rooms.

But seldom did they appear to choose utter silence during this intimate hour of the late day when the world was shut away from them by more than darkness. At

[268   ]

first there would be the good-natured stamping, patting and grunting that accompanied the building of their nests of clean fresh hay, the moving of the beds close to the barred window for companionship, shaping it into piles where they could touch each other. There was some good-natured stamping, too, as long as we remained a disturbing element. But principally this was the time when these two became most vocal.

I have read that gorillas are the most silent of all the anthropoid apes. I have even found the word mute applied to them. But judging from our own ape colony, where all four families of the anthropoid apes are housed and treated as nearly alike as their different natures will permit, I once more find myself forced to disagree, for the two gorillas were much more given to vocal expression than the adult orang-utans or even our juvenile specimens. The captive Man of the Woods is nearly mute; the Hairy Man often speaks, and his voice is flexible, having a wide range of notes. Most of his sounds come past closed lips and only now and then does he open his great mouth when conversing with his cage-mate.

These sounds are as difficult to describe as they are impossible to interpret. There was the first high note I ever heard them make when they recognized Osa Johnson; and as she whined, or sort of whinnied, at them they answered her in the native tongue she had learned from them in the wild, and during their own first year of captivity. Then when they had been here through a winter and we had begun to think they were becoming quite acclimated we gave them greater and greater variety of food. Late in the spring the first green corn was added to their diet. Henry told me he was going to feed it to them and, anxious to see what they did with it, I waited for them to enter their house after their usual

[269]

evening romp. Ngagi was handed the first ear of corn, from which we had removed part of the husk. He tore into it with his teeth and then, before Mbongo received his, gave a low grunt to voice his satisfaction with what was apparently a favorite form of food, perhaps always a rare treat. He began almost to sing, so quickly his voice lightened and slid up the scale. He had, it seemed, asked a question to which Mbongo, having just taken up his ear, answered in a grumbling, grunting and completely satisfied series of sounds, deeper in tone, as you would expect of the answer to the rising inflection of the question. It got to be quite a habit of mine to slip in to dinner with the gorillas and from appearing to resent our presence, they became so accustomed to eating before company that to be invited to "dinner with the gorillas to hear them talk" became a favor reserved for persons of scientific distinction or importance.

And so many have heard those two in adjoining rooms — after they outgrew their original bedroom —speaking to each other through the barred window between them, which was kept closed so they could each have the balanced meals we planned for them, but through which they could touch each other and see each other at will. There we would stand as they each discovered the delicacy for the evening, and "*Hmmmmmm?*" asked Mbongo over a fine fresh pineapple, and "*Hmmmmmm*" answered the older and slightly smaller gorilla as he too found that favorite article of diet, and deep satisfaction, contentment, and well-being was expressed in those voices so singularly small, gentle and pleasant from two such great and untamed beasts. I have heard and read of the murmurs made by gorillas feeding and am convinced that it is partly to keep them in touch so that they may not become too widely scattered through the dense jungle in the search of food, for always there must be that caution to keep the band together for complete protection.

There was little except humming in these voices, nothing that sounds like words, no vowels, no break of shorter or longer sounds, just the sliding inflection and tone up and down — *singsong*, for want of a more descriptive term. But there were other voices. One morning about a year ago, clear over at my office a good quarter of a mile away, I was startled out of an absorbed reading of the mail by a sharp, thin, penetrating bark which ended in a quavering high note which was a wild sound I had never heard before. I never hear ordinary zoo noises but I became instantly alert at this one and listened intently. Again I heard the high, queer, rumbling staccato bark, not a sound of distress in itself, but again it ended on that quavering, shrill, odd high note. I walked out into the grounds and listened; twice more it was repeated, and it seemed to have come from the heart of the zoo. I walked rapidly to the primate mesa, thinking it might have been some new creature calling for the first time, or some familiar one in serious trouble.

Since all seemed in order, down the long line of anthropoid-ape cages I hurried. There was nothing amiss, except that the chimpanzees, all high in the top of their cage, seemed to be giving more than usual attention to the gorillas next door on the west. Mbongo sat calmly on the ground beside what we call the salt lick, sucking his big finger, then sticking it through the wire to rub it against a block of stock salt fastened in a tight box on the outside of the wire. He raised his chin and grunted at me as I approached the cage. Ngagi, sitting near the pool at the opposite end, was very erect, his straight back pressed against the wall of the sleeping room and facing

[271]

directly to the south. He did not look at me as I approached, and just then Moore came around the corner of the house. "Did you hear him?" he asked. "Was it Ngagi?" I queried in return. "Yes," said Moore. "I can't think what is the matter with him. He has been active and restless for several days. Last night he didn't eat all his supper and this morning he was anxious to get out, as though something was disturbing him." That was the first time either of us had heard that particular cry but it was not the last, for during the past year, two or three times the older gorilla has had these rather sulky spells which always precede the days when he makes this peculiar call.

It must have some meaning and yet so far as Mbongo showed any reaction, it had no significance. He paid no attention to the dominating Ngagi; they never had any of their infrequent battles during the two or three days when Ngagi was calling his wild, piercing cry, and when he ceased and did approach his cage-mate, there was nothing aggressive or hostile in his action, or cringing and fearful in Mbongo's reception. I frequently saw him sit close to Mbongo after calling once or twice and lay his hand calmly and with the customary appearance of friendliness on the younger gorilla. Sometimes he would sit erect as he was the first day I heard him, and opening his mouth in two or three sharp, rather high staccato barks, follow them with the long-drawn-out quivering scream. At other times he stands on all fours and with the first note dashes forward two or three feet and then stands still, holding his head high, his shoulders elevated, and with flexed muscles holding the hair erect on the great forearms and over the enormous symmetrical crest.

Because he does not seem disturbed by any outward sound or condition we have attributed it, probably wrongly, to some inner urge or need, possibly sexual. And I have wondered if in the wild he would not long ago have been either forced from the troop or compelled to seek a mate or to fight for control of his native troop with an older leader. For there has never been any doubt in my mind that Ngagi is a born leader. His magnificent physique, his indomitable will, his complete independence and his intelligence would fit him for such a position. In descriptions of gorilla sounds I have sought for something that adequately describes this new cry that will always be strange and somewhat exciting to me; this thing which rightly or wrongly Moore and I believe is the call of the hairy man for his mate. And once more I find what I seek, mentioned by Yerkes in his account of the vocalization of the young female gorilla, Congo, in a much better description of the last notes of this peculiar cry than I could devise. I take the liberty of using his words. Ngagi's great bark, sharp, deep and louder than any voice of a huge dog, was followed by a "shrill, tremulous and also tenuous cry similar to the distant neighing of a horse or the call of a screech owl." This, it seems to me, is the cry that explorers may have heard at night during periods of long silence in the gorilla country. I believe it can have no significance as a danger signal to an organized troop or as a guiding sound to hold the band together.

Once when we were conditioning our camels to take part in a desert movie we led them past the great ape cages and both gorillas became greatly excited and showed every evidence of terror. They rushed close to each other as if for reinforcement and courage, then barked with sharp, loud roaring barks which could be heard in every part of the zoo and which had a tendency to frighten and excite all of the other anthropoids to a much greater degree than the sight of the camels had done. In fact, neither the orangs nor chimpanzees showed any real fright at the first appearance of the camel parade but when the gorillas set up their clamor the orangs, too, swung to the top of the cage and, pursing out their lips, hissed and fumed at the indifferent camels walking sedately by. The chimpanzees set up their shrill screaming, but it was the roar of the gorillas that disturbed the camels and made them swerve against the man leading them and break into a trot which could easily have become a stampede. The real stampede was the rush of the visitors to that end of the primate mesa, drawn as one man by that roar of the two usually silent beasts.

As a rule I have a feeling of resentment when people stand and make remarks about how hideous gorillas are and how fierce they look, and claim that they would hate to meet them loose anywhere. When I have given talks to organized groups in the vicinity of the ape cages, trying to present the great fellows of all the apes in their true colors, I have emphasized that the gorilla is a creature of a retiring nature which has been driven back and back to the last confines of the deepest jungle, where at last he has been forced to make a stand to protect himself and his dependents. But I, with all the others, stood aghast at the strength and overpowering volume of sound that these two made over so simple and harmless a creature as the camel, and at least for a few minutes I had something in common with the people who said, "Boy, I should hate to meet them on a dark night."

At times of lesser stress and more transient alarm the two would issue rapidly, and somewhat constantly, their series of warning grunts, so loud that they could be heard by visitors behind the guard fence twelve feet from the front wall of the cage. This sound is one of such plain significance that nobody can mistake it for anything dangerous or aggressive. They were conferring with each other and agreeing that danger was near and they would draw close together and by being each very alert almost seem to protect each other in every direction from an approaching disaster.

With the very recent acquisition of two young female gorillas of the lowland race, I have heard a new gorilla voice, nothing like the singing sliding tones of the two males when they are contented, and I am not sure that this is a contented noise. For these two were pitifully afraid of man; they dodged and winced at our every move; but when they finally were in their snug little sleeping quarters — each on her big bed of hay and with her stomach full of warm milk — and ready to be closed in together without any human being present, the older one muttered in a deep, guttural monotone to the youngster who clung to her for comfort and guidance in the new life. And this was a deep throaty clucking sound — almost as though it issued from the stomach rather than the larynx of the young gorilla. I cannot say it was a warning like the grunts of Ngagi when he and Mbongo took up their abode with us; it was not the satisfied, contented message over acceptable food, for Kenya, our older female, did not find the manhandled food much to her taste as yet; but Kivu, the younger, would listen and move closer and the sound had a certain amount of companionship in it for her and surely some meaning. Was it perhaps just an older sister whispering something to the younger that she herself in turn had learned from older gorillas of her troop and hoped to keep alive in this

[275]

new, strange and difficult world where she was not yet at home?

I was anxious to be near their cage if Ngagi should start his weird call, and see if they recognize it as part of their social background. I now hope that sometime the small gorilla will join with Ngagi when he beats upon the drums or that I again may be lucky enough to be near the big fellow who as yet does not appear to know that separated from him by one big wire cage and fifty feet of space is his future mate. I am wondering if they will challenge each other over that space with the calls of the wild gorilla or the beat of the native drums. For now Ngagi has only that one chance of gorilla response.

Did I say that no story of the zoo is ever complete? That is true, but now and then there comes an end. And so one blustering March day when the life of Mbongo here with us had gone on for ten years, five months and ten days, the buzzer sounded just once. Automatically I switched the telephone onto the soft bell and said, "Hello." Dr. McKenney was saying, and saying with dreadful reluctance, "He is gone; just lay over on his side and went to sleep."

No need to ask who *he* was. To all of us, for three weeks, *he* meant only Mbongo. He had been seriously ill with a mysterious sickness that had come on with little warning; a few days of not being very hungry, fewer days of appearing loath to go out into the crisp early morning he had loved, and then a day when he decided all by himself that he would loaf in bed.

I was on vacation, but the next day it was decided that he was really sick, and a conference of specialists from the Research Committee was called. Accurate diagnosis was impossible; nothing seemed very wrong — no appetite, a little fever, rarely a deep cough, no other appearance of cold, general indications of infection somewhere, but nothing to indicate pain or distress.

Comparisons with any of his former illnesses or those in the primate colony brought to light nothing fruitful or comforting. And so the weary days went on, with Mbongo drinking freely, taking milk now and then with evident relish even though it contained sulphadiazine and banana powder and other things which would have been given either in pneumonia or intestinal infections; mild in their reaction as must be when given to an ape, and yet ample to help him over a development of pneumonia or infection in brain or body.

The fever increased to 103, then suddenly waned. Then I came home and on hearing the bad news rushed to see my sick friend. He looked at me out of lackluster eyes — no sign to show he wanted to see me. The skin on his black face was drawn and shiny. I extended my arm through the bars separating his sleeping floor from the main room and touched his face. It was cool. He opened his eyes again at my touch, without recognition. I turned and went out, with a heavy heart.

Late in the day one of our consultants came in from the Scripps Hospital and stopped to discuss Mbongo's illness. Frankly, he said, they were baffled. There was no way to determine the cause or seat of the infection if that were the trouble. To move him forcibly or restrain him in the cage would be a greater hazard than the disease. They had been keeping him warm and quiet, with the temperature of the room a little over seventy, since his first day's illness. Each day he had with effort moved into the adjoining room. We hoped, and hoped desperately, that whatever it was would pass off without an attack of pneumonia.

The next day, Sunday morning, when I hurried to his cage, he grunted slightly and looked out of eyes much brighter, and I knew that he recognized me. His eyes followed Moore in his movements back and forth cleaning Ngagi's quarters. I felt his hand; it was cool and moist. His face had regained much of its usual velvety softness. Moore and I were happy beyond all reason. And when it came time for him to move into the adjoining cage he did it with much more ease and assurance than he had shown at any other time.

The doctors all hoped with us that he was better. We knew that at best the way back was going to be a long, tedious one, and for two or three days our hopes fluctuated as Mbongo was in turn brighter or more listless; as he turned and slept normally on his back with his short legs erect against the wall or slipped back to rest more comfortably in his habitual position, supporting himself on knees and elbows with the huge abdomen resting on the soft straw, the back of his right hand holding up his chin; as he drank his milk or poured it into the gutter, and all the while the specialists came and went, hoping for something upon which they might place their finger and say "That is what we must fight."

But suddenly without many words we all understood he was not so well. He too was impatient with our attempts to help him; he was restless, turning and rolling on his fine clean bed of straw, and turning on his side or holding his heavy body erect for a matter of seconds. Respiration was a little rapid, but not labored; 26, then 28, and finally about 30. He breathed through nostrils from which there was no discharge. The devoted Moore came back late each evening to see how he was, and one night found him with a severe nosebleed. It was apparently merely local, but again the gorilla had obviously lost ground. My own terrible desire to be with him fought with the feeling that I could do nothing but bother Moore, who practically spent the night in his cage. For the first time in our ten years together the responsive Mbongo gave no sign that he knew I was near. Each night Moore called me faithfully to report "No news." At last I knew when he had given up hope for Mbongo, without need of words between us, but I could not admit even to myself that I had. So beautiful in his excellent flesh, so full of life, it seemed he could not be this despondent creature who failed to respond even to his companion, Ngagi. In his anxiety, Ngagi watched us through the tiny peephole in the door as the doctor and Moore gave Mbongo inhalations under a hastily rigged tent. There was nothing to indicate that oxygen was needed, but he sighed as though in comfort from the damp, moist air of the inhalator.

Monday he dragged himself on his knees off the bed of straw so it could be cleaned, and crossed the threshold into Ngagi's room. Twice Moore suggested that he return. He knew that voice through the dimming of his senses and tried to obey. Once he got his head over the threshold but sank back in discouraged weakness. I coaxed Moore to put his room in order and let him go back when he wanted to badly enough to try harder. While Moore went out to prepare a pan of warm milk, I reached through for the second time in an hour to lay my hand on the huge black one. The dull eyes opened and looked into mine; the hand under mine moved slightly. I offered him a drink. He wanted it but was too tired, so I slipped my other hand under the great head and supported it for him. He opened his eyes again, looked at me with more recognition for the touch than he had before during the whole day, and again barely moved the cold hand on which mine rested, but the great lips trembled as he dropped his head once more on the back of his great fist. I hurried out before Moore should return, knowing that I would not see Mbongo again.

I tell myself over and over that we were lucky to have had him so long; that I have no right to feel as I do; but I find myself dreading to go by that cage when visitors are there, flinching from sympathy, knowing in spite of everything that the scientific loss is great, a grand entertainer has gone, and I have lost a rare friend indeed.

Even if we had known everything that the autopsy revealed, we would still have been helpless, for his death was due to Coccidioidal granuloma, a growth of a fungus, *Coccidioides immitis*, peculiar to our own climate and almost entirely confined to human beings, known principally in the agricultural centers of California. The spore, being received from the earth, possibly from clods in his hay bedding, develops rapidly, destroying the lungs much in the same manner as tuberculosis, and spreading to other organs; it causes death in human beings within a period of two weeks or less. No effective cure has so far been found, nor a single recovery reported. It is not communicated from one animal to another, therefore we do not expect a repetition.

And Ngagi. He had paid little attention to the fact that Mbongo was not out in the cage until, as I said, the day before his death. That day and the next he was restless and disturbed. That night, when we turned him into the open cage, he refused to enter, but when Moore returned after dinner and opened the door he went in, gazing curiously into Mbongo's room. He ate his regular meal and was ready to go out next day. He searched the cage, going immediately to the always open door of the

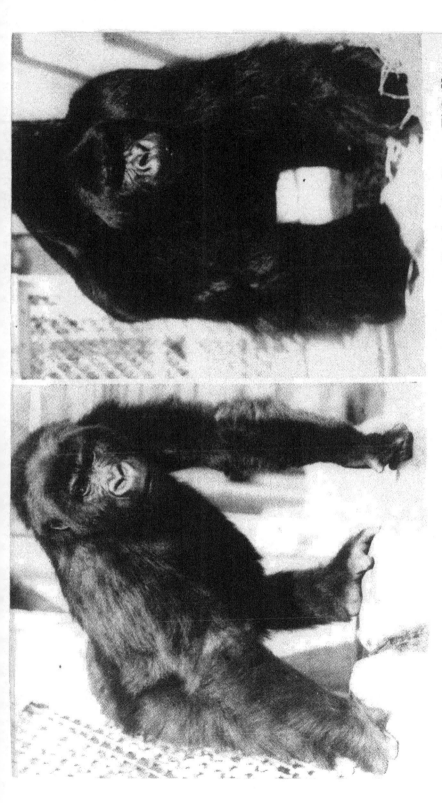

Ngagi in 1941, Showing the Changes Eight Years Wrought

Ngagi in 1933

unoccupied sleeping room across the safety cage from their quarters. Later I saw him up high on the steel framework watching the activity in the adjoining cages. Yesterday I walked over to the corner of the cage where he was lying and, poking my fingers through the wire, pressed them against the hard muscles of the great gray back. It had been many months since he had welcomed my attention, or even endured it, but at the first touch he shifted closer to the wire, turned his head toward me and permitted familiarities greater than he had for a very very long time. He held perfectly still while I poked or not too gently scratched him, rubbing him with the ends of my spread fingers as he used to like me to do. Some way I was sure that our mutual affection and understanding sympathy needed nothing audible, nor even a glance to pass between us.

But Hope! Ah, that is a different matter. I can find no means of communicating to him a hope which stirs in my heart on occasions as I pass the second cage to the east and watch Kenya, the rugged little female gorilla acquired last fall, hugging little Georgie, the chimp, to her fat stomach. She gives an excellent imitation of motherhood, reminding me of a stout, awkward little girl with a doll. When I see her bounding over the bars after him or hear her beating her chest with the hope that Georgie will respond, I also see her in the not too distant future in a screened off section of Ngagi's great cage, getting acquainted with her future mate.

This new gorilla companionship must be promoted judicially, for while we doubt seriously, since the autopsy on Mbongo, that even Ngagi has reached his sexual maturity, still we must not take any chances with either of these two. The hazards might be, for her, her youth, for she cannot be more than six or seven, and her

[281]

weakness due to her recent arrival, which might lead to her physical injury; for him, that she might still be in-fested with the communicable parasites that have already caused the early death of some of the little gorillas that arrived in America with her, including our own little Kivu.

And so we must wait and proceed slowly. Meanwhile we are watching carefully lest Ngagi might become too depressed or agitated by nothing better than our com-panionship. In such an emergency we will immediately put a dividing screen through the center of the big go-rilla cage and move Kenya and Georgie down there. These two are such fun that we would not think of separating them except in dire necessity. They love each other and play together like two chimpanzees. It has been amazing to me that they never play like gorillas. Does this fact indicate that the older Kenya is more in-dulgent to her little playfellow, so follows his lead? Is she quicker to learn his ways or more imitative? If she suits her ways to the imperious Ngagi as she has to Georgie, we may strongly hope that when she has outgrown the days of dolls and playing at motherhood, we may ac-complish that upon which our hearts are set and present to the world a baby gorilla.

PART FIVE

Simia quam similis turpissima bestia nobis
ENNIUS (239–169 B.C.)

A nasty beast the Simian;
How dreadfully is he like to man.
Translation by HAROLD J. COOLIDGE, JR.

CHAPTER XV

AND NOW you have met them — my friends, the apes. I dare not ask you how you like them — I am too much like a mother presenting her darling to the public, or a young girl bringing her first beau home to meet the family — too fearful that you will not see in them the endearing and interesting qualities that I have tried to show you. I realize more than I have ever done how feeble is the written word to portray the life, the sparkle and the beauty of motion that is the gibbon, the Oriental patience, the cunning and persistence, the strength and ugliness that is the orang-utan, the clever, comical, trying, and at the same time affectionate and jealous clown that is the chimpanzee and the dignified, poised, indifferent and sensitive personality that is the gorilla's.

From my ape friends I have not tried to make a composite picture of one, but rather have I given you the pieces in the hope that you might have the patience to fit each into its place in a magnificent jigsaw which would give you not only a creature hampered by men and steel and wire, but also one that would fit into a beautiful background of trees and vines and murmuring streams of the jungle, with men in the deep background, sympathetic and understanding, bridging the space between the treetops and the ground or penetrating the mountain mists.

These are not all of my friends the apes; I could take

each large group and add a dozen more creatures, either from my own or other collections. Gibby and her supine mate were not my favorites among our gibbons, but they taught me so much about their kind and were so long a part of my friendly association with the anthropoids that I wanted you, too, to know and enjoy them. Perhaps Old Mom, the toothless old crone, loved me the best of all the apes, but only her daughter Blackie can hold the top place always as everything that a siamang gibbon could possibly be. But even then I wonder at times if one of the gentle little gray gibbons known to the trade as "silver" who did not stay with us long did not hold a deeper place in my affections than any of the ones I have told you about.

And of all the chimpanzees I shall ever meet, I could not love one more than I do little Georgie, who just now is suffering the deepest pangs of jealousy because a little black sister must have his mother's attention and Moore and I are sharing his petting with the young gorilla Kenya and playing with her and responding to all of her shy advances. Soon these two will become pigeonholed in their proper place in the attention of us all — now they are far more important than they will be later — and then Georgie will have no cause to complain that his adored master and I have passed him by.

It would be useless to deny that Maggie will always be my dearest and closest friend among the orang-utans, for when you get to that degree of understanding which enables you to see a friend's faults and mistakes with no lessening of your affection, that person is the rare friend which you do not often find. And now at last I come to gorillas. I have had so few to choose from that there can be no question of my friendly feeling for the two leading characters among the hairy men. But if you can know which one was my favorite, you are wiser than I am. It was only in a surface way that I loved Mbongo best; when anything happens to disturb Ngagi I am panic-stricken; and when anyone maligns his character or disposition I demand what more could they expect of a gorilla; for he is, I must insist, everything that a gorilla should be physically and mentally. Mbongo had been much more susceptible to the ways and conditions of civilization, which is neither intelligence nor character. I could easily imagine Mbongo leading forth a band of adventuring souls like himself, while Ngagi would stand threatening but cautious on the edge of the primeval jungle. Ngagi would turn at last, all hope gone that the wanderers would return, and jerk up his chin in that expressive gesture typical of both our old and young gorillas and, uttering that warning guttural grunt, elevate his shoulders, flex his muscles until every hair on the forearms and great crest stood erect, and lead his band back into the safety of the jungle.

I hope in spite of the fact that each has been a personality and as such I have presented them, they are still apes to you, even though since their discovery they have been called by names implying their physical likeness to men and I have so designated them. The fact that we keep them strictly on the plane of other animals should neither lessen your interest in them nor diminish their importance to man in the study of their habits and lives in their bearing on himself.

Their greatest and most obvious physical or external likeness to man is their lack of tail. There is something very like primitive men in their faces and posture, and each of them differs from all others almost as much as he does from the human form. For instance, the three smallest apes, the gibbon, the chimpanzee, and the orang, have their slender, pinched pelvic regions, narrow backs without hips but legs jointed at the lower part of the torso without the full abdomen, wide pelvis, and the substantial hips which mark both man and gorilla. All of them differ boldly from man in the tremendous length of their arms as compared with the rest of their stature. The gibbon has the flattest face and standing erect as it moves upon the ground holds its head and chin in something very closely resembling the posture of man. The gorilla, the orang-utan and the chimpanzee are characterized by the protruding jaws and flat lips which are greatly extensible, far beyond anything human — even the thick lips of the Negro tribes of Africa.

Whereas the foot and hands of the gorilla are so distinctly like those of man that I insist upon calling him a biped and not quadrumanous, the long fingers and toes of the chimpanzee, orang and gibbon place them distinctly in the four-handed class. Their feet are as flexible, their toes nearly as long, as their fingers, and they hold, grasp, and work with their feet almost as deftly as they do with their hands.

The chimpanzee and gibbon become gray with age apparently as does man, but there are no decided hair-pattern changes during their life, nor any physical protuberances which come with age. The chimpanzee in some instances does become gray in marked patterns but this is not characteristic of the race, but of the individual. Our two mature males have differed greatly: Timmie began to turn gray on his lower back and legs at about seven years; Bondo, still living in San Francisco and at least in his early twenties, is glossy black as when I first saw him sixteen years ago.

Male orangs and gorillas differ greatly from the others and man, in that with physical maturity most if not all of them acquire great crests of fleshy gristle which rise above their heads in a most imposing structure, adding to the grotesqueness and ferocity of their appearance. The orang in maturity also acquires, except in unusual individuals, an enormous pouch which would in a human be considered a foreign growth, and in addition the great cheek callosities of which I have told you.

Even in their maturity all apes have many childlike qualities which are most endearing. One is their acceptance of conditions so calmly, and their ability to be playing, tearing about vigorously one second and the next to drop completely relaxed into a childish posture of deep untroubled sleep.

The gibbon, the gorilla and the chimpanzee have little physical endurance or mental fortitude when it comes to pain or illness. They go to pieces so quickly that if anything serious happens to them you have very little chance to aid them. They show the least upset, mental or physical, at once, and make a big fuss over it. At such times they usually become very gentle and seem to know instinctively that you are there to help them. The orang, on the other hand, is the stoic, and endures terrible illness and pain without a murmur. Our only remarkable cases of successful medical treatment among the anthropoid apes has been with the orangs. It is true that we have cured gibbons of wounds now and then, but more often they have succumbed to slight injuries, which may be due to their reaction to captivity or to a lack of physical stamina. The others have been nursed through slight colds with simple treatment such as constant use of citrus juices, sunshine and wise administration of proper laxatives. But when I think of the serious difficulties we have encountered among our orangs, the dreadful illness of old Mike with his hemorrhagic ulcers, the punishment

[289]

little Bujang suffered and all but conquered with his compound fracture and badly bitten leg, the severe treatment needed for Katjeung's gangrenous ulcer and one serious bout Maggie had with pneumonia, I feel that the orang at least in his reaction to medicine and nursing most nearly approaches the human body.

The mothers among the anthropoid apes have a sense of responsibility that is natural and expected; that is what a mother means. But in the wider sense, none of the apes shows a feeling of responsibility for the safety and welfare of the others in the cage except the gorilla — probably the foundation of their organized troops. Always Ngagi feared the impetuous Mbongo. He was so much more cautious, perhaps because of his age, that many times each day he prevented Mbongo from doing something he wanted to do. This protective control led to a domination over the younger gorilla that continued to Mbongo's death, although he outweighed the older fellow by at least forty pounds, and recently I smiled to see the protective feeling of the older of our young female gorillas as displayed constantly for the younger one. We do not know that they ever saw each other before they arrived in New York. The mixed group that came in with them probably represented several troops of gorillas. But beginning with that tender and unmistakable effort to comfort the smaller child when she emerged into her last big home on the day of their arrival there was a series of actions which leave no doubt that the older gorilla was alive to danger, and not only for herself but for the little Kivu. For several nights we had no trouble getting Kenya to come into the sleeping rooms while Kivu remained outside; and then the older one suddenly seemed alarmed at the crash of the heavy iron door. This started when one

[290]

night we separated them, and ever since that night we had difficulties getting them into their sleeping rooms. Kenya was not eating well and we were anxious to see just how much she did eat, so the doctor suggested that we close the barred door between them.

The boys had been held so late after their day's work and had been so patient that I went out to help, as it had seemed at first that the gorillas came in more quickly with me inside the house coaxing them a bit with voice and food. But coax as I would, and threaten as the boys did, waving slender bamboo twigs and motioning at the door to show what was needed, the two sat on the sand just outside the door looking first at the men and then at me. I tipped up the pan of nice warm milk, I held out a big orange enticingly, but Kenya sat on the ground and Kivu, who had climbed up on the shelf before the door, looked at her and then at me. Suddenly she stepped almost inside the door, reaching for the orange, and as she did Kenya's slender hand reached out and touched her on the foot with the same quick warning touch I had seen Ngagi use on Mbongo a thousand times in the past ten years. Kivu jumped out from under the door and we had to begin again.

Gibbons and gorillas seem to be little interested in mechanical devices. Neither of them build any sort of shelter except of a most transient nature. The gorillas do pile a mass of litter about them for their greater comfort and to hold them off the wet ground. The gibbon, as I have said, selects for his bed a crotch of a tree, which keeps him from falling. Chimpanzees and orangs build substantial nests in the wild and in our zoo; they like sacks, which they work with, rolling and shaping them into some sort of nest. For many years Timmie took an old tire to bed with him each night and in this he piled his sacks, and upon this queer contrivance he slept. In the morning he carried it out with him and used it during the day. As Georgie grew older he grabbed or pushed the tire out of position each time Tim left it; especially if it were high upon the cross arms of the trapeze. And so one morning with many a backward glance, Tim left his sleeping room without his precious tire. That night he looked inside his room and the tire was missing, for Moore, thinking he had tired of it, had removed it while he cleaned the room and left it against the wall in the back of the safety cage. Tim stood on the threshold and whined and fussed but refused to come in. Moore did everything he could think of and suddenly a great light dawned upon him. He picked up the tire and pushed it under the grill onto the floor of Tim's bedroom. Timmie grabbed it, grinning from ear to ear, and picking up his sacks tucked them snugly in. The whole situation with its reasons for the change in plan was perfectly clear to the understanding Moore.

Among their many characteristics, as we have stressed about all animals, there are many which are called man-like. Perhaps we have learned them or inherited them from the beasts for again I must emphasize that they are not confined to man but are widely distributed. We have listed them before so will not again. But there are out- . ward evidences of some of the qualities which are more highly evident in man than many beasts. While I am convinced that all of these animals have a sense of humor and a sense of play, it remains for the chimpanzee and orang really to laugh as man does. Little George breaks into a grin that shows every tooth in his head at the second he sees me stop my car and get out on his side. But on a Saturday afternoon a few weeks ago I saw something in the way of changing expression on Georgie's expressive little face that I would have given almost anything to have recorded pictorially.

Byron Moore, who had been his one human friend since his birth, the only person Katie had ever trusted to take him out of her arms, was recalled into the navy in September as instructor in machinist classes at the Naval Training Station and all the apes, and especially Georgie, had missed him greatly. Georgie began to suffer from a severe dysentery, which became so alarming that finally we decided we would have to catch him and separate him from his mother. Knowing this would be a difficult and heartbreaking task at best, we called Moore and asked him to come down to help on his first free day. All morning George sat miserably in the top of his cage, refusing to come down for anybody. Even for me he would move forward a little at a time and come part way down the wire, then crawl back to sit hunched up into a ragged, dejected-looking bundle.

I called him and he started across the cage toward us, and slowly down the wire. He had glanced at the group but apparently had mistaken Moore for the new head keeper, Pete March, still a comparative stranger to him. As he climbed down, his little face was long and pale and his eyes sunken deep in his head — a really sick little chimp. But suddenly as I looked to see if he was going to recognize Moore, he dropped far enough to see Moore's face below his cap. With one flash his face broke into the widest grin you ever saw. As he jumped at the wire, both tiny arms came through, grabbing frantically at Moore, kicking at the wire on the inside, grinning, pulling Moore toward him in an ecstasy of pleasure, showing more life than he had had for several days.

I can't tell which was happiest, Moore, Georgie or I.

[293]

It was one of those rare moments in a zoo in which the perfect understanding between man and ape is completely unfolded. Georgie did not want to let Moore go. Katie, realizing something was happening to her son, came over and, recognizing Moore, set up such a screeching that soon the whole ape colony was in pandemonium.

Kok-Kok and Maggie have the most engaging grins among the orangs; few children could change expression so quickly. Unlike the change of expression on the faces of dogs, which is largely in the eyes, or horses, which show temper or anger by laying back their ears and baring teeth, the whole face of these anthropoids seems mobile in the matter of expression. I have seen gibbons frown or scowl and pout; chimpanzees and orangs both scowl and grin, and the gorillas, by pulling down their brows in displeasure, leave no doubt of what they mean. Mbongo had the most expressive face and the most changing of all the apes I have known, but since others failed to see this as plainly as I did perhaps it was partly imaginary.

I have watched anthropoid apes in other zoos, in shows and circuses, and I have seen as many characters as I have seen apes. Among gorillas alone there is the great Bushman at Chicago, who is a comedian, and I judge that he would thoroughly enjoy the changing, surging crowds that have made the heart of Ringling's Gargantua rankle with hate. But the female Toto is obviously a smarty who loves the crowd and plays to it. She wants you to laugh with her and loves to be funny. Susie, at Cincinnati, is another gorilla who wants to have an audience for her act, but I felt she resented it when Dr. Sol Stephans took me into her sleeping room to show me how she slept in a hammock off the floor. There could be no greater differences of character

[294]

among human children than I noticed among the young gorillas at Brookfield Zoo, where the three were playing in one big cage. One wanted everything either of the others chose to play with. One was displeased with the visitors, and rudely threw dirt at them, and little Sultan, just awake from his nap, came straight into my arms as though he had known me all his life, youngest and most confident of my friendly intent. I should like a real opportunity to try to make a friend of Gargantua and the two huge male gorillas, Bamboo and Massa, at Philadelphia, for I cannot believe that they are really as hostile as the reputations they have built, partly by copying each other's antics and largely because it is such a lark for them to scare people by appearing violent.

Yes, apes do have many traits which we call human and childish ones, and it is fun knowing them just as it is a privilege to know children, just as it is to know dogs and horses and some cats. If we know them well and long enough perhaps we shall someday discover factors which will make for better understanding not only of the apes but of ourselves. Meanwhile research in many fields goes on and because of the similarity in their needs, and illnesses and reactions to ourselves, there can be no better beginning for investigation into the foundation of the mind and body of man than through these anthropoids.

But I am thankful that that side of the animal world does not too directly concern me. I am glad that when I go down the row of anthropoid-ape cages in the early morning of each day at the zoo, I hear first the high and sweet call of Negus, my lovely gray gibbon, whom I have not even mentioned in this book; that Goola swings over and sticks out her long thin hand and wiggles her fingers to me in greeting; that Georgie leaves what he is doing to cross the twenty feet of cage, hoping I am coming in this morning; and that the great beast in the last big cage leaves the pile of orange and grapefruit skins which he has been sorting over since breakfast and runs along the front of his cage to his favorite corner to wait for his very special good morning. They know me, each one of them, the whole score which make up our anthropoid-ape colony, and I am proud that they like me, for to me they are neither low-grade half-humans to be loathed and feared, nor dangerous brutes of animals to be shuddered at without sympathy and understanding; they are my friends, the apes, and to them I am and hope I shall remain, as Smitty who helped me so greatly to understand them always called me, "Your lady boss, fellows, and here she is."